ALSO BY DAVID HIRSCH

with the Moosewood Collective

New Recipes from Moosewood Restaurant

Sundays at Moosewood Restaurant

THE MOOSEWOOD RESTAURANT KITCHEN GARDEN

DAVID HIRSCH

A FIRESIDE BOOK PUBLISHED BY SIMON & SCHUSTER

NEW YORK LONDON TORONTO SYDNEY TOKYO SINGAPORE

FIRESIDE

SIMON & SCHUSTER BUILDING

ROCKEFELLER CENTER

1230 AVENUE OF THE AMERICAS

NEW YORK, NEW YORK 10020

FIRESIDE AND COLOPHON ARE REGISTERED TRADEMARKS

OF SIMON & SCHUSTER INC.

DESIGNED BY BONNI LEON

GARDEN PLANS DESIGNED BY DAVID HIRSCH

ILLUSTRATED BY MARTIN BERMAN

MANUFACTURED IN THE UNITED STATES OF AMERICA

10 9 8 7 6 5 4 3 2 1

10 9 8 7 6 5 4 3 2 1 PBK

LIBRARY OF CONGRESS CATALOGING IN PUBLICATION DATA

HIRSCH, DAVID P.

   THE MOOSEWOOD RESTAURANT KITCHEN GARDEN/DAVID HIRSCH.

     P. CM.

   "A FIRESIDE BOOK."

   INCLUDES BIBLIOGRAPHICAL REFERENCES AND INDEX.

   1. VEGETABLE GARDENING.   2. HERB GARDENING.

3. ORGANIC GARDENING.   4. VEGETABLES.   5. HERBS.

6. COOKERY (VEGETABLES).   7. COOKERY (HERBS).

8. MOOSEWOOD RESTAURANT.   1. TITLE.

SB324.3.H57   1992

635—DC20   91-37181

                                                            CIP

ISBN: 0-671-69239-9

    0-671-75597-8 PBK

ACKNOWLEDGMENTS

I would like to thank the following:

Allan Warshawsky, with whom I shared my first garden, and so much more, at Lavender Hill; my friends and fellow Moosewood members for their wisdom, culinary or otherwise, warmth, and cocreation of an enjoyable livelihood, especially Bob Love, for recipe testing, Susan Harville and Nancy Lazarus, for editorial assistance, and Ned Asta, for aesthetic considerations; Arnold and Elise Goodman, for their thoughtful and caring advocacy as our agents; Sydny Miner, who edited with encouragement and clarity; Ashley Miller, Linda Burton, and Karen Orso for various information; Steve Edminster, who intrepidly word processed my scribbly handwriting; and David Deutsch, for editorial process, daily support, and sweet companionship.

CONTENTS

INTRODUCTION

I moved to the country outside of Ithaca, New York, in the early seventies, when a "back to the land" movement was at its height. Until then, I worked in New York City, in an upper-floor office facing the Hudson River. Through the winter and early spring, I would get up from my drawing board and gaze wistfully at the sunset, wishing I were somewhere "out there." Not necessarily in New Jersey, looming on the horizon, but somewhere. The then popular vision of a "country lifestyle" was a romanticized mixture of simplicity and directness. While halcyon days of festivity and coming together awaited us in our new lives, so did the normal everyday difficulties of sustaining a livelihood and nurturing relationships. Few of us who have stayed in the countryside became the self-sufficient farmers we'd hoped. Instead, we are people who prefer the open spaces and delight in the privilege of relating closely to the earth.

My first encounter with Moosewood Restaurant, aside from that as a diner, was as a gardener with a surplus of fresh basil. We negotiated a barter arrangement: herbs for meals. A few months later, I heard from my neighbor Linda Dickinson, who was then and remains a member of the collective, that Moosewood was looking for new employees. It seemed to be a job I was suited for. I had always loved to cook. As a teenager, I watched Julia Child on television and took notes. The flexible work schedule was another incentive. I'd have time to work on a cabin I was building and to garden.

This was in the fall of 1976, which I guess makes me one of the collective's "senior" members. I immediately felt at home. I enjoyed learning and contributing to the ever-changing cooking repertoire and appreciated the casual yet structured worker-managed environment. After a series of brief jobs and pleasurable semi-nomadism that began after graduating architecture school in 1968, cooking at Moosewood became my first and only job of any duration.

Gardening and cooking are two of my favorite pastimes. Both are physical, sensual activities that offer tangible, relatively immediate rewards. I find it very satisfying to be involved in the entire process of creating food, from planting to cooking. The child in me enjoys gardening's playing-in-dirt, messy aspects, while my adult side favors the more aesthetic considerations of garden design and food preparation. An interest in architecture makes me curious to explore spatial possibilities in gardens, what different environments feel like, and how gardens can open up, frame, or enclose a given site. I think for most gardeners there's an unconscious connection to the archetypal myth of re-creating our own little Eden —a bountiful, sumptuous place of beauty where you gather the harvest.

The reality, of course, is quite different. But determined gardeners don't give up. I've endured early frosts, hail, snow, swarms of grasshoppers and gypsy moths, herds of deer, and the usual onslaught of assorted bugs, beetles, mites, grubs, voles, caterpillars, and larvae. Through it all, the gardener perseveres and learns to accept that not every seed sprouts and even the most carefully nurtured plant might die. And yet, as clichéd as it may sound, it is still miraculous to see, in a matter of short weeks, a ten-foot-tall sunflower emerge from a quarter-inch-long seed.

Time in the garden always goes quickly for me. My life has grown busier in the last few years, so garden time feels more precious. Yet, like other zealous gardeners, there's always time and room for new beds and borders that will need care. Even when there isn't.

Over the years, I've supplied the restaurant with herbs, flowers, and rare specialty produce. New types or varieties of produce can be tested both in the garden and in the restaurant, stimulating curiosity and interest in both pursuits. This year, along with old favorites, my garden includes: lemon basil, scarlet runner beans, Chioggia striped beets, curly endive, bronze fennel, pearl onions, anise hyssop, Lemon Gem marigolds, Pirat and Arctic King lettuces, kohlrabi Gigante, Shungiku (edible chrysanthemum), and Lipstick early red pepper.

There is no one Moosewood kitchen garden. Rather it is a network of local individual gardens and small farms that supply us (as well as other restaurants and markets) throughout the brief, bountiful growing season. We buy much of our produce from Finger Lakes Organic Growers, a local twenty-four-farm cooperative. In addition, several of the Moosewood staff have gardens that provide the restaurant with herbs, edible flowers, and vegetables.

With very few exceptions, we use fresh produce the year round, with a particular emphasis on locally grown foods. Anyone who has tasted homegrown tomatoes, corn, or peas knows that store-bought vegetables just can't compare. Produce from afar must be bred, grown, and harvested with an eye to its perishability, appearance, and yield rather than aesthetic appeal and taste. Superior quality and flavor result from harvesting foods as close to ripeness and the kitchen as possible. In addition, the nutrient and vitamin content of freshly picked food is always higher. Home-growing can also expand your cooking repertoire to include interesting vegetables and herbs that may not be available in local markets or simply are impractical to grow commercially.

At Moosewood, we try to cook with as much organically grown food as possible, and also to avoid packaged foods prepared with preservatives. Public consciousness about pesticides, herbicides, and food additives appears to be increasing, and we look forward to a time when a higher percentage of agriculture is devoted to organic growing.

I'm a confirmed organic gardener, because I feel there's an undeniable connection between our own physical and spiritual health and how we treat the earth. Growing at least part of your own food and purchasing organic produce give your body a break from the plethora of pesticides and herbicides used in most of commercial agriculture. Eating from the lower end of the food chain—plants, grains, seeds, nuts, and dairy products, with little or no meat—reduces the consumption of unwanted toxins. Meat from livestock whose diet consists of grains grown with herbicides and pesticides contains toxins in greater concentrations than the grain itself. There are also the ecological concerns. It takes nine pounds of grain to make one pound of meat. Grazing livestock creates deforestation and soil erosion in many parts of the world.

Our restaurant kitchen is surprisingly small and basic: no grill, no griddle, no microwave oven. Most of the techniques necessary to produce our meals are straightforward and can be applied in the home kitchen. What I think defines our style as "Moosewood" is the use of fresh foods prepared daily for an ever-changing menu that reflects the variety of the seasons. Our eclectic mix of recipes has been influenced by both international and American regional cooking styles and reflects the rich diversity of flavors and tastes that can be achieved with a full range of vegetables, herbs, grains, beans, nuts, and soy and dairy products. Many cuisines that we have drawn from, particularly those of Asia, traditionally feature superb meatless, protein-sufficient dishes.

The restaurant work can be physically exhausting, but we take pride in the meals we create and enjoy our time together in the kitchen or dining room philosophizing, gossiping, and entertaining ourselves.

This book is a guide for cooks and gardeners who want to feel the compounded pleasure of growing and cooking their vegetables and herbs, even if their "garden" is a windowsill of potted herbs. I hope to share our enjoyment of these two creative, life-sustaining processes.

In the chapters to follow, you will find discussions of vegetables, herbs, and edible flowers (pp. 11–138) that we have enjoyed using at the restaurant. Each entry includes ornamental aspects, growing requirements, harvest information, and culinary tips.

I have always admired gardens that share a sensitivity to their environment and reflect individual personal style. The Design chapter (p. 139) is intended to help outline planning decisions for new or experienced gardeners. In it are examples of various possibilities for kitchen gardens in a range of sites. The Gardening Techniques chapter (p. 173) is a guide of basic information especially useful to first-time gardeners. Beginners may find it helpful to read these chapters before learning about individual vegetables, herbs, or flowers. Recipes (pp. 205–270), many of which are Moosewood or personal favorites that feature specific herbs and vegetables, are included.

Since this book is not intended to be "the complete garden primer," the curious gardener may be interested in consulting other resources. The Bibliography (p. 275) and Mail-Order Sources (p. 271) will provide you with a wide selection of gardening and cooking information as well as resources that I have found to be helpful.

VEGETABLES

I t's not often that we think about a seed being sown while we're rushing about the kitchen chopping and cooking vegetables. Yet that is how the process starts for cooks and gardeners alike.

The growing season begins with choosing which seeds to sow. Seed catalogs list a confusingly wide array. Talk with gardeners in the neighborhood, at a local farmers' market, or at a Cooperative Extension office to learn what varieties perform best in your region; gardening magazines, such as *Horticulture, National Gardening, Organic Gardening,* and *Fine Gardening,* are helpful as well. An often overlooked resource is your local newspaper's gardening column. Ultimately, your own experience will combine with outside information to form a unique and individual body of knowledge.

Included in the Mail-Order Sources (p. 271) are seed and nursery catalogs that I have found to be reliable and informative. Many clearly indicate such valuable information as: how many feet of row a given quantity of seed will plant, the best season for sowing, disease-resistant varieties, and which plants will thrive in a specific region or are widely adaptable.

Gardeners with limited space or time may choose to buy seedlings at a local nursery or garden center. This can be particularly helpful for plants that require an early start indoors, such as onions, leeks, or spring broccoli, or that need specific conditions, such as heat-loving eggplant. I always buy a few greenhouse-started tomato plants to get a jump on the season, in addition to starting my own plants from seed. Local nurseries usually sell plants that have proven to be successful in your area.

In this chapter, I recommend varieties of plants that have, in my experience, been vigorous and healthy, as well as possessing culinary appeal. Unless specifically noted, these varieties are widely available. The listings in the Mail-Order Sources will help you locate sources for these varieties.

Admittedly, some of my prejudices appear, or do not appear, throughout this book. There is no discussion of celery, which I find far too difficult to grow and not that much better tasting than store-bought; nor of ordinary radishes, whose chief asset is the speed with which they produce many more than one could want.

Each year brings new varieties, usually improved for vigor, disease or pest resistance, shipping ability, physical appearance, or a desirable trait, such as a leafier dill with fewer flowers. Rarely, a genuinely new type of vegetable appears, like the snap pea.

Hybrids do have their distinct advantages as improved, often disease-resistant, high-yield varieties. Since their seeds may be sterile or revert to manifest an undesirable characteristic of a parent's strain, they can be reproduced only by a controlled pollination of the original parent selections and not from their own seeds. Hybrids are usually more expensive and need to be purchased, since the process above is not one the home gardener can easily deal with.

There is a current movement to preserve heirloom and other open-pollinated varieties that are in danger of being lost forever, as new hybrid plant varieties push them out of the marketplace. Open-pollinated varieties will produce seeds that are true to type. Over the years, farmers have selected the most desirable plants and saved their seeds for the next year's crop. Heirlooms are specific strains that have been planted by farmers and gardeners for generations. The concern here is for the loss of a broad genetic base as more old varieties are lost when fewer are grown. This creates a narrow, less diverse source of food crops that may not be adaptable to changes in climate, insect population, or disease. Many of the heirloom or open-pollinated varieties are still desirable plants for home gardeners. Some of the recommended vegetables that follow are heirloom varieties.

There are no hard-and-fast rules as to which type, hybrid or open-pollinated, will be a better plant. One stand-out exception is sweet corn; hybrid varieties are markedly superior. I have also had particularly successful crops with hybrid members of the cabbage family, onions, spinach, and carrots.

Purchased seeds saved from year to year will be most viable if kept in a cool, dry place below 70°F., but above freezing. Most will keep between three to five years, but buy fresh sweet corn, leeks, onion, parsley, and parsnip seeds every year.

Culinary tips are included with each vegetable in the following listings. In most cases, measurements or detailed instructions are not given, as they are meant to be a guide, or a jumping-off point for a cook's inspiration.

Gardeners may find that their soil becomes more fertile as the seasons go by. This is the result of good gardening practices that include the addition of compost, decomposing organic mulches or manures, and crop rotation. Subsequently, plant spacings may be closer than indicated in the "Starting" discussion for each vegetable that follows. Those with very limited garden area may want to choose varieties that are suited to close spacing; see Container Gardening (p. 168).

ASIAN SPECIALTY VEGETABLES

The cuisines of Asia have strongly influenced Moosewood's cooking style for a variety of reasons:

- The vegetables' fresh, clean flavor is enhanced with just a few seasonings, such as soy sauce, ginger, garlic, and sesame oil.
- Because the vegetables are cooked quickly, they retain nutrients and texture.
- Low-fat and low-calorie meals are possible using vegetarian protein sources such as tofu, tempeh, and wheat gluten products.

The vegetables listed below not only will widen your cooking and gardening repertoires but provide greens and roots that are rich in flavor, vitamins, minerals, and other nutrients.

chinese cabbage resembles green cabbage but with thinner, frilled, lettucelike, crisp leaves. Both the Napa (which is blocky and barrel-shaped) and Michihli (taller and cylindrical) share a sweet, mildly tangy taste, while Napa varieties store better. Most crops are grown late spring to mid-summer for fall harvest. Cool summer areas call for specific, bolt-resistant spring-planted varieties for summer harvest, such as Nerva (from Johnny's Selected Seeds).

daikon, an important ingredient in Japanese cooking, is a crisp, white, long (12 to 18 inches) radish. They're sweet yet hot and spicy. Varieties are available for spring, summer, and fall planting. Tokinashi (Abundant Life, Fedco) is a good variety for spring planting in most areas and early-fall planting where winters are mild. Omny (Shepherd's) has done well for me with spring-through-summer seeding.

edible chrysanthemum (shungiku) is grown for its leaves' aromatic flavor, which recall the pungent fragrance of ornamental garden chrysanthemums. Plants not picked as greens for cooking can be left to produce delicate orange and yellow button flowers.

mizuna is a mild Japanese mustard with fringed, lacy, foliage and white stems. The leaves make an attractive edible garnish. Plants can be harvested all season from one sowing.

pak choi (bok choy) is used widely in Chinese dishes where it lends a crunchy texture and sweet but mildly pungent flavor. An excellent new variety is Mei Qing Choi. Widely available, it's a "baby" type with pale green stems and darker green, veined leaves. The compact plants are mature at 6 to 8 inches tall and would make an attractive edging plant. In addition to being a good size for small households, they're heat and cold tolerant. Standard varieties are about 15 to 18 inches tall, somewhat resembling Swiss chard.

tatsoi has a flavor similar to fellow cabbage-family member pak choi. Its abundant small, deep-green, spoon-shaped leaves radiate from a central rosette. Attractive and low growing, tatsoi is heat and cold tolerant, which allows for a long growing season. I've harvested tatsoi well into December by covering late-summer-sown plants with a plastic tunnel in mid-fall.

STARTING

All of the above vegetables thrive in soil within a pH range of 6.0 to 7.5. Early spring planting is possible for daikon, edible chrysanthemum, mizuna, pak choi, and tatsoi. Chinese cabbage varieties for spring planting should be seeded in the garden after the last frost, or started indoors in peat pots. Seedlings exposed to frost and cold may bolt to seed before forming heads.

Chinese cabbage, daikon, and the standard-sized pak choi are seeded in rows 18 inches apart, with plants thinned to 6 inches apart for daikon and 10 to 12 inches for cabbage and pak choi.

Smaller-sized pak choi and tatsoi are seeded in rows 12 inches apart, with plants thinned to 4 to 6 inches apart.

Fall crops are possible for all of the above since they can tolerate light frosts. Winter crops can be grown in the South, Pacific coastal areas, or by anyone with a cool greenhouse or sunspace.

CULTURAL REQUIREMENTS

Flea beetles have been a major problem in growing all but the chrysanthemums. Row covers (p. 191) applied before seedlings emerge and the insecticides pyrethrum and rotenone can be effective controls.

HARVEST

chinese cabbage — Full-sized heads can be stored refrigerated or in a cool cellar for several weeks.

daikon — Roots harvested in the fall can be stored like carrots (p. 27).

edible chrysanthemum — Pick greens while plants are quite small, up to 6 inches tall.

mizuna — Pick individual smaller leaves for a long season of harvest, or whole, 6- to 12-inch plants.

pak choi—Can be stored like Chinese cabbage above.

tatsoi—Pick individual leaves or harvest whole plant.

CULINARY TIPS

- *The tender, young, raw greens of Chinese cabbage, mizuna, pak choi, and tatsoi can be used in salads.*
- *Bob Love is a Moosewood cook with a wonderful facility for the cuisines of Southeast Asia, where he lived for many years. This is his fast and delicious stir-frying technique for greens. Prepare the greens by thorough washing; chop coarsely. Cut garlic cloves into pieces large enough to be removed with a slotted spoon or mesh strainer. Heat some oil in a wok and fry the garlic until it's golden; remove and reserve. Stir-fry the greens until they're tender. Older or bulky greens will take 5 to 10 minutes; young or delicate, soft greens may be cooked in 1 or 2 minutes. The rinse water that clings to the leaves should provide sufficient moisture. Add a few splashes of soy sauce, Chinese oyster sauce, rice wine, and rice vinegar. Sprinkle the reserved crisp garlic over the completed dish.*
- *Daikon radishes are traditionally used in salads, soups, stews, dips, and pickled condiments. Pickled daikon is used to cleanse the palate.*
- *Grated daikon is an excellent addition to a dipping sauce for spring rolls, tempura, or grilled kabobs. Combine ½ cup vegetable stock or water with 2 tablespoons tamari soy sauce and 2 tablespoons sake or cream sherry. Simmer for 5 minutes. Remove from heat, add 1 teaspoon each of honey and apple juice, ¼ cup grated daikon, and 1 teaspoon fresh gingerroot.*

ASPARAGUS

Garden-grown asparagus is tender, sweet, and a delightful surprise to those who've only tasted it from the market. It's an unusual vegetable in that it's a perennial; yearly maintenance is all that is necessary to keep plants bearing well. The mature plants make a lush 4- to 6-foot screen or hedge for the summer landscape. Its finely cut, lacy foliage provides a handsome background for lower-growing flowers, herbs, or vegetables. The nonflowering male plants give higher crop yields than female plants, as all their energy goes to producing spears. Jersey Giant and Supermale are two newly developed varieties of this "macho" breed. This is a crop for gardeners with room to spare; two 20-foot-long rows will supply four people with fresh spears through the growing season.

STARTING

Most gardeners buy one-year-old crowns (roots) from the local garden center or by mail order and plant in early spring. Choose a spot where the tall, fernlike foliage will not shade sun-loving plants or be disturbed by rototilling or deep cultivation; this should be a permanent bed. Asparagus grows well throughout the continental United States and Southern Canada, except Florida and the Gulf Coast. Soil should be well-drained, fertile, with a pH range between 6.0 and 7.0.

Dig an 8-inch-deep trench, piling the soil to one side. Space trenches 4 feet apart, measured center to center. Remove large stones and supplement the new bed with compost, well-rotted manure, or peat moss to ensure a nutrient-rich home for the 10- to 15-year lifespan of the plants. Refill the trench with 2 inches of soil and supplement, then gently space the crowns 15 inches apart, with their long, snaky roots pointing down, on top of this bed. Cover the plants with 2 inches of soil. As the new shoots emerge, simply fill in with more of the supplemented soil, completing the job by early summer. This keeps the plants from pushing themselves to the surface as they grow.

CULTURAL REQUIREMENTS

Yearly maintenance would include providing adequate moisture, nutrients, and protection from invasive weeds. Asparagus is a heavy feeder; it will thrive if the soil fertility is kept high with early-spring and post-harvest applications of compost or well-rotted manure. Additional organic mulch applied during the growing season would help to maintain moisture and keep weeds from being a problem.

HARVEST

At the start of the second year, after one full year of growth following planting, a few spears may be cut for sampling. Spears are ready to cut when they're 6 to 8 inches tall and the tips are closed tight. Snap off the spears at ground level and refrigerate what is not to be used immediately. By the third year, harvest for a period of only 3 weeks and in succeeding years, harvest can continue for up to 6 weeks, or until the size of the newly emerging stalks are less than ½ inch in diameter. Pick often (two to three times a week), as stalks will leaf out and slow down production of new spears.

CULINARY TIPS

- *Snap off the tough bottom end by bending a spear with both hands until it snaps. Or, if you have the time and patience, peel the lower stem end to remove the tough, fibrous portion.*
- *At Moosewood, we don't use any special pots for cooking asparagus. Spears can be blanched in boiling water in 2 to 3 minutes, or steamed for slightly longer.*
- *The wonderful, delicate flavor of fresh asparagus calls for the simplest preparations. Steam and toss with butter and lemon, or sesame oil and a little grated fresh ginger.*
- *Asparagus adds class to any salad or marinated vegetable dish.*
- *Stir-fry sliced asparagus with just one or two other ingredients, such as tofu and mushrooms.*
- *Serve cooked spears with a smooth and tangy dressing that's half yogurt and half homemade garlic Herbed Mayonnaise (p. 248).*
- *When using chopped asparagus in a soup or stew, add the tips toward the end of cooking time for best appearance and texture.*

BEANS

A satisfying crop for the kitchen gardener, beans produce abundantly, yielding more per square foot than most other vegetables. They're valuable in garden rotations, since as legumes, they add nitrogen to the soil. The familiar immature seedpods (snap, green, or string beans) or seeds (dried beans) are one of the world's most important food sources. There are bush, pole, and fresh or dried shell beans for virtually every growing, eating, or storing situation. For ease in preparation, look for stringless snap beans.

bush bean plants average about 2 feet tall, need no other support, and are usually green or wax types. Bush Blue Lake and Provider are flavorful, easily grown green beans; Roc d'Or is a buttery wax bean. French filet beans, another bush variety, are long and slender and must be picked when they're no more than ¼ inch in diameter. Vigilant gardeners will be rewarded with tender beans of delicate flavor. Triumph de Farcy is an heirloom variety we have enjoyed. Purple bush beans are easier to pick, as they stand out against the green foliage, and are attractive on a platter of multicolored raw vegetables for dips or salads. When cooked, however, they turn green. Royal Burgundy is a tasty purple bean that also tolerates cool soils. Roma II is a Romano or Italian bean with thick, rich "beany"-flavored pods.

pole beans will give the highest yield for the amount of space required and can be grown along fences, trellises, or poles. Poles have always seemed unwieldy to me, requiring lots of work to get in the ground, only to be pulled up at season's end. Portable trellising (p. 46) is somewhat easier to deal with. Scarlet runner beans serve a dual purpose, covering arbors or trellises 8 to 10 feet tall and bearing hundreds of bright red (and sometimes white) flowers followed by extremely large (6 to 12 inches long) snap beans. Northern or cool-weather gardeners will have more success with this variety; they perform poorly where daytime temperatures are regularly above 85°F. Emerite, available from The Cook's Garden or Shepherd's Garden Seeds, is a productive, slender pole bean of excellent flavor.

shell beans include green soybeans, limas, French flageolet, and many other varieties traditionally popular both here and abroad. Home gardeners can enjoy the tender, buttery sweetness of freshly shelled beans that are rarely available in markets. King of the Garden is an excellently flavored pole lima bean offered by Stokes Seeds and Park Seeds. Flambeau (Johnny's Selected Seeds) is a flageolet bean with a delicate flavor similar to limas, but easier to grow in cool climates.

The pastel green shelled beans make a delightful side dish. Tongues of Fire (Johnny's Selected Seeds, Abundant Life) have red-striped, cream-colored pods with large, delicious beans. Seeds for this were originally collected in Tierra del Fuego, at the tip of South America. Shell beans that have fully matured and dried are stored for winter use. Kitchen gardeners with lots of space may want to grow their own kidney, pinto, black, navy, or other kinds of beans for drying.

STARTING

After the last expected frost date, sow seeds in well-drained, warm soil between pH 6.0 to 7.5. Soils cooler than 65°F. will result in poor germination and possible seed rot. For bush types, sow seeds 1 inch deep, 2 inches apart in rows 24 to 36 inches from other plantings. Pole types should be sown 1 inch deep with 6 to 8 seeds per pole, thinned later to the 4 strongest vines. Plant seeds 3 to 4 inches apart alongside a fence or trellis. Northern gardeners should start lima bean seeds indoors in peat pots or soil cells at 70°F. or higher. Outdoor seeding, when soil and air temperatures are warm enough for good germination, may be too late to mature a crop of beans before the cooler weather returns.

Nitrogen legume inoculant, harmless and beneficial bacteria, will greatly increase the yield of all beans by encouraging nitrogen-fixing bacteria to grow on the plant's roots. Lightly dust the seeds with inoculant, moisten, and plant as usual, or simply pour a small amount into each seed hole or row as you sow.

To avoid vast quantities of snap beans maturing at once, plant 3- to 4-foot rows 1 to 2 weeks apart as late as 2 to 2½ months before the first frost date.

CULTURAL REQUIREMENTS

Overfertilized beans result in lushly foliaged plants with few beans. The nitrogen-fixing properties of the plants themselves allow for lighter fertilization. Avoid working around bean plants after a heavy dew or rainfall, since dampness encourages a damaging foliage rust disease. Also, rotate bean beds from year to year to thwart any overwintering diseases or pests.

It may be necessary to guide the young vines of climbing varieties; they're easily distracted and will ramble everywhere.

HARVEST

The bean plant's speedy, prolific growth may surprise the inexperienced gardener. A few days out of the bean patch and you return to find a mess of big, tough beans. Fresh snap beans should be picked often, ideally every other day. Climbing varieties offer the advantage of some of the harvest being at eye level. I don't like to bend over the plants while picking bush varieties of beans so I leave sufficient room between rows to lounge comfortably on the mulch while hunting for beans amongst the foliage.

Shell beans are picked fresh when the pods are full and somewhat lumpy, and the beans firm but not dry. If it's rainy and damp at harvest time, hang the whole shell bean plant upside down in a dry, warm spot to dry.

CULINARY TIPS

• *Only the stem end of green or wax beans needs to be cut; the curly end is tender. The fastest way is to line them up on a cutting board and chop about ten at a time. Folks with more leisure can snap off one stem at a time, bean by bean.*

• *The year's first tender pickings are at their best quickly blanched or steamed and tossed with plain or herbed butter (pp. 254–256). When there's an abundance, use them as supporting players in soups, stews, stir-fries, casseroles, and marinated in salads.*

• *For marinated salads, add the dressing to the hot cooked beans for best flavor absorption.*

• *All beans have edible flowers. Scarlet runner blossoms make showy, vivid garnishes.*

• *Fresh shell beans (limas, soy, green, or flageolet) are simmered in stock or water until just tender. Flageolets are traditionally simmered with thyme, bay leaf, onion, clove, parsley, garlic, and tomato.*

• *For fast cooking and tender dried beans, withhold salt until the beans are almost done.*

• *To preserve nutrients in dried beans, cook them in their soaking liquid. To minimize gastric disturbance, soak beans for 3 to 4 hours and change the water before cooking. Boil for 30 minutes and change the water again if more cooking is necessary.*

• *Purée cooked beans with olive oil, garlic, and savory herbs. Serve on a bed of steamed kale or other greens.*

BEETS

Beets provide a "double" harvest: nutritious greens and ruby roots. The rich, earthy sweetness and brilliant color of the roots are unique among vegetables. Detroit Dark Red is a reliable beet with deep-red, sweet flesh. For good flavor and unique color, raw Chioggia beets have alternating interior rings of deep rose and creamy white; golden beets are vibrant orange.

STARTING

Seeds can be sown 1 month before the last hard frost, when the soil is workable. As the seeds are part of a thick, papery husk, you can encourage germination by soaking them in water for 12 hours prior to planting. Seedbeds should be worked to about 8 inches, well spaded and free of clods and stones that cause misshapen roots. A soil pH between 6 and 7 will give the best results. Sow seeds ½ inch deep in rows 12 to 18 inches apart every 2 weeks until midsummer for succession planting.

CULTURAL REQUIREMENTS

Thin seedlings to 4 to 6 inches apart, using the thinnings as edible greens. Beets resent extreme heat and need ample water during hot, dry periods to prevent the development of woody, tough roots. In areas with very hot summers but relatively frost-free winters, grow beets as a fall and winter crop.

HARVEST

Beets are ready to harvest from 8 weeks on; the optimum sizes for tender, juicy roots are from 1 to 3 inches in diameter. Flavor will deteriorate if the roots remain in the ground after maturity. Store in a cool root cellar (35°F. to 40°F.) or pit for the winter months. Cut off the greens, leaving a 1- to 2-inch stub.

CULINARY TIPS

- *Dismayed by the poor quality of winter tomatoes at Moosewood, we frequently use tender, shredded raw beets in tossed salad garnishes.*
- *The young, tender beet leaves make a fine salad green.*
- *Cook unpeeled, scrubbed beets whole. When the roots are slightly cool, it's easy*

to slip off the skin and cut into the desired shape. This avoids messy peeling and bleeding of raw beets.

• For a perfectly pink Scandinavian salad, we mix cooked beets with new red potatoes, sour cream, mayonnaise, snipped dill, and chives. Serve on a bed of ruby lettuce.

• Joan Adler, our resident cooked-greens enthusiast, likes to serve steamed beet greens tossed with an Herb Butter (p. 254) and topped with diced, cooked beetroot.

• Sauté beet greens with garlic and oil; toss with soy sauce and a few drops of rice vinegar.

• Try roasting whole baby beets alone or with new potatoes, pearl onions, and small globe carrots.

BROCCOLI

Like other members of the cabbage family, broccoli is a nutritious cool-season crop for spring or fall planting. Choose early-bearing hybrids for crops you can harvest before the heat of summer. Romanesco types have mild flavor and a chartreuse head of florets spiraling in a pattern that can only be described as psychedelic. Green Comet is an early, heat-tolerant broccoli producing a large center head followed by a long season of abundant side shoots.

STARTING

For spring planting, start seeds indoors about 2 months before the last frost. Transplant the 1- to 2-inch seedlings to individual pots.

Place seedlings in the garden in fertile soil of pH 5.5 to 7.0 about 3 to 4 weeks before the last expected frost. Space plants 18 inches apart in rows 30 inches apart. See page 197 for protection from cabbage-family pests and diseases which, though nasty and prevalent, are easy to control.

Broccoli plants eventually become quite large, at least 2 feet square; however, interplanting is possible with a row of early spring greens, such as spinach or lettuce, or a dwarf snow pea. These could be seeded down the middle of a double row of broccoli, 15 inches from either side. The plants or vines will have matured by the time the broccoli is reaching full size.

Midsummer or fall (in warmer climates) planting for fall or winter crops can be direct seeded or started indoors. Seeds can be sown directly in the garden, ½ inch deep, and thinned to stand as above. Seedlings are more tolerant of summer heat than older plants, which could bolt (go to seed) without forming usable heads.

CULTURAL REQUIREMENTS

Broccoli thrives in a cool, fertile, well-mulched, and well-watered soil. The addition of limestone and/or wood ash also helps to keep the soil alkaline and deters clubroot and root maggots. Crop rotation for cabbage-family members (broccoli, brussels sprouts, cabbage, cauliflower, collards, kale, kohlrabi, mustard, turnips) is crucial to disease control; select a spot where none of the above have grown for 2 to 3 years.

Cabbage-family members are heavy feeders that benefit from applications of compost or organic fertilizers three or four times during the growing season.

HARVEST

Harvest the heads while buds are fully formed yet tight. After the central head is cut, plants will continue to send up smaller side sprouts for several weeks' extended harvest.

CULINARY TIPS

• *Broccoli leaves and stems are frequently tossed into the compost. However, stems pared of the leathery peel and small leaves are as delicious as the familiar flower head.*

• *Cabbage worms are the offspring of white butterflies that lay their eggs on plant leaves. Broccoli harvested from unprotected plants (p. 197) may need to be processed in salt water to avoid the embarrassment of serving the well-camouflaged green worms. Soak the heads in well-salted water for 15 minutes. Dead worms will float to the top. Rinse the broccoli and prepare as usual.*

• *Broccoli is crisper if stir-fried or steamed. Boiled or blanched broccoli tends to hold moisture and be soggy.*

• *Slightly undercook broccoli, since it tends to continue cooking even when removed from the heat.*

• *Lemon juice or vinegar will turn broccoli a drab olive color if allowed to sit for more than a few minutes. For marinated dishes, we reserve the lemon or other acidifying agent until right before serving.*

• *Cooked broccoli goes well with gomasio, a seasoning made of toasted sesame seeds ground with sea salt.*

• *Broccoli will impart a strong unpleasant taste if cooked too long in slowly simmered soups or sauces. Add it toward the end of the cooking time.*

BRUSSELS SPROUTS

The first time I saw Brussels sprouts growing, I was amazed at its odd growing habits. Mature plants look like exotic miniature trees with clusters of sprouts hugging a fat, stocky stem topped with big umbrellalike leaves. Rows of the leafy, blue-green columns add architectural, visual interest to the garden, and provide nutty, sweet sprouts from fall into winter. Jade Cross E is a widely adaptable variety with good-quality sprouts.

STARTING

Brussels sprouts require a long growing season of 90 to 110 days from seedling to harvest. Start seeds in June, indoors or out, and transplant in July to a permanent spot, 18 inches apart in rows 3 feet apart.

CULTURAL REQUIREMENTS

Brussels sprouts have the same needs as broccoli (p. 24). Maximize space by interplanting early-maturing vegetables or herbs between rows of Brussels sprouts.

HARVEST

Sprouts are ready when they're the size of ping-pong balls, about 1 inch in diameter. Pick the lowest sprouts and leaves first. Removing these will encourage the plant to grow new ones at the top. The flavor will greatly improve after one or two light frosts. Plants can stand in the garden until temperatures stay below freezing, at which point the leaves are removed, and the sprout-filled stalks are cut and stored in a cool place for 4 to 6 weeks.

CULINARY TIPS

- *For faster cooking, cut x's in the bottoms of the biggest sprouts.*
- *Cut Brussels sprouts in half for an unusual stir-fry addition.*
- *Cooked rounds of carrot, parsnip, or sweet potato will add sweetness and color to cooked Brussels sprouts.*
- *Serve cooked sprouts topped with crisp bread crumbs that have been toasted in an Herb Butter (p. 254).*
- *Cheese sauce and Brussels sprouts are a classic combination.*

CABBAGE

Cabbage was a mainstay in the kitchen gardens of the past because of its excellent keeping qualities. In addition to the standard green varieties, try growing some red and savoy types for their color and texture.

The bright, frilled-leaf heads of ornamental cabbage accent the darkening days of late fall. Mature plants are very frost-tolerant. Seed in the late spring.

Cabbage does best in a cool, moist growing season. For a long period of harvest, choose early, mid-season, and late varieties. Early: Early Jersey Wakefield is an heirloom variety with crisp, tender heads for fine flavor. Midseason: Perfect Ball can be harvested over a long period since it holds good quality in the garden. Late: Danish Roundhead will store well for fall and winter use.

STARTING AND CULTURAL REQUIREMENTS

Seed starting and cultural requirements are similar to broccoli (p. 24). The cabbage feeder roots grow close to the surface, so avoid weeding or digging deeply into the surrounding soil.

HARVEST

Harvest when heads are firm and solid or before hard frosts. Late-season varieties are best for storage in a cool, dry root cellar or pit. To hold mature cabbage heads in the garden for late harvest, twist the whole plant sharply. By breaking some of the roots, you stop the growth of the head. Cabbages will taste sweeter after a light frost.

CULINARY TIPS

* *Use a stainless steel knife for cutting red cabbage. Iron knives or cleavers will turn it a washed-out blue.*
* *For a sweet, mild flavor, steam or sauté cabbage over low to moderate heat. High heat breaks down sulfur components in the cabbage, resulting in a strong taste and smell.*
* *Sauté onions, apples, raisins, and cabbage in butter for a fall side dish.*
* *Use savoy cabbage for a light, mild flavor. The large, ruffled leaves make nifty beds for platters of salads or dips as well as snazzy wrappers for stuffed cabbage rolls.*

- *We make a light, tangy cole slaw with the young, tender vegetables of early summer: shredded cabbage, carrots, kohlrabi, turnips, and Dill–Red Onion Vinaigrette (p. 245). Red cabbage makes a lavender-pink cole slaw.*
- *L. D. (the dean of Moosewood cooks) has a simple, delicious family recipe for sweet and sour cabbage: Slow-cook cabbage and onions in butter until they are decidedly brown (not burnt). Add sugar and vinegar to taste toward the end of the cooking time.*

CARROTS

Freshly dug carrots are crisp, sweet, and juicy. Their ferny foliage softly edges a border or bed.

The ideal soil for carrots is a loose, deep, sandy loam, with a pH 5.5 to 6.5. In heavier clay soils, short, blunt varieties such as Chantenay or Planet will be more successful than other types. I recommend A plus, a deep orange, sweet carrot high in vitamin A, and Parmex, a small, early round carrot best served whole in marinated salads or as a side dish.

STARTING

Sow seeds ½ inch deep in rows 12 to 16 inches apart, or in a band 1 foot wide, in well-dug, stone-free soil. Seeds should be two years old or less. To avoid soil compaction, plant in a raised bed or stand and kneel on a plank laid alongside the seedbed to distribute your weight. Ensure a good supply by making successive plantings every 3 weeks until early August or until whenever temperatures consistently exceed 88°F. Soils enriched with bonemeal, wood ash, and rock phosphate will increase available potassium and phosphorus to yield sweeter and more flavorful roots. Avoid manure that is not thoroughly aged and decomposed, as it will damage the roots.

CULTURAL REQUIREMENTS

Carrots can take up to 3 weeks to germinate. To maintain surface moisture and avoid crusting of soil, try one of the following:

- Cover seedbed with straw or moistened burlap.
- Sow radish seeds with the carrots. They germinate quickly, break up the soil surface, and keep a crust from forming. This method has its drawbacks for those of us who don't care for radishes, but there's always the compost heap.
- Pregerminate seeds by placing them between two damp paper towels; store in a dark place until the tips of the first leaves just emerge from the seeds. Handle carefully and plant as above without breaking the tiny seedlings.
- Wait until soil has warmed to at least 65°F. for faster germination. Many sources indicate early-spring planting for carrots, but in my experience they just sit and wait for some warmth. The higher temperatures call for greater moisture.

Mulching will keep weeds down and moisture levels high. Plants should be thinned to stand 2 inches apart. Although it's difficult, beginning gardeners must be ruthless when it comes to thinning. An overcrowded carrot bed will yield only disappointment.

HARVEST

Around the maturity date, pull up a carrot and check it. Carrots are mature when they're bright orange and the appropriate length for that variety. Pale carrots will lack flavor. Harvest may continue for about 3 weeks after maturity; later, cracking and quality loss may occur. Containers filled with sand work well for winter storage. Cut the tops and store the roots in a cold, but not freezing, humid location. Stored carrots will not be as tasty as fresh.

Late-maturing carrots grown in cold-winter areas can be mulched with a foot or so of dry straw to prevent them from freezing. Push aside the straw for midwinter harvests. Gardeners in snow country should mark the row with a sunflower stalk or some other device.

CULINARY TIPS

- *Carrots will retain more nutrients if they are scrubbed and not peeled. They will stay crisper longer if the green tops are removed immediately upon picking.*
- *Add grated carrots to cornbread, muffins, pancakes, and yeasted and quick breads for color, sweetness, and nutrition.*
- *We serve raw carrot salads as light accompaniments to rich dishes, or as part of multifaceted combination plates:*
  Mix grated carrots with yogurt, chopped fresh mint, nutmeg, and a few drops of lemon juice.

> Toss grated carrots with a little sesame oil, rice vinegar, finely grated fresh gingerroot, and a bit of honey or brown sugar.
>
> Chives, chervil, raspberry vinegar, and olive oil tossed with grated carrots makes a delicate, aromatic salad.
>
> • Add Marsala wine to sautéed carrots for a fragrant glaze.
>
> • Parboil carrots to be roasted or grilled to cut cooking time.
>
> • Carrots puréed in soups, stews, or sauces impart a golden hue and a hint of sweetness.

CAULIFLOWER

Cauliflower grows best in cool weather, with ample rainfall or irrigation. Choose varieties according to your growing season: early, mid, or late. Snow Crown has been a dependable all-season type that is widely adaptable to variations in climate. Gardeners with limited space should consider that individual plants cover an area about 2 feet by 2 feet, yielding one head per plant. Purple-headed types add an unusual color, as a raw vegetable, for salads or dips, but turn green when cooked. Violet Queen is an easily grown, mildly flavored purple variety.

STARTING AND CULTURAL REQUIREMENTS

Seed starting and cultural requirements are the same as for broccoli (p. 24). Heads exposed to sunlight and heat will turn yellow unless protected by a technique called blanching. This simply requires tying the plant's large outer leaves over the newly emerging white head. Bear in mind, though, that a "wrapped" head makes a cozy hideout for pests. Carefully open and check the growing heads periodically. Purple varieties do not require blanching.

HARVEST

Harvest while the head is crisp and compact, before it opens up and becomes "ricey."

• At Moosewood, we frequently include cauliflower in our marinated vegetable salads. Steamed until tender but crisp, it holds its shape, doesn't discolor, and absorbs the marinade.

• Roseann Trapani, a friend who is an excellent Italian cook, introduced me to a favorite side dish: steamed florets dipped in beaten egg and herbed bread crumbs, drizzled with oil or garlic butter, then baked on a cookie sheet at 350°F. until golden.

• Cauliflower curries are a regular feature of Moosewood menus. The florets absorb the seasonings and hold up well in slow cooking.

• Caraway seed and chopped fresh dill with yogurt or sour cream gives steamed cauliflower a Scandinavian flavor.

• Vary a standard cheese sauce for cauliflower by adding chopped shallots, tarragon, and parsley.

• Serve composed platters of alternating florets of cauliflower, purple cauliflower, and broccoli, stems cut at varying lengths and assembled floret side up to form a dome.

• Susan Harville and Tony Del Plato are Moosewood cooks with a special interest in Italian cuisine. Pasta is one of their at-home favorites: Put up a big (1 gallon or more) pot of water to cook pasta. Choose a bite-size shape, such as ziti or shells, and cut the cauliflower into roughly similar pieces. Cut garlic cloves into pieces big enough to scoop out with a slotted spoon. Sauté the garlic in olive oil; remove when just golden and reserve. Start to sauté the cauliflower in the seasoned oil when the pasta goes into the pot. Spoon on a little of the hot pasta water to help steam the cauliflower. Toss the drained pasta with the cauliflower and reserved garlic, top with freshly grated Parmesan cheese, and serve.

COLLARDS AND KALE

When we say "Eat your greens," this is the stuff we're talking about. High in vitamins A and C, iron, calcium, and other minerals, this duo is at their sweetest and tastiest when cool weather arrives.

Collards and kale are related closely enough to be grouped together.

collards resemble a nonheading cabbage, have a slightly different flavor, and are a popular winter green in the South. Champion bears sweet, dark-green leaves over a long season.

kale The curly and crinkly blue-green foliage of kale makes it a desirable ornamental in the garden and an edible garnish. Red Russian is an heirloom variety with purple-red veins and stems and flat, gray-green leaves. Unlike other kales, the young leaves are tender, and not bitter in the warmth of summer. Winterbor is a hardy, vigorous, ruffled-leaf kale good for fall and winter harvests.

STARTING AND CULTURAL REQUIREMENTS

Seeds should be sown approximately 3 months before the first frost, in soil of pH 6.0 to 6.8, ½ inch deep, in rows 20 to 30 inches apart. Thin kale plants to 12 inches apart, collards to 24 inches. Both can be grown all winter in mild climates.

Cultural requirements are the same as for broccoli (p. 24).

HARVEST

Harvest the young leaves of both collards and kale without disturbing the uppermost point of new growth. The very hardy plants can be picked when there's snow on the ground, but before temperatures are consistently below freezing.

CULINARY TIPS

• *Add shredded or chopped greens to soups, stews, or stir-fries for additional heartiness, flavor, and nutrition.*
• *Stir-fry greens with garlic and olive oil Mediterranean-style, or with ginger and a splash of soy sauce Asian-style, for a quick and savory side dish.*

> • *Add sautéed greens to pasta, mashed potatoes, or rice. Season with an Herb Butter (p. 254).*
> • *Sara Robbins, a Moosewood cook with an extended Southern family, makes tasty greens using well-washed collard greens with the tough stems and leaf spines removed. The leaves are coarsely chopped and simmered in water to cover until they're tender. Toss with butter, salt, black pepper, vinegar, and Tabasco or other hot-pepper sauce. The piquant flavor of this dish is a good complement to rich foods.*

CORN

The unsurpassable quality of homegrown sweet corn makes it one of the most popular garden vegetables.

Though seed catalogs list a staggering number of varieties, there are just three basic types of sweet corn: "normal," "sugar enhanced," and "supersweet," or "extrasweet." Genetic differences determine each variety's sweetness and tenderness, and the rate at which sugar is converted to starch following picking.

normal sweet corn quickly converts to starch after picking. Isolation from other varieties of corn is unnecessary Silver Queen is a time-tested, late-maturing variety of superb tenderness and flavor. Early Sunglow and Sundance are two reliable, delicious varieties that tolerate cool weather.

sugar enhanced (se) and Everlasting Heritage (EH) gene varieties have increased sugar and tenderness. Isolation from other varieties of corn is unnecessary. Sugar Buns was my favorite corn of this type the past season. It's sweet, with a good "corny" flavor that some of the sugar-enhanced varieties lack.

supersweet, or extrasweet, corn has a "shrunken" (SH 2) gene, named for the shriveled appearance of the dried kernel. This corn has the highest sweetness and the slowest conversion of sugar to starch. Honey and Pearl is a bicolor variety prized for its extra-sweet tenderness. As delectable as the supersweets are, they have special requirements:

• Plantings must be isolated by at least 25 feet from non-supersweet, to avoid cross-pollination. Alternatively, stagger planting dates to ensure a minimum 12-day difference in projected maturity.

• Soil temperature should be quite warm, ideally 75°F., but no less than 60°F.
• The "shrunken" seeds need more moisture for germination than other types.

When choosing a corn variety, note recommendations for early, mid-season, and late types. Early varieties are bred for higher germination in cooler spring soils. Northern gardeners should look for short-season varieties.

Untreated seeds will rot or germinate poorly in cold, wet soil. Gardens that are mulched over the winter should have the hay or mulch pulled back to allow the soil to warm. A covering of black plastic will prewarm the soil. Cover the seedbed 2 weeks before planting and either remove the plastic or cut slits in rows where the seeds are to be sown. To get a head start in colder climates, sow seeds indoors in a seedling flat composed of cells no smaller than 2 inches in diameter. Keep in a warm, well-lit spot until seedlings are 2 to 3 inches tall and the weather is settled and frost free. Plant hardened-off seedlings as directed below.

STARTING

Outdoors, seed is planted in rich, fertile soil of pH 6.0 to 7.0, 1 inch deep (1½ inches in very hot weather), 4 inches apart, in rows 30 inches apart. Thin seedlings to eventually stand 6 to 10 inches apart. To ensure pollination, 3 or 4 parallel rows must be planted simultaneously. In the small garden, plant rows that are just 3 to 4 feet long. Corn can also be grown in a minimum of 4 hills, 2 feet apart, to make a square. Sow 6 seeds per hill, thinned to the 3 strongest seedlings. Corn plants have deep, extensive roots that require generous space.

All plant growth slows in late summer's shorter days. Schedule midsummer plantings to provide extra days. For example, in an area with an expected first frost of October 15, plant an 80-day variety no later than July 5, allowing 20 extra days for 100 days total.

CULTURAL REQUIREMENTS

The rapid, lush growth of a towering corn plant requires ample moisture and fertile soil. Shallow cultivation is necessary to avoid damaging surface roots. When the weather turns hot and soils begin to dry, apply mulch to maintain moisture and choke weeds. "Suckers," the side growth at the base of plants, do no harm and need not be removed from corn plants. In windy locations, you can prevent toppling by hilling up 2 to 3 inches of soil at the plant base.

Squash and pumpkins are good companions for corn and will shade out weeds if their vines are encouraged to run in the corn rows. This is only an effective technique where the beans and squash can be planted later than the corn. If planted at the same time or earlier, the vigorous bean and squash vines could smother the young corn seedlings.

To aid pollination for small plantings, clip off the pollen-bearing tassels atop each plant and shake them over or lay them across the corn silks. This will also relieve old frustrations for those never chosen to be on the cheerleading squad.

HARVEST

Harvest when corn silks are brown and dry and the kernels are full. Peeking is okay, but not encouraged, since loose husks invite pests and birds. Regular varieties of sweet corn should be picked while the cooking water is boiling. Supersweets will keep their flavor and sweetness refrigerated for up to 10 days. Some of these varieties are actually sweeter 24 hours after picking than at harvest.

Cornstalks should be removed and shredded or composted after harvest to discourage disease and pest tenancy.

CULINARY TIPS

- *Try roasting corn for a nutty, different flavor. Pull off the outer husk, but leave the inner leaves and bake at 375°F. for 15 minutes.*
- *To grill corn, soak ears with inner husks on, in water for half an hour. Drain and grill over a low fire for about 10 minutes, rolling ears about for even cooking.*
- *Add corn kernels to omelets, cornbread, muffins, waffles, and pancakes.*
- *Make simple corn fritters with 2 cups of corn kernels, sliced off the cob, 2 beaten egg whites, ¼ cup cracker or matzoh meal, and ¼ cup milk. Drop onto a lightly oiled hot skillet, turning once. Serve with maple syrup.*

CUCUMBERS

Cucumbers add a refreshing, cooling note to salads and chilled soups. Sweet, firm, and crisp, with an edible, unwaxed peel, garden-grown cukes are far superior to supermarket fare. They are also remarkably easy to grow and quite prolific.

The four basic cucumber types are slicing, pickling, burpless, and mideastern. Look for disease-resistant varieties.

american slicing cucumbers are mostly vining types, 4 to 6 feet long, producing fruit best used fresh. Spacemaster is a dwarf variety, suitable for containers and small gardens, with vines that have a 2- to 3-foot spread. Marketmore 80 has been successful for me, with sweet fruits and vigorous, healthy vines.

pickling cucumbers are specifically bred to make crisp, flavorful pickles. Fruits are picked small, no longer than 4 to 5 inches. French Cornichon types should be picked when 1½ to 2 inches long.

burpless varieties produce thin-skinned, sweet fruits that are slow to mature and develop seeds. The larger fruits can be up to 15 inches long. Vines and fruit will perform best on a trellis. Try Rollinson's Telegraph or Suyo Long.

mideastern (beit alpha) varieties are particularly juicy, thin-skinned, and nonbitter cucumbers. Pick when 4 to 5 inches long, before seeds have hardened. Hylares is a refreshing, delicious cuke of this type that is not generally available commercially because it doesn't ship well. Seeds can be obtained from Shepherd's or Fedco.

STARTING

In short-season areas, start seeds indoors 1 month before the last possible frost date or when garden soil temperatures are consistently 65°F. or higher. Seedlings resent transplanting, so start seeds in peat pots or soil cells.

Outdoors, sow seeds or plant seedlings in a rich soil of pH 5.5 to 7.0, in rows with plants 12 inches apart; or in hills, 3 plants per hill, hills 4 feet apart. Train vines to grow up a trellis or fence to conserve garden space, hasten ripening, and avoid fruit rot. Rows that run from east to west will get the most available sunshine for quick growth and ripening.

CULTURAL REQUIREMENTS

Young seedlings are very frost tender. Hot caps or plastic jugs with the bottoms removed make good covers for early spring or cold nights.

With a water content of 95 percent, fruits require consistent watering during dry periods.

HARVEST

Harvest cucumbers often; like their cousin zucchini, they grow at an amazing rate, especially in the heat of summer. Pick fruits when they are no larger than the size indicated for that variety. All are at their best when the seeds haven't fully developed and the fruits are uniformly green without pale or yellow patches. At season's end, remove the vines to prevent them from harboring diseases and pests.

CULINARY TIPS

* *A remedy for bitter cucumbers is to cut off the stem end and peel the cucumbers including a thin layer of the white flesh just beneath the skin.*
* *Stuff seeded cucumbers with an Herbed Cheese Spread (p. 259).*
* *We like to serve cucumber salads as a refreshing counterpoint to hot spicy dishes. Toss cucumber slices with one of the Vinaigrette Dressings (p. 244).*
* *Chilled potato or tomato soups get a refreshing lift from puréed or diced cucumber.*
* *Toss linguini or thin Asian noodles with sesame or peanut butter dissolved in warm water and combined with minced garlic, chopped fresh cilantro, scallions, mild vinegar, hot chilies, diced cucumber, and soy sauce.*
* *To keep cucumber slices crisp, salt. Then place in a colander and weight with enough pressure to squeeze out excess juices. This will also remove any bitterness.*

EGGPLANT

The eggplant is a decidedly ornamental vegetable, with its shiny, pendent, black-purple fruits and star-shaped lavender flowers.

The most familiar types are the Mediterranean eggplants, cylindrical with fat bottoms. Asian varieties, smaller and more slender, are worth growing in short-season areas for their early bearing and ability to set fruit in cooler weather. I've had good results with Orient Express, available from Johnny's Selected Seeds. Some exotic types ranging in color from pure white to stripes are available from The Cook's Garden; Violette di Firenza is a lustrous lavender- or white-striped variety. Casper, from Stokes Seeds, is a white-skinned and -fleshed eggplant with markedly sweet flavor.

STARTING

Eggplant seeds germinate best in soil temperatures between 80°F. and 90°F. If necessary, sow seeds indoors 8 to 10 weeks before planting using heating cables, mats, or lamps for consistent warmth. After germination, 70°F. soil temperatures will suffice. Transplant to the garden when nights are consistently above 50°F., in soil of pH 6.0 to 7.0, 24 inches apart in rows 30 inches apart. Grow where other nightshade-family plants (tomatoes, potatoes, peppers) have not grown for 2 years.

CULTURAL REQUIREMENTS

Black plastic mulch and heat-retaining row covers help extend the warm conditions on which eggplant thrives. Remove row covers periodically in the daytime so that pollination can occur.

HARVEST

Pick fruits as soon as they're ripe; they'll be glossy and full. A dull finish indicates overripe eggplants of inferior flavor and quality. Use a sharp knife to cut the fruits from the brittle, easily damaged stems.

- *Presalting eggplant before cooking is a common technique to remove bitter juices. Ripe fruits from the garden should not need this treatment. Exceptions would include dishes where a dry eggplant is desired, such as breaded, fried slices for eggplant parmigiana. Lightly salt slices and place in a colander, with some plates or other weight on top to express juices. Allow to drain about 1 hour. Rinse, pat dry, and proceed with your recipe.*
- *Eggplant is one of the few vegetables that we prefer to slightly overcook. Crunchy eggplant ranks with raw potatoes for unappetizing texture and taste.*
- *Skinning eggplants will yield a more delicate flavor, but it's not a crucial step in most dishes.*
- *Marinate strips of steamed or baked eggplant in one of the Vinaigrette Dressings (p. 244).*
- *We could bake and stuff eggplant with a different filling every day of the week. Prebake eggplant on a covered baking tray until the flesh is tender. Mash it a bit with the tines of a fork and scoop filling on top. Bake again to heat through. A few filling possibilities:*

  Couscous, pine nuts, currants, scallions, mint, and parsley
  Sautéed mushrooms, bread crumbs, tarragon, and Dijon mustard
  Bulgur wheat, tomato, bell and chili peppers, cilantro, and olives
  Sautéed tofu, rice, shiitake mushrooms, soy sauce, ginger, and garlic
  One of the Herbed Cheese Spreads (p. 259) and rice
  Sautéed chopped fennel bulb and basil, croutons, and Parmesan cheese
- *Mix puréed roasted eggplant (p. 215) with lemon juice, tahini, and minced garlic to make Baba Ganoush, a dip for pita bread and veggie sticks.*

THE
MOOSEWOOD
RESTAURANT
KITCHEN
GARDEN

38

FENNEL

Fennel, or *finnochio,* is a common vegetable in Italian markets from late summer through winter. Its popularity has widened recently as part of an increased awareness of Italian cooking. Feathery, divided foliage tops celerylike stems that widen at the base to form a bulb. The bulb has a sweet anise flavor, with a background taste of celery. Zefa Fino, from Johnny's Selected Seeds, and Romy, from Shepherd's, are two varieties of this uncommon vegetable. An herb, *Foeniculum vulgare,* is also known as fennel (p. 97).

STARTING

Sow seeds in late spring for an early-fall harvest, allowing 3 growing months before harvest. Plant seeds in rich soil, ½ inch deep, in rows 18 inches apart. Thin plants to 8 inches apart.

CULTURAL REQUIREMENTS

Keep plants well watered during dry spells. When the stalks are a foot tall, blanch the stems by hilling up the soil around the base. This will result in a more tender vegetable.

HARVEST

Bulbs are ready for harvest when they're 2 to 3 inches in diameter.

CULINARY TIPS

• *Thinly sliced raw bulb is a classic ingredient of antipasto platters. Include them in tossed salads for an unusual touch.*
• *Combine thin-sliced rounds of fennel and orange with a few drops of lemon juice and chopped mint and lemon balm leaves for a refreshing salad.*
• *Blanch fennel halves for 5 minutes in water or stock and then broil, topped with Parmesan and mozzarella cheeses and chopped oregano or marjoram.*
• *Add fennel to soups, sauces, stews, and roasted and marinated vegetables for a light anise flavor.*

KOHLRABI

An odd-looking member of the cabbage family, kohlrabi looks like a leafy turnip growing aboveground. Its nutty-sweet flavor and crisp applelike texture make this unfamiliar, underappreciated vegetable well worth growing.

STARTING

Sow seeds in early spring in soil of pH 6.0 to 7.5, ½ inch deep, in rows 18 inches apart. Thin plants to stand 4 to 6 inches apart. In warm-winter areas sow in late summer to fall for winter harvests.

CULTURAL REQUIREMENTS

Kohlrabi is a cool-weather crop; its culture is the same as for broccoli (p. 24).

HARVEST

"Bulbs" (which are actually thickened stems) are ready for harvest when 2 to 2½ inches in diameter. Thicker stems will be tough and fibrous. An exception is an unusual variety, Gigante, offered by Nichols Garden Nursery. At 8 to 10 inches in diameter, Gigante will generously serve a large gathering of kohlrabi fanciers. With all kohlrabi, cut the plants instead of pulling, to spare neighboring roots.

CULINARY TIPS

• *Peeled and grated bulbs are a crunchy, sweet addition to leafy and raw vegetable salads. Mix with grated carrots, apples, or beets and dress with a Vinaigrette Dressing (p. 244) or Herbed Mayonnaise (p. 248).*
• *Thin slices make an excellent crudité with other vegetables for dips.*
• *For a simple side dish, steam slices and top with butter and chives or dill.*

LEEKS

Leeks are the gentlest and sweetest members of the onion family. Their subtle flavor harmonizes with and creates a good background for more dominant notes. Long popular in Europe, leeks command high prices in U.S. markets and are still considered a specialty vegetable. They're not difficult to grow, but require some special attention. The 2- to 3-foot-tall plants have blue-green straplike foliage that contrasts nicely with the rounder, softer foliage forms of lettuce, cabbage, or other vegetables and herbs. King Richard is a nicely flavored, early-maturing leek for summer and fall use. I grow Nebraska for late-fall/early-winter harvest.

STARTING

In cold-weather areas, start seeds indoors from February to March, sowing seeds ¼ inch deep in flats. Seeds can be sown outdoors in early spring in soil of pH 6.0 to 8.0, in rows 18 inches apart; however, germination can be slow and uneven.

CULTURAL REQUIREMENTS

Leeks are more tender if the stems are blanched. This can be accomplished in a number of ways:
• Sow seeds or plant transplants in a trench 6 inches wide by 6 inches deep. As the plants grow, gradually replace the soil that was removed.
• Plant seedlings 2 inches lower than they were grown in the seed flat. Bank the stems with compost, well-rotted manure, or hay. Continue throughout the growing season.
• Plant seedlings in 6-inch holes, burying all but 1 to 2 inches of green leaf. Don't firmly tamp the soil around the plants, but allow it to fill in by the action of rain or irrigation.
  Regardless of which blanching method you use, the stalks should eventually be banked with 10 inches of soil (measured from root zone up).
  Mulching leeks keeps the soil evenly moist and weed-free.

HARVEST

Leeks can be harvested at any time. The whites and the greens of young leeks can be used like scallions. More mature plants, however, have tough, leathery outer leaves, so only the white blanched stem and tender inner greens are eaten.

In mild-winter areas, leeks may remain in the garden through the cold season to be picked as needed. Be sure to harvest them all before warm weather returns. Where temperatures consistently remain below freezing, harvest leeks and store refrigerated or in a cool cellar. You can also cover the row with about a foot of hay or straw to prevent the ground from freezing hard. Mark the row with an old cornstalk or sunflower stem or you might find yourself traipsing around through snow drifts trying to locate lost leeks. On a frigid, scentless winter day, it's a real treat to shovel away the snow, pick up the hay, and smell and feel the earth once again as you harvest leeks.

CULINARY TIPS

• *It's important to rinse leeks carefully, as soil and grit tend to lodge in the multilayered stem. Cut off the roots and tough leaves, slice the leeks in half lengthwise, then rinse, allowing the water to run through all the stem layers.*

• *Use leeks where a flavor more delicate than bulb onions is desired: in soups, omelets, sauces, fillings, stews, marinated salads, or as a side dish.*

• *Avoid using the green parts of leeks in puréed dishes, such as tomato soup, where the green will contribute to a muddied color. All of the green leaves, including the tough ones, are suitable as stock vegetables.*

• *Leeks are particularly good in puréed soups and cream sauces. As they cook and soften, they "melt" to a smooth texture.*

• *At Moosewood, we serve the first "baby" leeks of the season whole, steamed, and marinated, tied in bundles using a long green outer leaf as "ribbon."*

LETTUCE

Lettuce is the centerpiece of salads at Moosewood. When fresh local produce is available, our salads become celebrations of taste, texture, and visual appeal.

Seed catalogs list an increasingly wider variety of types: leaf or looseleaf, butterhead, romaine or cos, batavian, or crisphead (such as iceberg), with leaves that are wavy, curly, or frilled. Colors range from bright lime to dark green, some tinged with light to deep ruby reds.

Home gardeners can choose delicate varieties that aren't available in markets because of their difficulty to ship. Some that we have enjoyed include Red Boston, Canasta, Pirat, Merveille des Quatre Saisons, Royal Oak Leaf, and Lollo Rossa. Canasta and Royal Oak Leaf have done well in midsummer planting here proving to be genuinely bolt resistant and not bitter. Seed companies recommend varieties according to season: spring, summer, fall, and greenhouse, as well as those suitable for overwintering. For gardeners excited about lettuce possibilities, The Cook's Garden lists over fifty kinds.

STARTING

Seeds can be sown outdoors as soon as the ground can be worked, in soil of pH 6.0 to 7.0, ¼ to ½ inch deep (deeper in warmer weather), in rows 18 inches apart. Young thinnings can go into salads, particularly French "mesclun" salads that combine young multicolored greens, herb sprigs (chervil, parsley, tarragon), and wild greens (dandelion, chicory) (p. 61).

Plant short (3 to 4 feet) rows of each type if you're not planning on an abundant harvest all at once. Seeds can be sown throughout the cooler growing season, but lettuce doesn't germinate well in temperatures above 80°F. Lettuces quickly reach maturity in the first warmth of spring. For midsummer plantings, heat-resistant varieties could be sown in small peat pots or soil cells in a cooler, shaded area. Transplant seedlings on a cloudy, calm day and water generously.

Sow seeds for fall-winter types about a month before the first frost, or, in hot climates, when cool fall weather arrives. Cover the small plants with a floating row cover before hard freezes. Suprisingly, I have grown lettuce in my zone 5 garden through an erratic winter with little or no insulating snow cover and no more protection than a row cover. Only with varieties adapted to short-day growing, such as Winter Density, Rouge d'Hiver, or Winter Marvel, should this technique be tried in cold-weather areas.

Plastic tunnels (p. 191) are good season extenders for lettuce crops early in the spring or in the late fall.

CULTURAL REQUIREMENTS

Lettuce has shallow roots and benefits from a moist (but not soggy), rich soil. Mulching is advantageous in the heat of summer, but may attract slugs in damp, cooler weather. Summer plantings can be made where the lettuce will be partially shaded by taller plants such as corn, asparagus, tomatoes, or trellised beans or cucumbers. Shade netting will also keep lettuce cool. Frequent watering in hot, dry weather is crucial to avoid a stressed and bitter crop.

Lettuces can be interplanted in mixed flower, vegetable, or herb borders where their fringed, savoyed, or color-tipped leaves provide a foreground for taller plants. Follow a late-spring to early-summer harvest with bedding plant annuals or a later-maturing ornamental basil.

HARVEST

Heads of lettuce are best cut in the morning, plunged in cold water, drained, and refrigerated to retain sweeter flavor and crispness. Leaf lettuces can be cut whole, or by pulling off the outermost leaves, keeping the growing center intact.

CULINARY TIPS

• *Wash whole lettuce leaves in a large pot or basin filled with cool water. Allow them to dry in a colander or between dish towels, or use a salad spinner. Tear leaves by hand, or use a stainless steel knife. Iron knives or cleavers will leave a rusty stain on lettuce leaves.*

• *Use the most decorative large leaves of lettuce as beds on platters of other foods or as wrappers for grilled fish fillets, crepes, cheese spreads, and firm dips.*

• *Create a late-spring soup with spinach and lettuce cooked until they're wilted, then puréed with some of the cooking liquid, scallions, mint, tarragon, and milk or cream.*

• *When I'm in a hurry, the simplest, quickest, and tastiest way of dressing a salad is the Italian style—merely drizzled with olive oil and vinegar. Try extra virgin oil and an herbed, fruited, or balsamic vinegar.*

• *Here's a favorite vinaigrette dressing that won't overwhelm the delicate flavors of the greens:*

1 CUP VEGETABLE OIL (PART OR ALL OLIVE)

⅓ CUP BALSAMIC VINEGAR

1 TABLESPOON DIJON MUSTARD

1 TABLESPOON CHOPPED FRESH TARRAGON *OR* CHERVIL

1 TABLESPOON CHOPPED CHIVES OR GARLIC CHIVES

SALT AND FRESHLY GROUND BLACK PEPPER TO TASTE

MELONS

Refreshing and fragrantly sweet, melons are a late-summer, early-fall treat here in Ithaca. Though technically a fruit, melons are included here since they are planted annually as are most vegetable crops. The sprawling vines need a lot of room, since they can spread 6 to 10 feet.

cantaloupe We have gotten excellent melons from Laurie Todd of the Melon Foundation in nearby Lansing. Summit, Superstar, and particularly Gold Star are her recommended cantaloupe varieties for short-season areas. Seeds are available from Harris Seeds.

honeydew are tricky to grow in cool, damp climates; the fruits tend to crack open. I have had good luck with Earlidew, an early-maturing melon. Galia is a new, green-fleshed, sweetly aromatic melon that will set fruit in short-season areas.

watermelon Yellow Baby and Sugar Baby are two "Icebox" or manageably sized watermelons with sweet flavor and relatively early ripening for all areas. Mix Yellow Baby with red watermelon, cantaloupe, and honeydew for festive fruit salads.

STARTING

Gardeners in cool climates will need to start seeds indoors in 3-inch peat pots, 1 month before the last frost. Sow 5 seeds per pot, thinning to 3 plants per pot. Seeds need 75°F. soil temperatures for good germination. Transplant seedlings after last frost in rich soil of pH 6.0 to 7.5 supplemented with compost or manure. Plant 3 seedlings per hill, in hills 3 feet by 6 feet apart, or in rows with each seedling 18 inches apart, 3 feet between rows. In warm climates, seeds can be sown directly in the garden.

CULTURAL REQUIREMENTS

The use of black plastic, hot caps, and row covers will help maintain the warm soil that melons need. Soil moisture is more important when fruits are forming than after they have set, when dry conditions are better for ripening. Trellising (p. 46) is recommended in damp climates, because the fruit is better exposed to sunlight and kept away from moist soil. Each fruit must be supported in a "sling" made of a section of mesh produce bag, netting, or slightly tattered hosiery.

HARVEST

Cantaloupes are ready when they are aromatic and pressure applied to the junction of stem and fruit causes the fruit to separate.

Honeydews are ready to be cut from the vine when the rind begins to turn yellow. Allow the fruits to ripen in a warm kitchen for a few days, until they develop a fruity scent.

Ripe watermelons will make a deep, hollow sound when thumped, have a yellow spot at the base of the fruit resting on the ground, and dry brown tendrils closest to the junction of stem and vine.

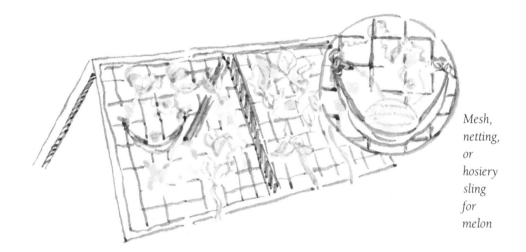

Mesh, netting, or hosiery sling for melon

Portable Trellis

CULINARY TIPS

• *Homegrown melons picked when fully ripe need no further attention or special procedures. They're a sweet, fragrant addition to fruit soups and smoothies.*

O K R A

Though long considered solely a Southern or hot-climate vegetable, okra can grow well in the North. Annie Oakley, available from Johnny's Selected Seeds and Burpee, is a compact, short-season variety for Northern growers. Clemson Spineless is an old standard that I like. Related to the hibiscus and hollyhocks, okra shares their pretty flowers and interesting leaf shapes. Plant height varies from dwarf 2-foot varieties to taller ones at 5 feet.

STARTING

In cool climates, start seeds indoors about 1 month before the last frost in 2- to 3-inch peat pots, 2 seeds per pot. Soil temperature of 80°F. to 90°F. is necessary for good germination, so use heat mats or coils. Thin seedlings to 1 per pot and place in the garden 2 weeks after the last frost, in soil of pH 6.0 to 8.0. Plant dwarf varieties 12 inches apart, taller types 18 inches apart, with 2 feet between rows. Direct seed ½ inch deep when soil temperatures are at least 70°F. Black plastic and row covers will maintain soil warmth in Northern gardens.

HARVEST

The immature seed pods are ready when they are between 2 and 3 inches in length. Frequent picking is necessary to ensure a long harvest and to avoid older, leathery fruits.

C U L I N A R Y   T I P S

• *Okra is indispensable in Creole gumbos and much of the cooking of tropical Africa. The sliced pods make a good addition to soups, stews, and sautés. Whole pods are a unique addition in tempura.*
• *Avoid overcooking. Mushy okra is not a pretty sight and has an unpleasant slimy texture.*
• *Cook okra in stainless steel or other nonreactive cookware. Aluminum or cast iron will give it an off-flavor.*
• *Dip okra in beaten egg and seasoned cornmeal; fry until tender.*

ONIONS

As Julia Child has so eloquently stated, "It is hard to imagine civilization without the onion." We always start off our day at Moosewood cutting onions: they're included in almost every dish on the menu!

Types of onions to consider growing include:

baby or pearl onions are quick-maturing small bulbs, elegant served whole with marinated vegetables, and in salads, brochettes, stews, and stir-fries, or pickled. Peel after blanching whole baby onions in boiling water for 1 minute. Sow seeds as for storage onions below.

red onions are mildly flavored bulbs that also lend interesting color to salads and sandwiches. Slice into horizontal rings for the prettiest effect. Sow seeds as for storage onions below.

scallions or bunching onions will not produce bulbs. Sow in early spring for summer harvest, midsummer for fall or winter harvest, and fall in mild climates for early-spring harvest.

spanish onions and other sweet varieties are available for different seasons and regions of the country. Short-day types such as Vidalia are grown in the cool winters of the Deep South. Seeds are sown fall through December for early- to late-spring harvest. Walla Walla Sweet is sown in late summer and harvested early the following summer. It can be overwintered in areas with a minimum temperature of 0°F.

Northern growers should sow seeds indoors from January through February, transplanting in early spring, as soon as the soil is workable. Sweet onions need to start in cool weather with plenty of moisture and low-sulfur soils.

Unless specifically noted, Sweet Spanish onions are not intended for storage.

storage onions are generally more pungent than sweet onions, because the chemical that irritates the eye also preserves the onion. A few Sweet Spanish types that store well include: Ringmaker, Ailsa Craig, and Sweet Sandwich (which mellows in storage). Copra is a standard storage onion that has proven to be one of the best long-term keepers. Seeds can be started in flats indoors or as early as the soil is workable outdoors.

STARTING

Onions can be started from seed or by purchasing "sets," small bulbs that will mature to full-size onions. Seed-grown onions offer a wider range of possible varieties, while sets are usually limited to what's popular and dependable in your area. Growing sets has the advantage of saving you time and yielding an earlier harvest.

Sow seeds in the garden (see list above for appropriate times) in a light, fertile soil of pH 5.5 to 7.0, 1 to 2 seeds per inch, ¼ to ½ inch deep, in rows 12 to 18 inches apart. Thin to eventually stand 3 to 4 inches apart or no less than 4 inches for larger Spanish types.

Sets are planted in early spring at a 3- to 4-inch spacing, in rows 12 to 18 inches apart. To have a harvest of both scallions and bulbing onions, plant sets 2 inches apart, pulling every other onion while it's young and green. The remaining onions can be grown on to "bulbhood" for storage or immediate use.

CULTURAL REQUIREMENTS

Onions are shallow-rooted and need ample protection from invasive weeds between rows. Mulch at the onset of hot weather to keep soil cool and moist; irrigate if necessary.

HARVEST

Onions are ready for eating at any point. To harvest for storage, check for tops that have yellowed and fallen over. When at least half of the crop has fallen tops, knock down the rest of them (with a hoe or rake) to promote ripening. When the leaf tops brown, pull up the onions and leave them uncut, covered by the tops, to cure in the sun for 3 to 5 days. If the weather is rainy, cure on a covered porch or in a well-ventilated shed or garage. When dry and cured, cut off all but 1 inch of the tops and keep in mesh bags or slatted boxes in a cool (ideally 35°F. to 40°F.), non-freezing, dry, ventilated spot. Don't store with apples, since the fruit gives off ethylene gas which will cause onions to sprout. Smaller onions can be braided at the brown-leaf stage and hung in a cool spot.

CULINARY TIPS

• *Short-term refrigeration of onions will reduce the pungency that provokes tearing.*
• *The easiest way to peel onions is to first cut off the root and stem ends, slice in half, and peel off the skin and one or two top layers.*

- *Use a separate cutting board for chopping onions or garlic. It can be deodorized with lemon juice or plain vinegar.*
- *Slow-cooked onions develop a mellow sweetness due to the caramelized vegetable sugars. Sauté onions on a low heat in a heavy skillet with oil or butter. Cook covered 20 minutes, then uncover and cook half an hour. They'll make a great filling for crepes, omelets, stuffed vegetables, and casseroles; a topping for pizzas; a base for onion soup; or a pasta sauce. Combine with other vegetables and herbs, or use as is.*
- *Finely chopped raw onions and minced chilies with some lime juice or vinegar makes a fiery condiment for foods needing an extra jolt.*

PARSNIPS

Parsnips add a sweet, earthy flavor to soups, sautés, and stews. We've noticed this nutritious root vegetable adds a homey, comforting quality to fall and winter dishes.

STARTING

Use fresh seeds every year and start early. Parsnip is a fall vegetable that requires a full growing season of at least 110 days. It's also slow to germinate; try soaking seeds overnight before early- to late spring sowing in a sandy, stonefree loam of pH 6.0 to 8.0. Sow ½ inch deep, in rows 12 inches apart. Thin plants to eventually stand 3 inches apart. To avoid a crust forming on the soil, cover with moistened burlap or lightly strewn straw or grass clippings.

CULTURAL REQUIREMENTS

A deep-rooted plant, parsnip requires a deeply cultivated soil that's not heavy. The use of manure or fertilizer may result in hairy or divided roots.

HARVEST

Dig parsnips after one or more light frosts, since extreme cold improves flavor by converting more of the carbohydrates to sugar, yielding sweeter roots. Parsnips should be dug carefully; pulling may break the roots from the crown. Roots not dug before the hard freeze can be harvested in early spring before growth restarts.

CULINARY TIPS

• *Bake sliced parsnips in a covered casserole with enough orange juice to barely cover them. When the parsnips are almost tender, uncover so the juices thicken.*
• *Cook parsnips and potatoes in water to cover until they're tender. Drain, then purée in a food mill or processor. If using a processor, quickly switch it on and off until the mixture is smooth. (Potatoes get "gluey" when they're continually processed.) Add butter and a pinch or two of freshly grated nutmeg.*

PEAS

For many gardeners, peas are the first vegetable planted each spring. Superbly flavored, fresh garden peas are also high in protein, and vitamins A, the Bs, and C. Peas do best with a cool, early start and will not set flower buds in hot weather.

Types of peas include: green or shelled peas, petit pois (baby peas), snap peas, snow peas, and soup or dried peas.

green shelled peas are familiar to all, more often than not, frozen or canned. Freshly picked peas are by weight a quarter sucrose, which rapidly converts to carbohydrates. This explains why so many peas are gobbled up in the garden before they arrive in the kitchen. Maestro is a disease-resistant, early, and delicious green pea. Wando extends the pea season by bearing crops in weather warmer than most peas will tolerate.

A new type of semileafless green shelled pea Novella has 18- to 24-inch vines with a preponderance of curling tendrils that hold the vines up off the ground without any other support. I've grown this pea and enjoyed having one less garden task in a season that's always too busy.

petit pois, the authentic tiny French peas, are available from The Cook's Garden, Shepherd's, or Burpee. They are particularly sweet.

snap peas are a relatively new vegetable. Like snow peas, they have edible pods but taste better when the peas are larger. Most varieties have strings that must be removed, an activity well suited for a comfortable rocker on a shady porch, or a good old movie on TV. Sugar Snap has an excellent sweet flavor and bears long and abundantly in my garden. It can grow as high as 5 to 6 feet and will need a fence or trellis for support. Sugar Ann is an equally sweet variety, but more compact at 18 to 30 inches tall.

snow peas, picked when the peas have just started to form in the pods, make a sweet, crisp, quickly cooked vegetable, delicious alone or in many Asian stir-fried dishes.

soup or dried peas are for gardeners with plenty of space and/or interest in putting things by for the winter months. Johnny's Selected Seeds' variety Holland Capucijners has the added bonus of being ornamental, with fragrant violet-red and pink flowers.

STARTING

Plant seeds in early spring as soon as the soil can be worked. Get a jump on the season by preparing the row on a sunny fall day. Soil should be loose and well-drained with a pH between 6.0 and 7.0. Use a nitrogen inoculant for all types of peas, since it will help fix nitrogen in the soil by introducing beneficial bacteria. Plant in rows or bands 18 inches apart for dwarf types and 4 feet apart for trellised, taller varieties. Sow seeds ½ to 1 inch deep (plant deeper in warmer, drier soil), with seeds 1 to 2 inches apart.

CULTURAL REQUIREMENTS

For bushy varieties shorter than 3 feet, insert pieces of brush along the row to help keep the vines off the ground. Rotate crops from year to year to avoid soil and plant diseases.

Sowings for a fall crop can be made in mild, cool-summer areas, about 60 days before the first expected frost. Crops will not be as bountiful in the shorter days of fall. Gardeners in frost-free areas can grow peas fall through winter if temperatures stay above 30°F. with average maximum day temperatures below 75°F.

HARVEST

Peas must be harvested often, at least every other day. I've always thought that genetic engineers should create a red-leafed pea plant to facilitate picking the green pods from the leafy vines. As consolation for his hard work, the pea-picker *does* get first dibs on all those succulent sweet peas.

• *Snow and snap peas will need to have fibrous strings removed. Grasp the stem end and pull down the string running along the pod's straighter side.*

• *Freshly shelled peas are best used in delicately seasoned dishes where their subtle flavor won't be overwhelmed:*

Combine them with the first small white onions, new potatoes, and a little chopped mint.

Toss with a "baby" pasta, such as pastina or orzo, butter, and a bit of grated Parmesan cheese.

Use as part of a filling for Timbales (p. 239), a savory baked custard.

Add to lightly seasoned rice or grain pilafs.

• *Snap and snow peas give a larger yield of vegetables per foot of garden row and can be used more lavishly than shelled peas. At Moosewood we use them in marinated salads, pasta sauces, stews, stir-fries, and sautéed or blanched on their own as a side dish. Blanched snow peas need less than a minute in boiling water; snap peas, being denser, perhaps 2 minutes. Cut the pods so they're in proportion to the other foods in a dish; for example, long pods would be awkward in a pasta sauce where other vegetables are sliced.*

• *Lemon juice or vinegar used to dress a salad containing green, snap, or snow peas will discolor them; reserve until serving time.*

• *Last spring in a San Francisco restaurant I sampled young shoots of pea vines, a tender, sweet delicacy. They were simply and quickly stir-fried with garlic and soy sauce. Since peas are planted early, when there's a lot of garden space, put in a few rows to be quickly harvested as 6- to 8-inch shoots. Make sure you are harvesting green pea vines and not those of flowering sweet peas. The latter are poisonous.*

PEPPERS

Peppers were cultivated in the New World long before the arrival of Europeans. Sixteenth- and seventeenth-century explorers brought hot and sweet peppers back to the rest of the world. Before then, there was no paprika in Hungary, nor any fiery chili peppers in the cuisines of Asia.

Pepper plants are a handsome addition to mixed borders of flowers, herbs, and vegetables. The medium-high bushy plants have glossy deep green foliage, white flowers, and fruit that can be green, gold, red, chocolate brown, or purple. Lipstick, available from Johnny's Selected Seeds, is a delicious, prolific variety for short-season, cool areas where red peppers aren't easily grown. We've also enjoyed Gypsy from Burpee and Sweet Chocolate from The Cook's Garden and Johnny's Selected Seeds.

Peppers require at least 2 months' warm weather after seedlings have been transplanted, before the first fruits are ready for harvest. They will not produce well where nighttime temperatures are regularly below 55°F.

STARTING

Sow seeds indoors, about 8 to 10 weeks before outside temperatures will be consistently warm. Seeds will germinate poorly in cool conditions, so soil temperature should be 75°F. or higher. When true leaves develop, transplant seedlings 3 inches apart in flats or into 3- to 4-inch containers. Plants grown at 70°F. day and 60°F. night temperatures will be sturdy and not leggy. Set plants in moderately rich soil of pH 5.5 to 7.0 when nights are generally above 50°F. and frosts are no longer a threat. Cold temperature causes bud drop, which may result in no fruit. Space peppers 12 inches apart and rows 24 inches apart. Rich soil that's too high in nitrogen will produce lush, green foliage with few peppers.

Plant hot peppers at opposite ends of the garden from sweet peppers to avoid cross-pollination. Hot peppers will be the spiciest in hot weather, but tend to be more tolerant of cooler and drier conditions.

CULTURAL REQUIREMENTS

High yields of fruit can be achieved with the addition of a high-phosphorus fertilizer such as rock phosphate. To minimize plant diseases, rotate crops and avoid growing peppers in the same location year after year.

Obtaining sweet, fully ripe peppers may depend upon the use of season extenders (p. 191) in cool areas.

Blossoms and young fruits will drop when the weather is extremely hot and dry, however plants will set new buds with increased humidity.

HARVEST

Bell peppers can be picked at any stage, but will be sweeter, thicker, and more flavorful at their ripest. Use a knife or shears to cut the fruits, as the brittle stems break easily. Here in the usually cool summers of Ithaca, far too few peppers reach the glorious, glossy red stage before the frosts. Harvesting some of the first peppers at the green stage will stimulate more fruit production. Then be patient and allow remaining fruits to ripen fully to red, orange, gold, purple, or chocolate brown.

Harvest chili peppers, green or red, when they are full-sized.

C U L I N A R Y   T I P S

* *Lisa Wichman is our chief advocate for cooking with fresh chili peppers. Some of us are tempted to use the more convenient dried cayenne pepper, but fresh chilies lend a fuller, more complex flavor. Her advice for handling: The seeds and inner membranes of chili peppers are the hottest parts. Make sure to wash your hands thoroughly after handling chilies. Some people wear rubber gloves when handling the hottest peppers.*

* *The hotness of chili peppers varies widely. These varieties are commonly available and listed in order of hotness from the volcanic to merely perky: Habanero, Serrano, Super Chili, Cayenne, Jalapeño, Mexi Bell, Anaheim, and Ancho.*

* *Small, very hot peppers can be added whole or halved to sautés and stir-fries. Toss with the warmed oil before adding other ingredients; they will season the whole dish but can be removed later by those choosing not to eat a very hot pepper.*

* *Chilies are traditionally used in the cuisines of the Caribbean, Latin America, Asia, and Africa, but can be incorporated into other dishes as well. We find that even a small amount of chopped fresh chili adds a zip that picks up food without making it spicy. Try using less salt and compensate with the chilies.*

* *For many years, Dixie Merilahti had a shop across the hall from Moosewood. This is a favorite snack of her invention that we shared together: crusty French bread, sweet butter, and sliced roasted peppers. To roast peppers, bake (p. 215) or grill (p. 237) and peel. The roasted peppers' lush smoothness and sweet flavor enlivens salads, fillings, sandwiches, or pasta sauces.*

• *The bell pepper's blocky, hollow shape invites stuffing. We often do, using a variety of fillings that include:*

> *Ricotta and Parmesan cheeses with bread crumbs, fresh basil, and grated nutmeg*
>
> *Corn and pinto beans with garlic, chili pepper, ground cumin, and coriander seeds*
>
> *Mushrooms, dill, and scallions, with cream, cottage, and cheddar cheeses*
>
> *Cooked, drained spinach with leeks, thyme, and Swiss cheese*
>
> *Rice pilaf with diced onions, carrots, parsnips, marjoram, pine nuts, currants, and a pinch of saffron*

Cut the peppers in half lengthwise and seed; leave the stems on to help the peppers hold their shape. Stuff the raw peppers with the cooked or prepared filling and place in a baking dish, adding about ½ inch of water or tomato juice to the bottom. Bake, tightly covered, at 375°F. for 40 minutes, or until peppers are tender.

• *Peperonata is a simple Italian stew with onions, peppers, and tomatoes sautéed with a splash of red wine and balsamic or herbal vinegar. Cook uncovered in a heavy skillet or pot until the vegetables are tender and most of the liquid has cooked down.*

• *Have a multicolored sauté using green, red, and gold peppers.*

• *Peppers sautéed with onions until softened on a gentle slow heat are a fragrant addition to omelets, fillings, open-faced sandwiches, sauces, and frittatas, or as a pizza topping.*

POTATOES

Originally from South America, the potato returned to the New World with Irish immigrants in the early eighteenth century. This most humble of vegetables is now generating a lot of attention as a specialty crop.

Gardeners with ample space and a cool growing season might want to try varieties not easily available in markets.

german yellow fingerlings Small potatoes good for salads, stews, or boiling, where their firm, waxy texture is an asset.

irish cobbler An early, all-purpose white variety that bears well and stores until March from a fall harvest.

peruvian purple A small purplish-white potato planted primarily by people with a penchant for purple.

red pontiac A red-skinned, all-purpose, reliable performer that keeps well.

yukon gold Wonderful new potatoes with a firm, yellow flesh. Adds a golden hue to mashed potatoes or puréed soups.

STARTING

Choose a spot where other nightshade family members (potatoes, tomatoes, eggplant, and peppers) have not been grown for a year or two. Ideal soil would be sandy, acidic loam, with a pH between 4.8 and 6.0, that is not overly fertile. Lime soils are hospitable to a scab fungus that damages the tubers.

Plant in the spring, as soon as the soil is workable. Buy seed potatoes that are certified disease-free; supermarket potatoes are usually treated to prevent sprouting. Cut potatoes to egg-size pieces with 1 to 2 eyes each. Allow them to dry in an airy location for 4 to 5 days before planting. Space seed potato pieces with the eyes pointing up, 1 foot apart, 3 to 4 inches deep, in rows 3 feet apart.

CULTURAL REQUIREMENTS

An acidic mulch of peat moss, pine needles, or pine-leaf mold will help conserve moisture, fight weeds, and prevent potatoes from developing the toxic green spots caused by exposure to light. If unmulched, potatoes should have dirt hilled up at the base of the plants. Potatoes are 75 percent water by weight, so ample moisture is important for good-sized tubers, but be sure the soil is well drained. Potatoes will not form at temperatures consistently above 85°F.

HARVEST

Pick new potatoes before the main crop by careful division. Gently dig at the base of the plant and remove a few spuds, leaving the rest to fully mature. Crops can be dug when the foliage has yellowed or died back. Potatoes can be left in the ground until hard frosts threaten, but earlier digging will prevent burrowing vermin damage. Dig on a sunny day, allowing the tubers to dry on the ground before storage. Store in a cool, dark location at 35°F to 45°F.

CULINARY TIPS

- *Organically grown potatoes need only be scrubbed in preparation for cooking. But in some dishes the slight sacrifice in nutrition caused by paring away the vitamins contained in the peels may be justified by improved appearance and texture.*
- *The eyes and green sections of potatoes are toxic and should be cut off and discarded.*
- *Potatoes appear in every conceivable form from soups to desserts (New Recipes from Moosewood Restaurant, Ten Speed Press, 1987, has a Russian Chocolate Torte with mashed potatoes a key ingredient).*

  Toss new potatoes with chopped fresh basil and butter or olive oil.

  Stuff baked potatoes with any of the Herbed Cheese Spreads (p. 259).

  Roast potatoes with one of the marinades for Grilled Vegetables (p. 237). Slice, coat with the marinade, and bake in a 375°F. oven, with the pan tightly covered, for 35 minutes. Uncover and bake another 30 minutes or until tender, stirring often.

  Sauté small cubes of potatoes with a choice of cilantro, dill, marjoram, rosemary, sage, savory, or thyme, and use as a filling for crepes or omelets. Or use fresh chili peppers, seeded and diced.

  Blend minced or pressed garlic with mashed potatoes. For a nuttier flavor, sauté the garlic until golden in a small amount of oil or butter.

RHUBARB

Rhubarb is an ornamental, long-lived perennial. The unique tart flavor of the stalks makes a delicious addition to dessert pies, sauces, and crisps. A cold-winter dormancy limits its growth to the northern half of the United States.

STARTING

Plant rhubarb in the early spring from root divisions obtained from a nursery or from other gardeners who may be happy to divide a mature, overgrown planting. Set the root 3 to 4 inches deep in fertile, well-drained soil generously supplemented with compost or aged manure. Select a permanent location where it won't be disturbed and where its bright red stalks and large, wavy, green and red leaves will be shown off. Soil should be prepared deeply, since rhubarb is a vigorous grower; a single plant can be 4 feet wide and 3 feet high.

CULTURAL REQUIREMENTS

Rhubarb is carefree and easily grown. Plants will bear more abundantly if they're well watered, mulched, and fed.

HARVEST

Refrain from harvesting any stalks the first year. A few can be picked the second year, and by the third year, plants are ready for a 2-month picking season. Stalks should be at least 10 inches long and 1 inch thick. Pull the stalk from the base of the plant with a slight twist, separating it from the plant crown. *Rhubarb leaves contain poisonous amounts of oxalic acid and should not be used raw or cooked. Stems are edible only when cooked.*

CULINARY TIPS

- *Add diced rhubarb to apple pies, rice and bread puddings, or fruit crisps for a tart accent.*
- *Serve stewed, sweetened rhubarb and sliced strawberries as a topping for yogurt or ice cream.*
- *Make a dessert sauce for shortcakes or pound cakes with diced rhubarb, all-fruit berry preserves, apple juice, and sugar or honey to taste.*

SALAD GREENS

There is a whole universe of green salads beyond the traditional lettuce and tomatoes. Try some of the greens listed below singly, in combination, or as an intriguing addition to a tossed salad. Many of them can also be cooked or used as a seasoning.

STARTING, CULTURAL REQUIREMENTS, AND HARVEST

arugula (rocket, rugula, roquette) Arugula has deep green, softly serrated leaves and an unusual toasted sesamelike flavor that is both peppery and nutty. It adds a sharp accent to salads when used in small quantities with other greens.

Plant through the early spring and again in late summer. Arugula tastes and grows best in cool weather. Sow seeds ½ inch deep; thin plants to 4 inches apart. Harvest the young leaves when they're 3 to 4 inches long, or whole, small plants 6 inches tall, for milder flavored greens. Older plants, especially ones that have bloomed, will be very pungent.

corn salad (mache, lamb's lettuce) The very delicate, tender leaves of corn salad have a mild, sweet, almost perfumed quality.

Sow seeds for cool-weather growing in early spring, late summer, or fall. Plants will overwinter in Northern areas if covered with mulch.

Thin plants to stand 3 inches apart. Harvest leaves or whole plants before warm weather arrives.

cress

garden cress These flat-leaved or curly greens provide a flavor similar to watercress but require less work. Sow seeds from early spring through fall for outdoor harvest. Plants are ready to pick in less than 2 weeks, when they're 2 to 3 inches tall. Pots of cress can be grown on sunny windowsills all year long.

watercress This green's perky tanginess enhances soups, sandwiches, and salads. Seeds should be started indoors in moist soil. Transplant seedlings to large pots of well-limed soil (pH 7.0), or, ideally, to a flowing stream's banks where water depth is about 6 inches. Pots should sit in pans of water that are changed daily.

endive

curly endive, or *friseé*.
With its deeply cut, frilled, crispy leaves, this endive adds beauty and character to salads. Though not commonly grown in the United States, I would highly recommend *friseé* to anyone's seed list. Trés Fin Marchiere from Shepherd's, Salad King from Johnny's Selected Seeds or Fine Curled from The Cook's Garden are all excellent varieties.

escarole (batavian endive)
This decorative green boasts broad, wavy, dark green leaves surrounding a tightly folded, buttery yellow center.

Use the young greens or heart, in mixed salads. Sauté mature plants Mediterranean-style in olive oil and garlic until wilted, or add shredded greens to brothy soups.

Sow seeds both for endives in the early spring or late summer for cool-weather growing. Plant seeds directly in the garden ½ inch deep; thin seedlings to eventually stand 6 to 8 inches apart.

Blanching heads a few days before harvest yields more tender and sweet endive. Tie the outer leaves over the head, or cover each with a paper bag or cardboard.

mesclun
A salad composed of a mixture of young, tender greens and herbs. Originally from Southern France and Northern Italy, mesclun's popularity has spread to upscale North American markets and restaurants. Trendiness aside, mesclun salads can be delightfully varied in personality. Any of the salad greens in this section, along with baby lettuces, kale, mizuna, pak choi, tatsoi, chard, and tender herb sprigs, can be mixed and matched to create colorful delicious salads. Tart, robust salads made primarily of endive, mustard, arugula, or cress may only need a drizzle of a good-tasting oil to be ready for the table. One or two kinds of tender herb sprigs, such as anise hyssop, basil, chervil, chives, dill, lovage, tarragon, or thyme, can be added in moderation so as not to overwhelm the more delicate greens. Garnish salads with edible flower blossoms.

Mesclun seed mixes are available from The Cook's Garden or Shepherd's Garden Seeds. Alternatively, make your own mixture of greens by thinning whatever is at the "baby" stage in the garden at a given moment. Plant short rows of lettuces and greens every couple of weeks to keep a season-long succession of young, varied salad material.

Sow seeds at the appropriate time for cool-season growth (similar to lettuce) in your climate. Plants should be lightly shaded and frequently watered as spring turns to summer. Harvest greens by snipping off the baby leaves just above the soil line. Plants that are watered and fertilized will continue to grow for another harvest in a few weeks.

radicchio
A member of the chicory family, radicchio is grown for its deep burgundy red and creamy white heads. Radicchio's bitterness is mellowed by the cool weather of spring, fall, or mild winters.

Choggia is a type that forms rounded heads. Varieties include Marina, Giulio, Alto, and Augusto.

Treviso types form elongated, conical heads. Plants are cut back in the fall, then the new growth is harvested in winter to early spring. Gardeners in cold-winter areas can grow Treviso types only with a generous layer of straw or hay mulch to cover the cut-back plants. Treviso varieties include Rossa di Treviso and Rossa di Verona.

Spring-seeded summer crops are viable where night temperatures are cool, below 60°F. Fall crops from mid- to late-summer seedings are more reliably bolt resistant in most parts of the United States.

Sow directly in the garden or indoors, in peat pots or soil cells, barely covering the seed with soil. Seeding in pots or cells placed in a cool, shady spot will be more successful if the weather is hot and dry. Germination ideally occurs in soil temperatures between 65°F. and 70°F.

Space plants 10 inches apart, in rows 18 inches apart, in well-drained, fertile soil. Keep soil moisture consistent; water during any dry periods, but not to the point of sogginess.

Choggia types are ready for harvest when the small (6 to 8 inches) heads are firm and no longer growing in size.

Treviso types that have overwintered should be harvested before warm weather arrives.

sorrel The bright green leaves of sorrel are prized for kitchen use in early spring and late fall. A tart soup using the lemony fresh new growth of sorrel is an early-spring favorite at Moosewood.

Because sorrel is perennial, plant only where it can grow undisturbed. Keep seed heads cut in summer to avoid unwanted seedlings all over the garden and to assure tender new leaf growth. Plants form vigorous rosettes with 9- to 12-inch-long leaves.

Sow seeds ½ inch deep, in rows 1½ feet apart. Thin plants to 8 inches apart. Harvest leaves only the first year; subsequently whole plants can be cut above the crown. Established sorrel is easily divided to share with friends.

CULINARY TIPS

- ARUGULA: *Add small amounts of arugula to cheese sandwiches or dips, pestos, soups, and other sauces.*
- CORN SALAD: *Use corn salad with other more assertive greens that will contrast with its subtle nature.*
- CRESS: *Add small quantities of peppery cresses to dips, omelets, salad dressings, and sauces.*

* RADICCHIO: *Create a varied salad with the slightly bitter quality of radicchio and the sweetness of ripe pears and sliced fennel bulb. Sprinkle with olive oil and balsamic vinegar.*

Sauté chopped or shredded radicchio briefly, and toss with pasta, rice, or white beans and freshly grated Parmesan cheese. Or use it as part of a pizza topping with tomatoes, cheeses, and olives.

Quickly grill or broil quarters of a head brushed with olive oil, herbs, and garlic for a zesty side dish.

The outer leaves of radicchio make a beautiful, bowl-shaped "container" for salads.

* SORREL: *Use it to add a zippy touch to salads, soups, sauces, dressings, and herb butters.*

SHALLOTS

Milder than its *Allium*-family relatives onion and garlic but sharing qualities of each, shallots are a classy, easily grown vegetable. Each single bulb planted in fall or early spring will provide 4 to 10 new bulbs. French shallots are the best-flavored variety. Their distinctive pinkish skins and flesh separates them from other types.

STARTING

Soil requirements are the same as for onions (p. 49). Plant bulbs 1 to 2 inches deep, 6 inches apart, in rows 1 foot apart. Bulbs planted in fall should be generously mulched where winter temperatures drop below 0°F. Remove the mulch in early spring, when the ground is no longer frozen.

CULTURAL REQUIREMENTS

The small bulbs can be easily overwhelmed by weeds. Hand weeding is necessary before the greens are large enough to be well mulched.

HARVEST

When the tops turn yellow, pull up the bulbs and air dry them in the garden for a few days. Store as for onions (p. 49). Shallots can also be wintered over in the garden, with mulching in colder areas. Smaller bulbs can be replanted for next year's harvest.

CULINARY TIPS

- *Shallots cook quickly to a soft texture, making them ideal for speedy sauces, sautés, or omelet and crepe fillings.*
- *Use minced raw shallots in dressings and marinades for a delicate onion flavor.*

SPINACH

It's funny how spinach, formerly the bane of childhood dinners, is now a favorite. We enjoy it in salads and blended into our Moosewood House Dressing, and dozens of dishes are enhanced by its mildly earthy flavor and bright verdancy.

Seeds are available for both smooth- and savoyed-leaved types. The savoyed varieties are prettier for salad greens, but their crinkled texture requires more careful washing and rinsing.

Tyee is a vigorous, heat-tolerant variety that has performed well in my garden for spring and early-summer crops. Winter Bloomsdale is a good standard spinach for fall planting.

STARTING

Spinach likes a cool, fertile soil of pH 6.0 to 7.0. Sow seeds as early as the soil can be worked, ½ inch deep, 1 inch apart, in rows 1 foot to 1½ feet apart. Thin plants initially to 3 inches apart, then 6 inches apart. Thinnings can be used in salads or cooked.

Fall crops can be grown in mild-summer areas by sowing seeds from mid-July through August. Seeds germinate poorly in very warm soil, so try refrigerating them between moist paper towels for 5 to 6 days before sowing. Seeds can be sown in September for overwintered plants. A mulch of straw or hay is advised for Northern areas. Southern gardeners can plant spinach through the fall and winter if temperatures remain above 25°F. and daily highs remain below 75°F.

CULTURAL REQUIREMENTS

Keep plants well watered during dry periods. A side dressing of compost or rotted manure will help maintain soil fertility and result in bushier plants.

HARVEST

Plants will bolt to seed in hot weather. Harvest single leaves and small plants at the beginning of the season, followed by whole mature plants later on.

C U L I N A R Y   T I P S

- *For recipes requiring quantities of cooked spinach, blanch the whole rinsed leaves in a generous amount of rapidly boiling water for 2 to 3 minutes. Drain, squeeze out excess water, and chop. This is easier to chop than bulky, raw spinach.*
- *Cook spinach until it's just wilted and still bright green. Overcooked spinach has a strong bitter taste and unappealing drab green color.*
- *Cooked spinach is an excellent addition to soups, sauces, stews, quiches, pizza toppings, pasta, and crepe fillings.*
- *Purée fresh basil and cooked spinach and make a pasta sauce by adding chopped tomatoes, garlic, and olive oil. Alternatively, combine the purée with ricotta and Parmesan cheeses for a rich, fragrant filling for lasagna, stuffed vegetables, manicotti, ravioli, or stuffed shells.*
- *Fresh spinach leaves make a deep green bed for other vegetable salads or additions of avocado, croutons, feta cheese, chick peas, olive oil, and lemon.*
- *Freshly grated nutmeg goes very well with cooked spinach used as a side dish, on its own, or as an ingredient in other dishes.*
- *Andi Gladstone, our resident link to Japanese cuisine and culture, prepares this delicate spinach side dish: Blanch and chop the spinach as described above. Mix together small amounts of soy sauce, sake (rice wine), freshly grated gingerroot, honey, and toasted, coarsely ground sesame seed.* Toss with the spinach.*

* Toast sesame seeds in a dry skillet until brown. Grind in a spice or coffee grinder.

SUMMER SQUASH AND ZUCCHINI

Summer squash plants provide a bountiful harvest of zucchini and straight, crookneck, and scallop (Patty Pan) squashes. One hill of 3 plants can supply at least 3 dozen fruits in a season. I can't detect a difference in flavor between the various summer squashes and zucchini, so I pick colors and shapes that are pleasing. Most squashes are yellow; zucchini can be gold, gray, green, or black.

STARTING

Direct seed in warm soil (70°F.) of pH 6.0 to 8.0. Sow seeds 1 inch deep, 6 seeds per hill, hills 3 feet apart each way. Squash are heavy feeders and need fertile soil; dig in plenty of well-aged manure or compost. Thin seedlings to the 3 strongest plants per hill.

In short-season areas, start seeds indoors in 3-inch peat pots, 4 weeks before the last frost. Sow 3 seeds to a pot, thinning to 1 or 2 plants. Plant outdoors as above, after danger of frost has passed.

CULTURAL REQUIREMENTS

Young seedlings should be kept weed-free. The large, prickly leaves of older plants serve to shade out weed competition. Water during dry periods.

HARVEST

The tenderest and most flavorful squash range from baby-size (3 to 4 inches) to 8 inches long. Longer ones will be tough and seedy. Pick frequently to encourage production and extend the season. Unpicked squash will quickly grow to an impressive baseball-bat size and retard new fruits. Allowing a few fruits to uninhibitedly grow this big could be used as a technique to slow production when the pantry is overflowing, you've exhausted all available squash recipes, and the neighbors are trying to give you their surplus.

CULINARY TIPS

• *Sauté zucchini or summer squash Italian style with garlic, olive oil, tomatoes, and fresh basil or oregano.*

- *Stuff squash by scooping out the center pulp (use it in stock or other dishes) and fill with:*
  - *Feta, cottage, and cream cheeses, parsley, dill, and scallions*
  - *Cooked chick peas, rice, spinach, garlic, and lemon*
  - *Sautéed onions, toasted walnuts, bread crumbs, cheddar cheese, and sage*
  - *Cooked barley, mushrooms, red and green peppers, and marjoram*
- *Bake, covered, at 350°F. for 45 minutes in a pan with about ⅛ inch of water or tomato juice in the bottom.*
- *Small "baby" squashes look best if cut in half lengthwise for marinated salads, stews, or as a side dish. They cook very quickly; remove from heat when crisp but tender.*
- *Squash and zucchini are good additions to soups and stews for feeding lots of people. Their delicate flavor harmonizes with most foods, and the abundant yields enable the cook to use them without reserve.*
- *Squashes have lovely, bright edible flowers that can be stuffed, batter-fried, or sautéed. Use some of the male flowers, located at the end of short stems, since the female flowers, which yield the fruit, should not be used. You can recognize female flowers, since there will appear a small fruit between the flower's base and the vine.*

SWEET POTATOES

Gardeners with ample growing space can enjoy this luscious, nutritious source of vitamins A, the Bs, and C. Traditionally grown during the long Southern summer, sweet potatoes can also be a successful Northern crop. I've had good harvests by using the short-season variety Centennial, and by warming the soil with black plastic for 2 weeks prior to planting. Porto Rico is a mid-season type available in bush form for smaller gardens.

STARTING

A sandy, slightly acid (pH 5.5 to 6.8), not too fertile soil is best for good-sized tubers. Young plants, or "slips," can be purchased at local nurseries or through mail order. If slips appear particularly dry, soak overnight before planting. Resist trying to start with store-bought sweet potatoes. The slips will be of an unknown, possibly inappropriate variety, and the potatoes probably will have been treated not to sprout.

Prepare garden soil into ridgelike rows 6 to 8 inches high, 3 feet apart. When soil temperatures are 70°F. and frost danger is passed, plant the slips a foot apart along the top of the ridge. Set the slips so that 4 inches of each is buried in the soil. Two leaves should remain above the soil line; it's fine if others are buried.

CULTURAL REQUIREMENTS

In cool climates black plastic that has been used to warm the soil should be kept in place throughout the season to maintain warmth. Young plants must be kept well weeded until vines are robust enough to cover the rows.

Sweet potatoes do not thrive in a continually moist soil. Water only during extended dry periods.

HARVEST

Sweet potatoes can be dug after the first frost blackens the tips of the foliage, or, in warmer regions, when the foliage turns yellow. Tubers will be damaged if they sit too long in soil cooler than 55°F. Dig and handle carefully, since damaged skins will not store well. Dry in the sun for 3 to 4 hours, then cure in a warm place, 80°F. or higher, for 1 to 2 weeks.

Store at 50°F. to 60°F. in a well-ventilated, dry location. Sugar content improves with storage. Never refrigerate, as it encourages rot.

CULINARY TIPS

- *Use sweet instead of white potatoes for a deeper, richer flavor in soups, stews, or pancakes. Or serve simply fried, puréed, or roasted.*
- *We like to use sweet potatoes in vegetable curries; the sweet smoothness is a good contrast to the spicy, piquant seasoning.*
- *Try an unusual potato salad with:*
  Cooked sweet potato chunks, lemon and lime juice, vegetable oil, grated fresh gingerroot, parsley, and red onion
  Cooked sweet potato chunks, lemon juice, mayonnaise, apple, celery, and walnuts

SWISS CHARD

A cousin to the beet, Swiss chard has a similarly earthy, green flavor and yields over a long season. The plant's deep roots condition the soil as well. Rhubarb Chard (not to be confused with rhubarb) is an equally ornamental and edible variety with opulent ruby red stalks and veined wavy leaves.

STARTING

Seeds can be sown early or late in the spring. Soak the heavily husked seeds for 24 hours prior to planting. Plant seeds in soil of pH 6.0 to 7.0, ½ to 1 inch deep, 3 to 4 inches apart, in rows 1½ feet apart. Thin plants to stand 6 inches apart.

CULTURAL REQUIREMENTS

Swiss chard can be picked all summer if watered during dry periods. It makes a good hot-weather spinach substitute. Plants can be mulched to overwinter and provide early-spring greens.

HARVEST

Snip the outer leaves, leaving the new growth to continue producing greens. Whole plants can be harvested to make room for other plantings.

CULINARY TIPS

- *Tender young greens can be used in salads; stalks and medium-sized leaves, cooked as a green vegetable.*
- *Cooked Swiss chard can be used where spinach is called for, provided its more robust flavor would not be intrusive.*

TOMATOES

What praises can I sing to garden-grown tomatoes that haven't already been sung? Prized for their aromatic, rich, sweet flavor, fresh tomatoes shine in even the simplest of preparations. Slice and serve with classic companions fresh basil and golden olive oil, or simply eat them, warm off the vine, like an apple.

You can check with local sources for varieties proven in your area, but with hundreds of unique types available through mail-order seed companies, there's no reason to limit yourself.

Most tomatoes will fall into one or more of the following categories:

early/determinate types are so named because their vines cease growing once the terminal buds set fruit. These plants tend to be bushy and can be grown with or without support. New Yorker is a good-tasting early type for cool or short-season areas. Long Keeper, from Burpee, is best picked at season's end to ripen indoors. Though not as spectacular as a midsummer garden tomato, it is far superior to store-bought varieties in the fall or early winter. Marmande, available from Bountiful Gardens or The Cook's Garden, is a French heirloom that is semideterminate, richly flavored, and does well in cooler climates.

indeterminate/main crop are tall, continuous growing plants. They inevitably need support (see below) for best results. Vines will continue to bear until frost or cold weather. Nepal, from Johnny's Selected Seeds, is a large, juicy beefsteak that we have enjoyed. Early Girl and Supersteak, two luscious beefsteak types reputed to be widely adaptable to climate, are from Burpee.

low-acid tomatoes are milder and less acidic than most others. These varieties are frequently yellow or orange. Orange Queen is an early beefsteak, low-acid tomato from Stokes. We like to create salad plates with alternating slices of deep red and bright orange thickly sliced beefsteak tomatoes.

plum or paste tomatoes are drier and firmer than other types and so best suited for canning or sauces. Polish Paste, from Territorial Seed, is a tall-growing indeterminate that bears abundant, huge fruits for processing as sauce, paste, or ketchup. In particularly damp seasons, cracking does seem to be a problem. San Marzano is a delicious paste type that is just as good for eating in hand as for cooking purposes. It dries well, too.

small-fruited tomatoes include cherry and pear salad tomatoes, hanging basket, and container varieties suitable for gardeners with limited space. My friend and a former Moosewood member Ashley Miller recommended Sweet Million, available from Stokes Seeds, which I've found to be more crack resistant than the popular Sweet 100 variety. An indeterminate type, it needs staking. Yellow Pear is not as intensely flavored as Sweet Million, but nice to grow for its unique color.

In catalogs or seedling packs you will notice the letters V, F, N, T, A, FF, St, and L located next to a variety, e.g., Burpee's Supersteak Hybrid VFN. The above indicate genetic resistance to or tolerance of Verticillium wilt (V), Fusarium wilt (F), Nematodes (N), Tobacco Mosaic virus (T), Alternaria Alternata (Crown wilt) (A), Race 1 and 2 Fusarium (FF), Stemphylium (gray leaf spot) (St), and Leafspot (Septoria) (L). Varieties so marked should help avoid the worst diseases, particularly for tomatoes grown in the same location in continuing seasons.

STARTING

Sow seeds indoors 6 to 8 weeks before the last frost. For good germination, soil temperatures should be 75°F. or higher. After true leaves develop, transplant seedlings into individual peat pots or soil cells. Grow them in ample light with a soil temperature range of 60°F. to 70°F.

Seedlings can be set out when nights are above 50°F. and frost danger has passed. Plant outdoors in soil of pH 5.5 to 7.5, 1 to 2 feet apart, in rows 2 to 3 feet apart, depending upon the size of the variety. Rotate tomato crops from year to year to avoid diseases. Soil should be supplemented with a shovelful of compost for each plant, or with an organic fertilizer.

Young tomato plants can be devastated by cutworms. Before planting, wrap each seedling with a newspaper collar that will extend 2 inches above and below the soil level. (These will decompose by the time the plant is no longer vulnerable.)

To set seedlings horizontally in a shallow trench, remove the lower leaves and bury the stem up to the top 3 to 6 leaves. Cover with 2 to 3 inches of soil, making sure the top cluster of leaves is above the surface. Additional roots will form along the buried stem. The sun's heat will more readily penetrate to these roots than if the seedlings were planted vertically.

CULTURAL REQUIREMENTS

Tomato vines grow exuberantly, with little regard to order or decorum. I never seem to get my plants as neatly restrained as I would like. Your choices are:
• Leave plenty of room around each plant, allowing them space to sprawl on the ground or dry mulch. This is the least efficient method of producing well-ripened, unblemished fruits, but good for those in dry climates and/or with a laissez-faire attitude.
• Single stakes (below).
• Trellising (p. 46).

- *Fruits grow between leaf stems.*
- *Tie soft twine or yarn to vertical stem and stake 6-foot-tall stake, buried at least 1 foot in the ground.*
- *Remove "suckers"—shoots growing from junction of vertical and leaf stems.*
- *Plants grown on a single stake—spaced 18 to 24 inches apart and pruned or pinched to a single vertical stem—will have a more open manageable growth and earlier-ripening fruits than unpruned plants.*
- *Alternatively, space plants 3 feet apart and allow multiple stems to form that are tied to 3 stakes. Harvests will be later than above, but more abundant.*

- Cages, available at garden stores, work best with determinate or compact bushy varieties. A tall cage filled with tomatoes and heavy vines can easily topple, even in a moderate wind.

Hotkaps and poly-tunnels (pp. 190–191) are useful to protect seedlings from cold, late-spring weather. Make sure they are removed when the weather turns warm. Blossoms will not set fruit in excessive heat.

Avoid smoking cigarettes near tomato plants before handling them. This spreads mosaic virus.

All tomato plants need consistent moisture (not soggy soil) to avoid blossom-end rot, which first appears as a dark, leathery spot on the side of the tomato opposite the stem. Regular watering, especially with a drip-irrigation system or soaker hose, and mulching help maintain consistent soil moisture.

Plants will be neater if pruned to one or two main stems. "Suckers," the side shoots that grow between the leaf axil and the main stem, should be removed to maintain open plants with a minimum of unnecessary vegetative growth.

HARVEST

Pick the ripest fruits and store at room temperature for best flavor. Refrigerated tomatoes become mushy and lose their flavor. When frost threatens, green tomatoes can be picked, wrapped in newspaper, and stored in a cool, dark place to ripen gradually.

• Broil thick tomato slices with garlic, oregano, and a drizzle of olive oil until the tomatoes are just heated and the garlic is golden.

• Prepare tomatoes for stuffing by scooping out the inside (reserve for other uses), lightly salting, and draining upside down for 15 minutes. Fill with:

  Diced cucumbers, peppers, capers, and garlic Herbed Mayonnaise (p. 248)

  Diced avocado, minced chilies, cilantro, scallions, and Monterey Jack cheese

  Cooked rice marinated with one of the Vinaigrette Dressings (p. 244) and diced raw vegetables

  Crumbled feta cheese mixed with cottage cheese, basil, and parsley

• My friend and neighbor Ann Pitkin makes a quick meal by tossing hot pasta with chopped uncooked tomatoes, garlic, and olive oil. Serve with grated Parmesan cheese.

• An excellent sauce needs only some roughly chopped tomatoes, a clove or two of garlic, some bay leaf, and a touch of basil or oregano. After cooking the tomatoes just long enough to soften, remove the bay leaf and purée or process until smooth. Cook a bit more, uncovered, to reduce to desired thickness.

• At Moosewood, we use chopped fresh tomatoes as a tart-sweet topping for rich, creamy dishes such as cheese rarebit or ravioli with pesto. Chopped basil, oregano, marjoram, chives, or shallots may be added.

• We have a different pita sandwich every day. Try the suggestions below combined with juicy fresh tomatoes and a variety of lettuces:

  One of the Herbed Cheese Spreads (p. 259)

  Sliced mushrooms, grated carrots, and Golden Sesame Dressing (p. 246)

  Cooked chick peas, feta cheese, and Basil-Shallot Vinaigrette (p. 245)

  Hard-boiled eggs, chives, celery, and Herbed Mayonnaise (p. 248)

  Cubes of Jarlsberg cheese, minced pickle, and Dill–Red Onion Vinaigrette (p. 245)

  North African Roasted Vegetable Salad (p. 215)

  Sesame Baked Tofu (p. 235), cucumbers, and a Vinaigrette Dressing (p. 244)

• Make a quick gazpacho by puréeing peeled, seeded tomatoes, onion, garlic, fresh chili, and sweet peppers with a drizzle of olive oil. Serve at once or chilled.

• If you have the space, freezing tomatoes is easier and faster than canning. Whole tomatoes can be frozen in plastic bags or containers. Thaw only as many as you need. Once frozen, they can be easily peeled by rubbing off the skin under hot tap water.

• Fried green tomatoes are a classic fall treat. Dredge the slices in herbed cornmeal and fry in ⅛ inch of vegetable oil until each side is crisp. Drain, serve immediately.

TURNIPS

The tender, crisp roots of turnips are an essential addition to the soups and stews of fall and winter. Turnips are cool-weather root vegetables that will be mild and tender if grown in early spring, late summer, or Southern winter. Crops will be woody and bitter if temperatures are consistently above 80°F. Purple-Top White Globe is a standard variety that I've found to be mild in flavor and appealing in texture.

STARTING

Direct seed in loose, fertile soil with a pH of 6.0 to 8.0, ¼ to ½ inch deep, in rows 12 inches apart. Thin plants to 3 to 4 inches apart.

CULTURAL REQUIREMENTS

Floating row covers will help keep young plants free of damaging insects. Seedlings should be weeded regularly to avoid spindly roots.

HARVEST

Green tops, an excellent source of vitamin A, are ready to pick for cooking greens in 30 days, roots in 35 to 60 days, depending upon the variety and growing conditions. Roots are at their best when picked young, at 2 to 3 inches in diameter. Storage turnips should be picked before the ground freezes and stored, without the greens, in a root cellar or pit at 32°F. to 40°F.

CULINARY TIPS

• Grate raw young turnips into salads or mix with grated apple or carrot and a light dressing of lemon, oil, chives, and dill.
• Turnips add a sweet, earthy flavor to stews and hearty soups.
• Mash together cooked potatoes and turnips with butter and a pinch of nutmeg.
• Layer a casserole with slices of steamed or boiled turnips, sautéed onions, sliced apples, and cheddar cheese. Bake until the apples are tender and the cheese is golden.

WINTER SQUASH

Winter squashes add a warm, sweet touch to meals in the chilly, dark days of late fall and winter. Varieties range from the petite individual serving size of Sweet Dumpling to the mammoth 25-pound Blue Hubbard. My personal favorite is Delicata for its rich, sweet, dry-textured flesh. It stores very well and bears abundant, moderately sized fruits just right for stuffing.

STARTING

See summer squash (p. 66) for starting information. Winter squashes have more aggressive vines and should be placed in rows 3 feet apart, 2 feet between individual plants, or 3 plants to a hill, hills 6 feet apart. Plant squash where the possibly 12-foot-long vines can ramble without trampling smaller plants.

CULTURAL REQUIREMENTS

Row covers can protect small plants from damaging bugs. These must be lifted as the flowers form to ensure pollination. To save space, small-fruited vining types can be trellised (p. 46).

HARVEST

Squash is ripe when the fruit has a hard skin and dry stem. Harvest before a killing frost, since it could shorten the fruits' storage life. Cut fruits allowing 1 to 2 inches of stem to remain. Cure in the sun, if possible, for 1 week to 10 days. Cover well at night if a frost threatens. If the weather is chilly and damp, cure indoors in a warm spot, 80°F. or higher.

Store in a cool, dry location, 45°F. to 60°F., arranging squashes so that air circulates between them. Wash off any molds that may appear on the skin. Many varieties can be kept for at least 4 months.

CULINARY TIPS

* *Add cooked squash to soups, waffles, muffins, biscuits, and quick and yeasted breads for sweetness and a golden hue.*

* *Puréed winter squash with butter and nutmeg or cinnamon makes a simple, comforting side dish.*
* *Bake squash halves with a filling of:*
  Diced apples, cinnamon, and butter
  Walnuts, dates, lemon juice, and grated lemon peel
  Honey, butter, and raisins
  Orange juice concentrate, pecans, and dried apricots
  Cranberries and honey
  Sautéed mushrooms and onions
* *Baking squash brings out the sweetest and nuttiest flavor. For a quicker preparation, cut squash into rings or chunks and steam until tender.*
* *Cook whole spaghetti squash in a pot with water to cover. Simmer for half an hour after the water has boiled or until tender when pierced. Drain the squash and allow to cool. Cut in half, remove and discard the seeds, and scoop out the "spaghetti" strands from the pulp. Keep warm and serve with an Herb Butter (p. 254), pesto, sweet red pepper, tomato, or cheese sauce.*

HERBS

Throughout history herbs have been found wherever people have gardened. In the days before mass-produced chemicals and pharmaceuticals, the herb garden supplied nearly everything for cooking, making medicines, and various crafts such as dyeing and perfume making. I've thought it would be nice to bring back the old custom of strewing herbs across the floor as a primitive air freshener. The prospect of filling the house with the fragrance of mint, artemisia, lemon balm, or hyssop was appealing until I realized that the earthen floor of a cottage was far easier to sweep clean of trampled leaves and stems than a wall-to-wall carpet. But there remain countless ways to introduce the beauty of herbs: in cooking, in potpourri, and as ornamental plants interspersed in vegetable and flower gardens.

There's confusion regarding the difference between herbs and spices, perhaps because so many of us use the terms interchangeably. Generally, herbs consist of the plant's leafy parts. Herbalists further complicate matters by referring to seeds, barks, and roots as herbs as well. Spices are primarily of tropical origin: allspice, cinnamon, cloves, ginger, nutmeg, and peppercorns, to name a few examples. Spices are usually derived from seeds, fruits, barks, and roots.

GROWING HERBS

Most herbs are compact and so can easily be tucked into vegetable or flower gardens to fill an empty space or add an interesting note of color, form, or foliage. Some ambitious gardeners plant specific herb theme gardens composed of plants of similar fragrance, color, origin, use, or value.

Included in the herb listings that follow are a few solely ornamental species that are either very easy to cultivate or have a striking appearance, in bloom or leaf. Kitchen gardens need not be limited to edible plants; cooking and gardening share the ability to be more richly dimensioned when all the senses are treated as part of the experience. The few ornamental herbs mentioned represent a small percentage of the hundreds of interesting plants waiting to be explored and enjoyed.

Generally less fussy than vegetables, herbs will thrive in soil less rich than that of a well-tended vegetable garden. Commonly recommended for locations that are moderately dry, lean, or sandy, basil, lavender, marjoram, oregano, rosemary, sage, and thyme will have a stronger essential oil and taste than if grown in rich, moist soil.

Most herbs do best in full sun, with at least 6 hours a day of direct sunlight.

The following listings group together herbs that satisfy specific conditions. See the individual entries for their botanical names.

HERBS TOLERANT OF PARTIAL SHADE

angelica	hyssop	parsley
bee balm	lemon balm	sweet cicely
chervil	lovage	sweet woodruff
germander	mint	

HERBS FOR FRAGRANCE

basil	lemon balm	santolina
bee balm	mint	scented geranium
chamomile	rosemary	thyme
lavender	sage	

HERBS TO DRY FOR INDOOR ARRANGEMENTS

lady's mantle	lavender	yarrow
lamb's ears	santolina	

HERBS FOR COLORFUL, FRAGRANT FRESH BOUQUETS (USING SPRIGS, LEAVES, OR FLOWERS)

angelica	dill	mint
basil	hyssop	sage
bee balm	lady's mantle	santolina
borage	lavender	scented geranium
calendula	lovage	thyme
chamomile		

HERBS THAT CAN BE GROWN AS HOUSEPLANTS

basil	chive	parsley
bay	marjoram	rosemary
calendula	mint	sage
chervil	oregano	scented geranium

In homes with very sunny, cool (50°F. to 70°F.) rooms or with grow lights, herbs can be grown in pots. Hot, dry, stuffy rooms invite pests and disease that will reduce harvests. Plants that are brought in from the garden at summer's end should be acclimated gradually to the indoors beginning 2 or 3 weeks before the heat comes on. Before bringing any plants in, check carefully for insects (p. 192) and cut back leggy growth, including blossoms and buds, which will deplete the plant's energy. Pots of chives should be subjected to some freezing weather outdoors to break their dormancy before moving indoors (p. 94). Be careful, however, not to allow them to freeze in a clay or ceramic pot, since it will crack.

Pick herbs for freezing or drying when the essential oils are at their peak, ideally, when they're on the brink of their flowering cycle, early in the morning after the dew has dried but before the heat of the day.

Strip the leaves from the stems (the house will smell great for hours). Place the leaves on window screens, in mesh produce bags, or in paper bags with small ventilation holes. Alternatively, spread the leaves on aluminum foil in an oven set at the lowest temperature. Watch very carefully to avoid overdrying or cooking. I use a warm attic room for drying. Herbs are dry when they're just at the point of crumbling. Cool and then place in containers.

Store jars of dried herbs in a cool, dark spot. It may be convenient to store them near a stove, but you will sacrifice flavor for convenience.

Fresh herbs to be stored in the refrigerator should be loosely wrapped in plastic to avoid drying out or soggy decay. Sprigs of parsley, cilantro, mint, and dill can be kept for a few days in small jars of water if you've picked more than you need.

HERB FLAVORS BEST RETAINED BY FREEZING

basil	cilantro	parsley
chervil	dill	tarragon

HERBS WITH GOOD FLAVOR WHEN DRIED

basil	mint	sage
dill	oregano	savory
lovage	rosemary	thyme

In the herb discussions that follow, attention is paid to the culinary and landscape use of herbs. Consult the Bibliography (p. 275) for resources dealing with a wider range of herb subjects.

Pregnant or nursing women, and people in unstable health, should consult a physician before taking any herbal preparation.

PROPAGATING HERBS

Many perennial herbs can be propagated by simple division. For Northern gardeners, a good time to do this is in early spring, when the plants are still dormant. Gardeners with a long, mild fall or winter can divide in late summer. Divide large or overcrowded clumps with a sharp spade into smaller sections that can be replanted or given away. Bee balm, chives, lemon balm, marjoram, mints, oregano, creeping thymes, tarragon, sweet woodruff, and yarrow are all easily divided.

Cuttings are the best way to propagate woody herbs such as bay, lavender, rosemary, rue, sage, scented geraniums, winter savory, and common thyme. Cut 4- to 6-inch-long growing shoots from about ¼ inch below a leaf joint. Do a few at a time, since not all will root. Carefully remove all the leaves from the lower half of the stem using a sharp, clean knife or blade. Fill a small pot with moist vermiculite, perlite, or sand. Make a hole, 1 to 3 inches deep, with a pencil, insert a cutting, and gently firm the damp rooting material. Water and set in a bright spot out of direct sunlight. Keep the cuttings evenly moist but not soggy. If your room is very dry, cover the pots with lightly perforated plastic to retain high humidity. Use a coated wire hoop, bent pipe cleaner, or three sticks (Popsicle sticks, straws, or wooden plant markers) to hold the moisture-condensing plastic up above the leaves. Contact with the damp plastic can cause rot or mold.

POTPOURRI

Regardless of the season, potpourri will bring back the heady fragrance of a warm summer day.

Basically, potpourri is composed of a main ingredient, which supplies the dominant scent, usually derived from flowers, aromatic leaves, or roots. To this are added blending scents, fixative (to "fix" the scent), and possibly essential oils. Essential oils are highly concentrated substances that may be added a few drops at a time to intensify a particular scent in potpourri mixes. I use them only if the mixture's fragrance seems weak. A general formula for 1 quart of potpourri is: 2 cups flowers, 1¼ cups fragrant herbs, ¼ cup spices, 1 tablespoon fixative, and a few drops of essential oil (if desired).

Pick flowers for potpourri early in the day, after the dew has dried. Flowers should be in bud or just beginning to open, but not in full bloom or past their prime. Dry them on a screen in a warm, well-ventilated spot out of direct sunlight until they are just brittle. Use recently dried herbs and freshly ground spices for additional fragrance.

Potpourri ingredients not in your garden, including fixatives, other herbs, and essential oils, are available through Nichols Garden Nursery and Well-Sweep Herb Farm. Orris root, the ground rhizome of *Iris florentina,* is one of the most widely used fixatives.

Store potpourri in covered, nonmetallic containers to retain the fragrance. (Metal may alter the mixture's scent.) Add dried, colorful flower petals to mixes that will be kept in glass jars or bowls.

Sachets are potpourri mixes sewn into fabric bags to be placed in clothing or linen drawers. Use tissue paper as an inner lining for the bags to prevent small bits of crumbled potpourri from sifting out.

POTPOURRI RECIPES

ROSE

2 CUPS ROSE PETALS AND
  BUDS
1 CUP ROSE GERANIUM
  LEAVES
1 CUP LEMON VERBENA
  LEAVES

1 TABLESPOON GROUND
  ALLSPICE
1 TABLESPOON GROUND ORRIS
  ROOT

LEMON

1 CUP LEMON GERANIUM
  LEAVES
1 CUP LEMON BASIL LEAVES
1 CUP CARNATION PETALS
¼ CUP LEMON THYME LEAVES

½ CUP LEMON PEEL,
  CHOPPED
1 TABLESPOON GROUND ORRIS
  ROOT

SPICE

1 CUP NUTMEG GERANIUM
  LEAVES
1 CUP COCONUT GERANIUM
  LEAVES
½ CUP BASIL LEAVES
½ CUP PATCHOULI LEAVES
½ CUP MINT LEAVES

2 TABLESPOONS GROUND
  GINGER
2 TABLESPOONS GROUND
  CLOVES
2 TABLESPOONS GROUND
  CINNAMON
1 TABLESPOON GROUND ORRIS
  ROOT

WOODSY

2 CUPS SOUTHERNWOOD
  LEAVES
1 CUP VETIVER ROOT*
¼ CUP LEMON GRASS

¼ CUP BEE BALM LEAVES
¼ CUP MINT LEAVES
2 TABLESPOONS ROSEMARY
  LEAVES

LAVENDER

2 CUPS LAVENDER BUDS
1¼ CUPS SWEET WOODRUFF*
  LEAVES
½ CUP ROSE PETALS OR
  BUDS

2 TABLESPOONS GROUND
  NUTMEG
2 TABLESPOONS GROUND
  CLOVES

Combine the potpourri ingredients and store in a covered, nonmetallic container in a cool, dark spot for 1 month to blend the fragrances. Tired potpourri can be revived with a few drops of essential oil or 1 teaspoon of brandy.

Vetiver root and sweet woodruff leaves act as fixatives.

ANGELICA
(Angelica archangelica)

With an ultimate height of 6 feet or more and width of over 2 feet, handsome leafy stalks, and greenish flower umbels, angelica is a striking, dramatic presence.

A short-lived perennial, angelica frequently takes 2 or 3 years to flower and dies shortly thereafter. If the rounded flower umbels are cut off early enough, plants should live another year. Or, if you prefer, seeds can be left to self-sow or be collected and planted shortly after they have ripened. Seeds do not remain viable for long.

GROWING

Native to wet areas, angelica does best in a cool climate, moist, well-drained soil, and full sun to partial shade. Plants are best started from seed or seedlings.

Set plants 2 to 3 feet from one another or neighboring plants.

CULINARY TIPS

* *Angelica leaves and stems have an aromatic, licorice flavor. Add a few young leaves to fruit or leafy salads.*
* *The tender stems of new growth can be candied for an old-fashioned treat.*
* *Roots and seeds have been traditionally used in perfumes and liqueurs.*

NOTE: Angelica should not be ingested by diabetics or pregnant women.

BASIL

(Ocimum basilicum and other species)

I had my first taste of basil over twenty years ago at a friend's house in California. Rose had prepared a simple vegetable soup that she'd seasoned with something wonderful that I couldn't quite place. It turned out to be Bronx-grown basil, packed in olive oil and salt, that Rose's mother shipped all the way to Berkeley.

Since then the rest of the country has discovered and developed quite a love affair with basil. Pesto sauces (of which basil is the key ingredient) are almost a cliché. Still, summer without fresh basil would be dull indeed.

Though sweet, or Italian, basil is the variety most commonly known for cooking purposes, there are other spicy, fragrant, and colorful basils that can be used for cooking, garnishing, making teas and potpourri, or ornamental planting. These include:

anise basil (*O. basilicum*)—sweetly flavored, combining the licorice flavor of anise and the rich taste of basil. It is particularly popular in Southeast Asian cuisine.

cinnamon basil (*O. basilicum*)—strongly fragrant with attractive pink-mauve flowers. Grow these alongside a path, and as you brush the leaves, they will perfume the air. Dried leaves retain their scent and make good potpourri material.

holy basil (*O. canum*)—green- or purple-leafed types are ornamental plants with a sweet clove fragrance. Now grown primarily for potpourri, holy basil was historically used as a sacred herb in the temples of India.

lemon basil (*O. citriodorum*)—a unique lemon flavor adds a twist to any dish where sweet basil might be used. The fragrant leaves also enhance herbal tea mixes, potpourri, and iced drinks.

lettuce leaf basil (*O. basilicum crispum*)—large, mild-flavored leaves make pesto production, drying, and freezing less of a chore. The big leaves make nifty wrappers for hors d'oeuvres.

purple, or dark opal, basil (*O. basilicum*)—varieties include Purple Ruffles and Opal. The dark maroon-purple leaves and baby pink flowers make showy bouquet additions and culinary garnishes, as well as good foils for lighter garden plants. My favorite way of using this beautiful basil is in a brilliant, ruby red Herb Vinegar (p. 242). This strongly flavored basil should be used sparingly in cooking.

small-leaved basil *(O. basilicum)*— includes Minimum, Spicy Globe, Fino Verde Compatto, and Piccolo. These compact, mound-shaped 8- to 12-inch plants do well in pots and other containers, or can provide an attractive, dense, edible edging for flower or vegetable beds. Leaves are small but have the same flavor and fragrance as sweet basil. Include a pot of mini-basil in a sunny winter window garden.

GROWING

Start basil seeds indoors 4 to 6 weeks before the last frost or sow directly in the garden when the soil is warm and frost danger is past. Lemon basil resents transplanting and should be sown directly in the garden or in peat pots. Thin or plant seedlings to stand 1 foot apart (8 inches for mini-leafed types). Basil likes a hot, sunny, fertile location. The leaves will discolor and be damaged in cold weather, so cover plants if temperatures drop below 40°F. Keep flowers pinched to encourage new growth. Harvest basil before fall frosts or the onset of cold weather.

CULINARY TIPS

- *Basil is probably the most commonly used herb at Moosewood. We cook with it every day, using either the fresh or dried leaves in soups, sauces, stews, fillings, sautés, dressings, and dips.*
- *Wash and drain the fresh leaves gently; they bruise and blacken easily.*
- *Marinate juicy, ripe beefsteak tomatoes with chopped basil leaves, garlic, and extra virgin olive oil.*
- *Prepare a fast uncooked tomato sauce with garden-ripe tomatoes, a few cloves of crushed garlic, a small onion, a generous handful of basil, and a little mint and parsley. Purée or process until smooth, toss with hot pasta, and serve immediately with freshly grated Parmesan cheese.*
- *Make a quick "pizza" by cutting a pita bread in half horizontally to yield 2 "crusts." Top each half with chopped tomatoes, fresh basil, fresh oregano, garlic, mozzarella and Parmesan cheeses, and a drizzle of olive oil. Broil or bake until golden and bubbly.*
- *Toss pasta with a sauce of diced garden vegetables (carrots, zucchini, peppers, fennel, eggplant, or tomatoes) that have been sautéed with fresh basil, a splash of dry white wine, and some cream.*
- *Add basil to cheese fillings for tortellini, lasagna, crepes, omelets, stuffed shells, or manicotti.*

• *Fresh basil's flavor can be preserved only by freezing, canning with olive oil, or incorporating in an herb vinegar. Dried basil is a fine seasoning, but has a different, subtler, and less aromatic taste than the fresh herb.*
• *Purée or process fresh, stemmed basil leaves with olive oil and freeze or refrigerate in small containers for future use. Refrigerated basil will need a protective layer of oil at the top of the jar, and this should be replaced after each use. At Moosewood we also freeze plastic bags full of stemmed basil leaves when we're too busy for the blending method. Frozen basil will turn blackish when it's thawed, so use it in dishes where appearance will not be a problem.*

BAY LAUREL
(Laurus nobilis)

The bay tree's glossy deep green leaves and elegant form make it an outstanding ornamental as well as a popular culinary herb.

An evergreen tree native to the Mediterranean, bay is hardy outdoors only to zone 8. We have a potted bay tree at the restaurant that is many years old. Container- or pot-grown plants need a summer outdoors or a sunny window indoors. Plants can be easily trimmed; train young trees to a single trunk standard or allow them to form a shrubby bush.

The laurel wreaths of classical times were made from bay. Experience a sense of continuity with the ancient Greeks and Romans by presenting a homemade wreath on any number of occasions, victorious or not.

GROWING

Bay trees are difficult to start from seed. Buy plants from a nursery or root a cutting taken from the new, green growth. Trees can be grown outdoors in partial shade to full sun.

CULINARY TIPS

• *All Mediterranean cuisines make generous use of bay leaves. In the New World, Creole and New England cooking rely on bay as a primary seasoning.*

• At Moosewood we use bay leaves in combination with other herbs. Bay is like the bass part in music: perceived, but as a background to other dominant notes. Chowders, stews, vegetable or fish stocks, sauces, and marinades benefit from bay leaves. It's an herb that should be included early on in the cooking process, because heat draws out the essential oil.

• We also use bay leaves in storage containers for grains and beans; they're reputed to deter cereal moths. Continue the "relationship" by cooking beans or grains with a bay leaf or two.

• Always use whole bay leaves. Even hours of cooking will not soften small pieces of leaf and they will be hard to find. Thoughtful cooks try to remove bay leaves before serving a dish to prevent accidental ingestion. However, others claim that it's good luck to get a bay leaf in your dish.

BEE BALM, OR BERGAMOT
(Monarda didyma or Monarda fistulosa)

Drifts of bee balm make a brightly flowered background for sunny borders or partially shaded areas. The 3- to 4-foot-tall plants are topped with a unique pom-pom of tubular flowers in many shades of lavender, pink, white, violet, or red. The midsummer blooms attract butterflies and hummingbirds.

This American native was traditionally used as a tea by the Oswego Indians, and later by the colonists during their boycott of English imported black tea. It's also known as bergamot, and is the ingredient that gives Earl Gray tea its distinctive taste.

GROWING

You'll find bee balm identified as bergamot or monarda. Hardy in zones 4 through 9, bee balm is happy in sun or partial shade, but will do best in shadier locations in its Southern range. To obtain specific colors, buy plants or acquire divisions from friends, since seedlings may be variable in color and form. The offspring of one pink bee balm in my garden was a brilliant violet-purple, which I actually preferred to the pink.

Space plants 2 feet apart in a moist location with rich, fertile soil. Plants will tolerate dryness, but they may wilt and bloom poorly. Divide the vigorous clumps every 2 to 3 years. Colonies tend to form as a "donut" around the bare older center. Cut out wedges of the newer growth to replant, and discard the dead, woody center. Also be aware that most monarda can be quite invasive, so you may be dividing clumps as early as the first year.

CULINARY TIPS

- *Bee balm's vivid flowers and fresh leaves are edible. I find the leaves have an unusual flavor that I would describe as perfume-mint-oregano. Flower petals make brilliant garnishes or additions to multicolored salads.*
- *Bee balm is used in the manufacture of perfume. The dried leaves and flowers retain their essential oil, known as bergamot, for fragrant potpourri and herbal tea material.*

BORAGE
(Borago officinalis)

Blue flowers are my favorite. They're not as common in nature as yellows, reds, and pinks, and so they are highly prized for not only their color but the "cooling effect" they have wherever they appear. Borage's little sky-blue, star-shaped flowers open from nodding, pink buds in the spreading, 2- to 3-foot plants. In dramatic contrast, the large, sometimes floppy, gray and green leaves and stems sport bristly hairs.

Partaking of the edible leaves and flowers was traditionally believed to promote well-being and dispel melancholy. Borage is also a good plant for apiculturists, since the flowers will attract honeybees, which are excellent pollinators for the garden.

GROWING

A vigorous self-sowing annual, borage can be planted in their permanent spots from early spring to early summer. Plants do well in even poor, dry soil, but require full sun. When I grew a few in a fertile vegetable bed, the plants were gigantic and crowded all their neighbors. Thin seedlings to stand 1 foot to 18 inches apart. Because it self-sows so freely, you may be surprised to see where it turns up next year.

C U L I N A R Y   T I P S

• *The blooms, peeled stems, and tender fresh young leaves give a cucumber flavor to salads and soups. Try adding a few tablespoons of chopped leaves to chilled potato, tomato, cucumber, or gazpacho soup.*
• *Blossoms are exceptionally pretty arranged with other edible flowers on a cake with a cream cheese or white frosting.*
• *Freeze flowers in ice cubes for tall, cool drinks.*
• *If you've planted lots of borage, gather a couple of cups of blooms and make a lavender-tinted herb vinegar with a delicate borage flavor.*

CALENDULA
(Calendula officinalis)

Single or double daisylike flowers in all shades of cream to deep orange grace the 6- to 24-inch-tall calendula plants. The original species is somewhat floppy and 18 inches to 2 feet tall, with smaller flowers. The newer varieties range in size from the 6-inch dwarfs (Bon-Bon, Fiesta Gitana) to 18- to 24-inch plants (Pacific Beauty, Kabblouna).

Many British gardening books refer to calendula as "marigold" or "pot marigold." Calendula should not be confused with the very separate *Tagetes* species that we in the United States know as marigolds. The name "marigold" derives from a medieval association between the Virgin Mary and *Calendula officinalis*'s golden-rayed flowers. *Tagetes* have sharply pungent foliage and flowers and should not be used interchangeably with calendulas. Most *Tagetes* are not edible.

Historically, calendulas were used in Europe for myriad medicinal and culinary purposes. At Moosewood, Maureen Vivino makes a calendula ointment that's a time-honored and -tested remedy for burns and cuts, two mishaps not uncommon in a busy kitchen. It requires no arcane procedures or exotic (eye of newt, etc.) ingredients. Cut 2 or 3 calendula plants as they are budding, but before they bloom, when the essential oil is strongest. Either mash the stems and leaves with a mortar and pestle or roll with a heavy rolling pin between sheets of waxed paper until the juices flow. Put 1 cup of this pulverized mash into a 1-quart canning jar filled with ethyl alcohol or 100 proof vodka. Let it steep in a dark place, such as a kitchen cupboard, at room temperature. Shake the jar once a day for 2 weeks, then twice a week. The ointment will be ready about 100 days from picking the herbs, though you could sneak a little before then in an emergency. Strain and discard the pulp, and reserve the fluid, keeping the jar tightly capped. Generously apply with cotton to burns and cuts.

GROWING

Calendulas are hardy annuals that can be seeded as soon as the soil is workable. They will self-sow if they're happy in the location. The plants do better in cool weather, so grow them early or late in the season where summers are hot. They can survive light frosts and will do well in coastal California or Southern winters.

Space dwarf varieties 8 inches apart, taller types 1 foot apart, all in full sun.

CULINARY TIPS

• *Sunny, brightly colored calendula petals are having a renaissance in flower cookery. Fresh petals should be snipped off the flower center; hold the outside edges of the petals with one hand while cutting with the other. Cut so that the somewhat bitter whitish part remains with the discarded flower center. Use 2 to 3 tablespoons (less if dried) of fresh petals for subtle flavor and a golden hue in pilafs, breads, soups, salads, and egg dishes.*
• *Home-grown calendula petals can be substituted for saffron for a similar color but different flavor.*

NOTE: Pregnant women should avoid ingesting calendula.

CHAMOMILE
(*Matricaria recutita* and *Chamaemelum nobile*)

The term chamomile is applied to two separate genera of plants.

One, *M. recutita* (Sweet False or German chamomile) is a 2- to 3-foot-tall annual with feathery, divided foliage and small, apple-scented, daisylike flowers.

The other, *Chamaemelum nobile* (or Roman chamomile) is a perennial that grows 8 or 9 inches tall. Its similarly feathery foliage is more strongly scented than that of *M. recutita*, and its flowers can be single or double.

GROWING

Sow seeds for *M. recutita* in fall or spring in a sunny area. Plants will tolerate dry, sandy, and sunny locations. Harvest the flowers when they are fully open, allowing some to remain on the plant to self-sow.

C. nobile can be seeded in spring and prefers moist but well-drained soil in sun or partial shade. This species makes a feathery ground cover that releases a fruity scent when walked upon. Plants can be mowed to encourage denser growth, but should be well established first.

Both species do best in the cooler climates of zones 3 to 5 or the temperate areas of the Pacific Northwest and the California coast.

CULINARY TIPS

• M. recutita *flowers are the ones to grow and dry for chamomile tea. Tisanes (herbal teas) of chamomile have been and remain popular in Europe as a soothing, calming drink that is claimed can alleviate everything from colds to upset stomachs.*

NOTE: Pregnant women should avoid ingesting chamomile.

CHERVIL
(Anthriscus cerefolium)

The fernlike, delicately flavored foliage of this hardy 2-foot-tall annual is used in French cuisine. The taste is reminiscent of a mild tarragon combined with parsley. The plant's rounded form and feathery leaves are attractive in flower, herb, or vegetable beds.

GROWING

Chervil does well in cool seasons, quickly bolting to seed in hot weather. Sow seeds outdoors early in the spring, then thin plants to stand 6 inches apart. I've grown chervil between broccoli plants, letting the taller broccoli provide some cooling shade in the hotter months. Allow plants to go to seed. Chervil has generously reseeded itself in my garden from year to year.

CULINARY TIPS

- *Use fresh chervil leaves where their subtle bouquet won't be overwhelmed by more assertive tastes: in creamy dips, sauces, light soups, cheese spreads and fillings, vegetable purées, simple fish dishes, omelets, dressings, mayonnaise, and herb butter.*
- *At Moosewood, we use whole sprigs as a lacy, elegant garnish.*
- *Toss new potatoes with chopped mint and chervil.*
- *Put leafy sprigs into salads of multicolored lettuce leaves and zippy greens such as arugula, endive, or radicchio.*
- *Chervil will lose most of its flavor when dried; freeze sprigs for winter use.*

CHIVES
(Allium schoenoprasum)

Clumps of chives, with their deep bluish-green, grasslike leaves, make handsome foot-high edgings. In late spring, rosy-lavender, purple, or white flowers appear above the foliage, giving a beautiful mounded effect.

GROWING

Seeds can be started any time and will germinate best if kept in a dark spot with a soil temperature between 60°F. and 75°F. Get a head start by planting new plants or divisions. Chives are quick-growing hardy perennials that thrive in good soil. Set plants 6 inches apart in a sunny or lightly shaded spot. Divide clumps every 3 years or so, especially if neighboring plants are being crowded.

Leaves should be snipped, about 2 inches above the ground, never pulled, for harvest. Cut off the faded flowers; if allowed to go to seed, their progeny will crop up throughout the garden, and subsequent blooming will be discouraged.

Clumps may look a bit tired in a hot, dry summer, but should revive with cooler, moist weather.

For winter windowsill pots of chives, dig up a clump in late summer, place in a plastic pot, and let it remain in the ground for about 1 month of freezing weather. The plants will then have experienced the brief dormancy they need in order to send up new growth once inside.

CULINARY TIPS

• *With a flavor similar to but milder than either scallions or onions, chives can be used by discreet cooks without fear. Chives should be added at the very last minute to any hot foods; their flavor is diminished with too much heat.*

• *Chives can add a last-minute pick-up to dishes that need just a little something to spark the palate.*

• *Creamy, mild dishes such as dips, cheese spreads, white sauces, eggs, herb butters, plain steamed vegetables, grains or noodles, and dressings can all be enhanced with a few tablespoons of finely chopped chives.*

• *Use the edible flowers to garnish salads and soups (they float nicely), and to make a pale pink herb vinegar. Taste them first; some blossoms are quite pungent.*

• *Freeze chopped or whole chive leaves; home-dried plants lack flavor.*

CORIANDER (CILANTRO)
(Coriandrum sativam)

Few people are indifferent to the pronounced flavor of fresh coriander leaves, also known as cilantro; there are those who are fans, and those who are not. At Moosewood, we use it in a variety of dishes, where its pungent flavor is ethnically or traditionally appropriate, and in newer recipes that cross cultural borders.

Coriander seeds taste completely different from the leaves. They're more sweetly aromatic and flavor foods as diverse as hot dogs and butter cookies.

An annual, coriander will grow 2 to 3 three feet tall in a sunny, fertile spot. The vivid green divided leaves resemble a smaller, paler version of flat-leaved, or Italian, parsley.

Cultivated in Latin America, Asia, and the Middle East, coriander has only recently become popular as a fresh herb in American cooking.

GROWING

Sow seeds where they are to grow after all frost danger is past, in full sun. Plant often, as even the slow-bolting varieties will go to seed after a few weeks' growth. Thin seedlings to stand 6 inches apart.

HARVEST

Harvest the fresh leaves before the plant begins to flower. Pick the seed heads when they are dry and brown. In cold or wet weather, plants can be hung upside down indoors, and the seeds will continue ripening.

CULINARY TIPS

• *Add fresh leaves at the end of cooking time for best flavor.*
• *Spicy salsas with coriander leaf add a distinctive Latin American spark when served with bean dishes, soups, grilled fish or vegetables, chips, guacamole, and casseroles.*
• *The cuisines of India, the Middle East, China, and Southeast Asia use coriander leaf as a key herbal accent or final garnish. One or two tablespoons of chopped leaf make a cooling, fresh counterpoint to peppery curries, soups, or stir-fries.*
• *Serve a refreshing cucumber raita with fiery curries. Combine 1 diced cucum-*

ber, 2 cups yogurt, ¼ teaspoon ground cardamom seeds, and 2 tablespoons chopped, fresh coriander leaf.
- Dried leaves lack flavor; freezing is preferred.
- For the richest fragrance, we use freshly ground coriander seeds (a coffee grinder works well).
- Ground coriander seed adds a spicy (though not hot) bouquet to chowder, chili, bean dishes, tomato sauces, marinades, muffins, sweet breads, and cookie batters.
- Add a few whole coriander seeds to mulled cider or wine along with 2 to 3 whole cloves or allspice berries and a cinnamon stick.

DILL
(Anethum graveolens)

If basil is the most frequently used herb at Moosewood, then dill is surely the runner-up. With extremely fine blue-green foliage and chartreuse flower heads, the 2- to 4-foot-tall plants are suitable for the back of the flower border as well as the vegetable garden. The wide, upside-down umbrellalike flower heads of this easily grown annual give cut bouquets unusual form and color. I've enjoyed a planting where the early-morning sun shone through plants filigreed with dew.

GROWING

Dill does not transplant happily; sow seeds in good garden soil and full sun in early spring. Thin seedlings to stand 6 inches apart. I've had good luck with dill vigorously reseeding on its own from year to year. Curiously, these "volunteer" seedlings are taller and more robust than those from subsequently planted purchased seeds. Allow a few plants to stand in the garden until the flower heads have matured and dropped seed.

- *The fresh or dried dill leaf is referred to as dill weed in some recipes.*
- *We use dill weed anywhere its mellow herb flavor will enrich a dish, especially in Jewish, Russian, Greek, Scandinavian, and Eastern European cuisines. Try it with foods for which it has a particular affinity: potato dishes and soups, cucumber salads, eggs, sour cream or yogurt dips, sauces or dressings, hearty fall and winter stews, sautéed mushrooms, cheese spreads or fillings, with lemon butter and broiled fish, green beans, and in herb vinegars and butters.*
- *Dill seeds have a carawaylike flavor and can be used whole in rye or pumpernickel bread, or to top savory pastries. Add ground seeds to soups, stews, and pickled vegetables.*
- *Whole flower heads are flavorful, attractive additions to pickling marinades.*
- *Dried dill weed is an acceptable substitute for the fresh leaves. Frozen is even better.*

FENNEL
(Foeniculum vulgare)

A tall (4 to 6 feet), striking plant with feathery foliage, fennel (or sweet fennel) is a decidedly ornamental herb. The foliage resembles dill, but its flavor is similar to licorice or anise.

The varieties Bronze, Rubrum, and Copper feature maroon-purple young growth that later matures to bronze. These create a stunning contrast to lighter flowers and green plants. *F. vulgare* should not be confused with the bulb-forming vegetable, Florence Fennel, or *finocchio* (p. 39).

GROWING

Fennel is hardy to zones 5 or 6, but can be grown easily as an annual. It has naturalized with abandon in the mild climate of coastal California.

Sow seeds in the early spring, thinning small plants to 12 inches apart. Seedlings for the bronze-leafed varieties can be obtained from nurseries specializing in herbs.

HARVEST

Leaves are harvested for culinary use at any time. They do not retain their flavor when dried. Pick the seeds soon after they turn brown or they will self-sow throughout the garden.

> ## C U L I N A R Y   T I P S
>
> • *Use leaves and tender stems in dressings, marinades, salads, pilafs, stews, and fish dishes.*
> • *Fennel seeds add a nutty, anise flavor to breads, cookies, apple pie, Italian sweet biscuits (biscotti), soups, marinades, and tomato sauces.*
> • *East Indian meals are completed with* paan, *a mixture of fennel or anise that sometimes includes cardamom seeds. It serves as a digestive aid and palate cleanser.*

GARLIC
(Allium sativum)

Technically, garlic is considered a vegetable, a member of the onion family. Most people, however, use garlic as a seasoning, not a side dish, so I have included it in this chapter of the book.

The Moosewood kitchen exudes garlic-scented vapors when the cooks are busily prepping meals.

Planted in almost every country of the world, garlic is universally appreciated. This is due to both its popularity as a pungent seasoning and in recognition of the many medicinal and nutritive benefits attributed to it. Garlic *has* been proven to deter the growth of bacteria and fungi, as well as reduce serum cholesterol levels. Eating garlic can do no harm, unless you're the only one in a group who has indulged.

Raw garlic is more often the culprit in breath problems than cooked, because the aroma-causing agent in raw garlic enters the bloodstream and is exhaled with each breath. After an especially garlic-filled Bacchanalian feast, the ancient Romans ate raw parsley to cleanse the breath.

GROWING

The onionlike flat leaves grow 1 to 2 feet tall from cloves planted in fall or winter. Garlic needs a long, cool start and should be planted in the spring only in the coldest areas. Fall-planted bulbs can be twice as large as those planted in spring. Gardeners who live where winter temperatures regularly drop below zero should mulch fall-planted bulbs with 3 or 4 inches of hay or straw. Check with local gardeners or your Cooperative Extension office to learn what varieties do well in your area.

Space individual cloves 6 inches apart, 1 inch deep. Choose a sunny spot with rich, well-drained soil that is not stony. Keep plants well weeded or mulched for the biggest bulbs. Irrigate, if necessary, to keep the soil moist, but not soggy.

HARVEST

Remove most of the coiled flower stalks as they appear to avoid weakening the bulb, sparing a few for their elegant, Art Nouveau form.

To help the bulb ripen, stop watering once the foliage begins to yellow. Carefully dig the bulbs when the tops have withered and browned. If this has not occurred by late summer, bend the tops to the ground to induce dormancy. Dig as above.

Cure bulbs in a dry, shady, ventilated spot for a few days until any clinging dirt can be gently removed. To braid garlic, choose plants with supple foliage that is not too dry or brittle and with no tough, woody flower stalks.

Storage is the same as for onions: a cool, airy, dark location, ideally 50°F. Colder temperatures (in a refrigerator, for example) will cause the bulbs to sprout; hotter temperatures encourage rot.

CULINARY TIPS

- *To quickly peel garlic cloves, give them a good whack with the side of a sturdy, long knife or cleaver. Not so hard that you've got a pulverized mess all over the chopping board, but enough to loosen the skin. Practice.*
- *Garlic's intensity will vary depending on how it's prepared:*
  Whole garlic cloves added to soup, sauce, or stew for long, slow cooking will be mild and gentle.
  Finely minced or pressed garlic will be strong, as its potent oils are released in mashing.
  Whole or half cloves can be used to season cooking oil. Remove the cloves from the hot oil when they are golden; discard. The oil will be garlic flavored without being overpowering.

Rub a wooden salad bowl with a cut clove of garlic (which is then discarded) for a subtly flavored salad.

• Garlic should be carefully sautéed; it will taste harsh and bitter if allowed to brown or burn.

• Add small amounts of pressed or minced garlic to sauces, stews, or soups that need a boost.

• Garlic is a popular seasoning, but for variety and contrast, use it only in one or possibly two dishes in a given meal.

• Elephant garlic, actually the bulb of a type of leek, has cloves two to three times larger than regular garlic. I don't recommend it; the very bland taste requires using more of it, which defeats the size advantage.

• When we're talking garlic, we're talking fresh garlic. Avoid the bitter, artificial taste of dried or processed garlic powder, granules, or salt.

• Garlic croutons are a much-loved garnish at the Restaurant. The crisp, savory croutons perk up soups and salads while putting leftover bread to good use. Simply toss toasted bread cubes with garlic butter. Bake in low heat for a few minutes to crisp.

THE
MOOSEWOOD
RESTAURANT
KITCHEN
GARDEN

100

GERMANDER
(Teucrium chamaedrys)

Germander is an excellent visual foil for brightly colored flowers or the gray foliage of lavender, stachys, sage, and other herbs. The shrubby, deep green foliage can be pruned for a hedgelike effect in edging borders or traditional knot gardens. In summer, petite rosy-violet flowers appear atop small spikes on the 1- to 2-foot plants.

GROWING

Purchase small plants from a nursery that specializes in herbs, or propagate by cuttings and division. Plants can be started from seeds, but may take more than a month to germinate. Germander is a perennial and will grow in zones 5 through 10 in well-drained, good garden soil. Set plants 1 foot apart.

HYSSOP

(Hyssopus officinalis and Agastache foeniculum)

Used as a ritual cleansing herb in biblical times, today the sharply aromatic hyssop plant is grown predominantly as an ornamental. The 1- to 2-foot perennial has spikes of small blue, pink, or white flowers. Plants can be trimmed to a hedge; however, flower spikes may be cut off in the process.

A dwarf variety, *Hyssopus officinalis* Aristata, is a compact plant, no more than 1 foot tall and suitable for low edgings.

Anise hyssop (*Agastache foeniculum*) is a perennial that features showy 3-foot-tall purple flower spikes in summer.

GROWING

Both hyssop and anise hyssop are grown from seeds, divisions, or cuttings. Plants do best in full sun to partial shade in well-drained, average soil. Space dwarf hyssop 8 inches apart, *H. officinalis* 1 foot apart, and anise hyssop 1½ feet apart.

CULINARY TIPS

• *The flowers and leaves of anise hyssop are anise-scented and can be used as an edible garnish.*

LADY'S MANTLE
(Alchemilla vulgaris)

A spreading ornamental herb that grows 1 to 2 feet tall, lady's mantle's gray-green, fan-shaped leaves soften the edges of beds and borders. The "pleated" foliage is valued for its ability to hold sparkling drops of dew or rainwater. Stems of small but abundant yellow-green flowers appear in summer. These can be dried for winter arrangements.

GROWING

Lady's mantle is an easily grown perennial in zones 3 to 9. Plants will spread and possibly self-sow where it's moist (but not soggy) in full sun or partial shade.

THE
MOOSEWOOD
RESTAURANT
KITCHEN
GARDEN

102

LAMB'S EARS
(Stachys byzantina)

The velvety, remarkably soft foliage of lamb's ears forms a textured carpet of silvery green. Densely growing plants create a tight, weed-resistant ground cover or edging. The unusual foliage form and color contrast nicely with other garden plants.

Small purple-flowered spikes appear in summer. These dry for winter bouquets, but tend to be floppy and unattractive in the garden. A nonflowering variety, Silver Carpet, has no flower spikes to detract from the lush matlike effect.

GROWING

This perennial can be started easily from seed or divisions.

Hardy in zones 4 to 10, stachys prefers a sunny, well-drained, sandy soil. Established plants are drought resistant.

LAVENDER
(Lavandula angustifolia, also L. vera or L. officinalis)

Prized for the delicious, clean fragrance of the foliage and flowers, lavender adds grace to gardens. A native of the Mediterranean, lavender grows in fields that scent the air and color the hillsides of Southern France. Much of the lavender used worldwide for perfumes and cosmetics is grown and processed in Provence.

Varieties of lavender range in height from 1 to 3 feet tall, all with silver-gray foliage and flowers of lavender, pink, or purple. Its mounded, bushy habit makes it perfect for low hedges or aromatic edgings.

A sedative tea used to be made with the newly opened flower buds. Years ago, lavender smelling salts were used to revive delicate souls who had fallen into a swoon, something not as common in these tougher times.

GROWING

Lavender is a perennial shrub hardy in zones 5 to 9 grown from seed or cuttings. Plants raised from seed will take longer to produce good-sized plants and may not have the desirable characteristics of specific, cutting-grown strains.

There are many species of lavender; however, *L. angustifolia* is the most readily available and widely grown. Some common named varieties include:

Hidcote—1 to 2 feet tall, deep purple flowers, gray leaves.

Munstead—1 foot tall, with pale lavender flowers, blue-gray leaves.

Jean Davis—1 to 2 feet tall, with pale pink flowers, green leaves.

Lavender is drought resistant and requires a sunny, well-drained spot in light soil. Plants grown in sandy or stony soil will produce flowers with a more potent essential oil than plants grown in rich, moist soil. Good drainage will help lavender survive winter, as will a blanket of pine boughs during times of severe cold.

In the spring, prune off dead growth by trimming back to new buds. The attractive foliage will be evergreen in mild climates and needs pruning solely to maintain a neat appearance. Cut spikes of lavender for dried sachets when the buds are just about to open. Plants may rebloom if the spent flower spikes are pruned off (dead headed) soon after flowering.

CULINARY TIPS

* *Lavender makes an edible garnish and a violet-colored Herb Vinegar (p. 242).*

LEMON BALM
(Melissa officinalis)

The lemon-scented leaves of this 1- to 2-foot perennial are used as a fragrant herb in cooking and for teas. Plant lemon balm at the edge of a path, and its refreshing scent will be freely released when the leaves are brushed against or clipped.

The regular species is a bushy, vivid green plant that makes a good backdrop for other colors. Variegated and golden-leaved varieties (*variegata*) are also available.

All varieties have low spikes of inconspicuous white flowers attractive to bees.

THE
MOOSEWOOD
RESTAURANT
KITCHEN
GARDEN

104

GROWING

Start plants from seed or division, or purchase at a nursery. Lemon balm can be grown in zones 4 to 8, in poor to average soil with a sunny or partially shaded location. Space plants 1½ feet apart, where their vigorous growth will not interfere with small or delicate neighbors. Lemon balm has freely reseeded in my garden, almost to the point of being a pest.

CULINARY TIPS

• *Fresh lemon balm leaves can be added to fruit salads or green salads, herb butters, dressings, dips, pilafs, iced tea, conserves, and sorbets for a delicate lemon bouquet.*
• *Lemon balm loses most of its fragrance when dried. Freeze some leaves or pot a small plant to keep on a sunny windowsill.*

LOVAGE

(Levisticum officinale)

Considering its many virtues—its longevity, celery flavor, and dramatic appearance—it is surprising lovage is not commonly grown. The leafy growth forms a lush mound of dark green leaves with tall (4 to 6 feet) hollow-ribbed stems topped by flat clusters (or umbels) of minute, yellow-green flowers resembling dill.

Gardeners who have difficulty growing celery (which requires a long, cool season) should try planting lovage.

GROWING

Hardy to zone 3, lovage requires some winter chilling, limiting its Southern range to zone 8.

Plants do well in fertile, well-drained soil and full sun to partial shade. Start lovage from seed, division, or by purchasing small plants. Space plants 3 feet apart in anticipation of their future size. Seedlings will take a few years to reach full height.

To spur continuous leaf growth, pinch off flowers as they appear.

CULINARY TIPS

• *The leaves, stems, and seeds can be used anywhere celery would be appropriate, in soups, stews, salads, sauces, stuffings. Flower umbels can be used in pickling marinades or as a garnish.*

MARJORAM
(Origanum majorana)

A useful kitchen garden herb, sweet marjoram is a tender perennial best grown as an annual. Bushy plants reach about 1 foot and feature small, oval, gray-green feltlike leaves and tiny white or pink flowers.

GROWING

Start seeds indoors in late winter or buy small plants at a nursery. After danger of frost is past, space plants 6 inches apart in a sunny spot with light soil.

THE
MOOSEWOOD
RESTAURANT
KITCHEN
GARDEN

106

CULINARY TIPS

• *Marjoram is well suited to the cuisine of its native Mediterranean region, but we use it anywhere its aromatic, mild oregano flavor is desired.*
• *Add marjoram to herb butters, soups, stews, bean dishes, vinegars, dressings, and marinades for vegetables or fish. It keeps good company with basil, bay, dill, garlic, parsley, and thyme.*
• *Marjoram's flavor is well preserved by drying; however, potted plants can be grown indoors on a sunny windowsill.*

MINT

(Mentha species)

Deliciously refreshing, mint is one of the most popular and well known herbs. Vigorous perennials, plants in the *Mentha* family range from a creeping 2 inches to 2 feet tall. Most have square stems and all, opposite, highly aromatic leaves. Small white, pink, or lavender flowers appear in summer on slender spikes.

There are many species or named varieties of mint. Here are five of the most useful and popular:

apple mint *(M. suaveolens)*—The furry round leaves give a light, fruity mint flavor to cool drinks, fruit salads, sorbets, and tea mixes.

corsican, or creeping, mint *(M. requienii)*—A low-growing ground cover, this mint's tiny, deep green leaves release a peppermint fragrance when crushed. Not as hardy as other mints, it can be grown to zone 5.

orange, or bergamot, mint *(M. piperita citrata)*—Adds a citrus fragrance to potpourri and tea mixes and other beverages.

peppermint *(M. piperita)*—Menthol gives peppermint its distinctive, zingy quality. Best for teas, cool drinks, potpourri, frostings, sorbets, and ice creams.

spearmint *(M. spicata)*—One of the best mints for culinary purposes. The familiar, gentle spearmint flavor harmonizes with a wide range of seasonings.

GROWING

Specific mint varieties should be obtained from nurseries or friendly gardeners. Seed-grown mint may not be true to type, as varieties frequently cross-pollinate.

Space plants a foot apart in full sun to partial shade. Mints are happiest in moist soil, but they will survive dry conditions, though growth will be limited. Most mints are hardy to zone 4.

Avoid using manure to fertilize mints; it causes a rust fungus disease.

Mints are wildly invasive perennials and require either isolation from other plants or physical restraint. The latter can be in the form of a moisture-proof barrier of metal or plastic buried 1 foot down from the surface to keep wandering roots at bay. You can achieve the same result by planting mint in a deep container with drainage holes, then "planting" the container.

Cut mint frequently for more compact, bushy plants with tender new leaves. Mint will grow in pots on a sunny windowsill.

THE
MOOSEWOOD
RESTAURANT
KITCHEN
GARDEN

108

CULINARY TIPS

- *To preserve its fragrance and flavor, add fresh mint to hot foods when cooking is completed.*
- *Mint is widely used in the cuisines of the Middle East, Southeast Asia, and the Mediterranean. It adds a fresh, zesty quality to vegetable sautés, leafy or vegetable salads, pilafs, tabouli or other grain salads, bean salads, sauces, dips, dressings, preserves, and jellies.*
- *Vietnamese cooks use fresh mint as a garnish and primary seasoning for soups and stir-fries.*
- *Toss new potatoes, pearl onions, and peas with fresh mint, butter, and chives.*
- *Cucumbers mixed with yogurt and chopped mint is a cooling summer treat.*
- *Bottled, refrigerated, spring, or tap water gets a decided lift from a few sprigs of fresh mint.*
- *Mint dries well, retaining its essential aromatic oils. Pick leaves for drying when the flowers are just opening.*
- *For custards, dessert sauces, or homemade ice cream, steep chopped fresh peppermint leaves in warmed milk for 20 minutes, using about ¼ cup leaves to 1 cup milk. Strain out the leaves and discard; use the milk as your favorite recipe requires.*

MULLEIN
(Verbascum species)

With tall spires of furry stalks and foliage, mullein gives beds and borders a storybook or cottage-garden touch. One of my favorite ornamental herbs, it provides height, color, and textural interest. There are several named species, all long-flowering biennials or perennials.

V. bombyciferum (where *do* they get these names?) is a silvery, particularly woolly-leaved species with 5-foot-tall spires of yellow flowers.

V. olympicum is similar, with smoother foliage and a "candelabra" of spikes with yellow flowers.

GROWING

Mullein is hardy in zones 6 to 9, but can be grown further north in areas with reliable snow cover, or if covered with a generous mound of cut pine boughs.

Preferring poor, sandy, well-drained soil in a sunny location, mullein should be started in peat pots or seeded where it is to grow, since it resents transplanting. Mullein will not tolerate a wet, soggy soil.

The first-year plants produce a beautiful rosette of leaves; bloom stalks appear the second year. Plants content with the location will self-sow.

OREGANO
(Origanum heracleoticum)

Our oregano of choice is the Greek species, noted for its pungent aroma that most people recognize as a key ingredient in pizza sauce. Long before pizza was invented, Greeks were enjoying native oregano, a name that translates as "joy of the mountains."

Even among plant experts, confusion reigns as to just which "oregano" is truly oregano. In fact, most seeds and plants sold as oregano are nothing of the sort.

Though they taste something like oregano, they are frequently a wimpy, pallid variety lacking Greek oregano's bite and aroma. Stick to plants and seeds specifically labeled *O. heracleoticum*.

O. vulgare Auream is a golden-leaved low-growing ornamental. The bright foliage contrasts well with other herbs' various greens and grays.

GROWING

A perennial hardy to zone 5, Greek oregano forms 1- to 2-foot-tall vigorous, spreading mounds topped with sprays of small white or purple flowers. Space plants 1½ feet apart in a sunny spot with well-drained soil. Remove flower spikes to prolong new leaf growth. Oregano dries well, with most of its fragrance preserved.

THE
MOOSEWOOD
RESTAURANT
KITCHEN
GARDEN

110

CULINARY TIPS

• *Greek salads combine the sharp, aromatic flavors of feta cheese, chopped fresh oregano, red onion, and kalamata olives with mixed greens, dill sprigs, and tomato and cucumber slices. Serve with lemon wedges and olive oil.*
• *Add oregano to Mexican bean dishes for more robust flavor.*
• *A simple yet delectable open-faced sandwich can be made with crusty Italian bread and thin slices of fresh mozzarella cheese and tomato topped with chopped fresh oregano and a drizzle of olive oil.*
• *Oregano is de rigueur for pizza and most Italian tomato sauces.*
• *Add its assertive flavor to marinades for salads, kebobs, and roasted or grilled vegetables and fish.*
• *Season vinegars and oils with oregano.*
• *Olive oil, garlic, parsley, basil, dill, tomato, eggplant, and zucchini harmonize well with oregano.*

PARSLEY
(Petroselinum crispum)

Parsley is to Moosewood as fairy dust is to Tinkerbelle. Few of our dishes leave the kitchen without being ritually sprinkled with the chopped green herb. It's not only for the bright dash of color but also its clean, mild taste.

A powerhouse of nutrition, parsley contains high concentrations of vitamins A, B complex, C, and E, and the minerals iron and calcium.

There are three basic types of parsley: flat-leaf, or Italian; curly-leaf, and parsnip-rooted (Hamburg). Curly parsley makes an attractive garnish, but the flat-leaf type has a richer, more substantial flavor and is best used as a culinary herb. "What is this tasteless American parsley?" my Italian friend Luna disdainfully remarked when I suggested she cook with the curly parsley growing in my garden years ago. The roots of Hamburg parsley have a celerylike taste, useful in soups and stews.

The vivid green divided or frilled leaves make a handsome border or edging plant for vegetable and flower beds.

GROWING

Parsley is a biennial best grown as an annual. The seeds are slow to germinate; soak in warm water for 24 hours to speed the process. Start seeds indoors for a quicker crop or in the garden when the soil has warmed but before hot weather. Keep the seedbed moist (see Carrots, p. 27). Seeds do not remain viable for long; use fresh ones each year. Plant 6 to 8 inches apart in fertile, moist soil in a sunny or lightly shaded spot.

Plants can be potted for winter use after a couple of light frosts. They will do well in a cool, sunny room.

Parsley may survive mild winters but will send up flower stalks and quickly go to seed with the first warmth of spring.

CULINARY TIPS

• Use parsley as a seasoning as well as a garnish. A couple of tablespoons of chopped leaves give a mild, fresh green taste appropriate to almost any savory dish.

• At the end of the cooking time add some to soups, sauces, or stews that need perking up.

- *Noodles, potatoes, steamed vegetables, pilafs, and grains benefit from being tossed with chopped parsley.*
- *Mayonnaise, marinades, dips, spreads, dressings, pesto, and cheese fillings that feature a specific more assertive herb, such as basil or garlic, will be enhanced by parsley's milder, sweet flavor.*
- *An effective breath sweetener, parsley will help to counter the scents of raw garlic or onions.*
- *Use a few sturdy sprigs of parsley as an edible brush to swab marinades on grilled foods.*
- *Dried parsley has little flavor or appeal. Freeze the leaves for winter use; they will be sweeter when thawed.*

THE
MOOSEWOOD
RESTAURANT
KITCHEN
GARDEN

112

ROSEMARY
(Rosmarinus officinalis)

With its gnarled, twisted growth and gray-green needlelike leaves, my ten-year-old rosemary plant has the venerable presence of a windswept bonsai. I periodically prune off sprigs for cooking, keeping the plant compact and bushy. It winters in a cool, bright sunny room and flowers through the cold months.

Rosemary leaves have an aromatic, woodsy fragrance and a piney, resinous taste. This distinctive flavor can be wonderful used discreetly. However, I have sampled a few dishes overpowered and ruined by too much rosemary. Perhaps this is why some Moosewood cooks have hidden the rosemary jar at the back of the top kitchen shelf, a place you can reach only by standing on a stool and risking decapitation by an overhead fan.

Common rosemary (R. officinalis) is the best variety for cooking. It grows in an upright, shrubby form and is hardy to 15°F. Trailing rosemary (R. officinalis Prostratus) is the plant described at the beginning of this discussion. It is hardy to 20°F. and mildly flavored. With a picturesque form of trailing, twisting stems, Prostratus looks good in hanging baskets and containers. Arp is the hardiest variety of rosemary, reputed to survive temperatures of −10°F. without protection.

Except for the white-flowered Alba, most varieties have blooms in various shades of blue. Rosemary typically blooms in the winter.

GROWING

Rosemary is difficult to grow from seed, so buy plants at a nursery, or root cuttings from mature plants. Gardeners in much of the country will have to grow rosemary in containers that can be moved indoors in winter. Indoors or out, rosemary needs a sandy, well-drained soil and plenty of sun. It should be allowed to dry between waterings, but not to the point of wilt. The essential oils are more fragrant in plants grown in poor, dry soil. Leaves on overwatered plants will brown and may fall off. Keep indoor plants in a cool location away from heat.

CULINARY TIPS

- *The warm, piney taste and fragrance of rosemary highlight herb butters, marinades, cheese spreads, dips, soups, stews, grilled and roasted vegetables or fish, crusty bread, rolls, crackers, and potpourri mixes.*
- *Rosemary keeps good company with its Mediterranean cousins lemon, tomato, and olive oil.*
- *The brittle, dried rosemary leaves do not soften much in cooking; we try to infuse its flavor in oil or liquid. Warm the oil or butter to be used in a dish and add rosemary. Heat gently for a few minutes; strain and discard the leaves. For soups, stews, or other liquid-based dishes, rosemary can be added to a bouquet garni in cheesecloth or a tea/spice ball.*

HERBS

113

RUE
(Ruta graveolens)

Rue is grown for its ornamental, lacy blue-green foliage and provides an unusual counterpoint to other garden colors. This bitter herb of antiquity was once used to ward off evil spirits. Pugnacious qualities might have been attributed to rue because of its pungently fragrant leaves that can be toxic if ingested in quantity. Avoid the fresh leaves and their juice; they provoke dermatitis in many people.

Blue Beauty and Blue Mound are two varieties with richer blue-green foliage than the common species. Variegata has cream-edged leaves.

GROWING

Perennial in zones 4 to 9, rue is a 3-foot-tall evergreen in warmer areas. Start seeds in the winter, or buy plants. Plants should be spaced 1½ feet apart in average garden soil in a sunny location.

THE
MOOSEWOOD
RESTAURANT
KITCHEN
GARDEN

114

SAGE
(Salvia officinalis)

Sage deserves a second chance from people whose sole association with the herb is as a poultry seasoning cliché. Highly aromatic, pebble-textured leaves appear on a shrubby perennial that grows 1 to 2½ feet tall. The gray-green leaves and blue-violet flowers can be an ornamental addition to herb or flower gardens.

Variegated sages, with golden, purple, or tricolored leaves, are available but less hardy than the common species and will reliably winter outdoors only to zone 7.

Sage has been used as a medicinal and culinary herb for hundreds of years. The Latin *salvia* means "to save," testament to its healing properties.

Salvia sclarea, or Clary Sage, is a self-sowing biennial that bears impressive 3- to 4-foot spikes of showy, silver-pink flowers and broad, gray-green leaves redolent of pine and sage. The flowers make an elegant garnish, while the leaves can be used in potpourri.

GROWING

Sages do well in dry or average, well-drained soil. *S. officinalis,* perennial in zones 4 to 8, is the best culinary sage. Seeds have a short lifespan, so buy small plants or obtain divisions or cuttings. Space plants 1½ feet apart in full sun.

Evergreen in many climates, common sage can be picked through the winter, even here in Ithaca.

In the spring, cut back the woody growth of established plants by half to encourage new, bushy growth.

CULINARY TIPS

- *Fresh sage leaves have a more complex, milder flavor than dried.*
- *Sage enhances herb butters, pasta sauces, marinades, cheese dishes, breads, stuffings, beans, omelets, hearty soups or stews, polenta, and potato dishes.*
- *An aromatic tea made with sage leaves is a warming, soothing beverage.*

SANTOLINA
(*Santolina* species)

A shrublike perennial, santolina is a strikingly ornamental herb. The finely cut, evergreen foliage is elegantly filigreed, giving the plant a corallike appearance. Small yellow button flowers appear in summer.

Traditionally used as an easily pruned herb in knot gardens, santolina is also an excellent specimen for rock gardens or pots. The dried foliage of all species is highly aromatic and can be used in potpourri and decorative arrangements, or as a moth repellent.

Santolina chamaecyparissus is silvery-leaved with woolly foliage growing to 18 inches. A dwarf variety, Nana, is 10 to 12 inches tall.

Santolina virens has deep green, needlelike leaves and grows to 2 feet.

GROWING

Santolina can be started from seed, cuttings, or divisions. Space plants 1 foot apart for a dense, low hedge. It prefers a sunny location in light, sandy soil that doesn't stay wet in winter.

Reliably hardy to zone 6, Santolina should be covered with a protective layer of pine boughs in zone 5.

SAVORY
(*Satureja* species)

Savories are good candidates for low-growing edgings and knot or rock gardens. When brushed against, their aromatic essence is freely released.

Summer savory (*S. hortensis*) is an 18-inch annual bearing small, pale pink or white flowers, and gray-green soft leaves that are more suited for culinary purposes than the resinous, strong tasting perennial species.

Winter savory (*S. montana*) is a 1-foot-tall, woody, semievergreen perennial with small, deep green leaves and small, white or lilac flowers. This species is best used as a landscape plant.

THE
MOOSEWOOD
RESTAURANT
KITCHEN
GARDEN

116

GROWING

Plants can be started by seed, division, or cutting. Ordinary well-drained soil in a sunny location suits both savories, though summer savory will do well in partial shade. Winter savory is hardy to zone 5.

CULINARY TIPS

• *We use summer savory in bean dishes, split pea, lentil, and other hearty soups, herb breads, marinades, and cheese spreads. The robust flavor is reminiscent of a combination of sage and thyme.*
• *Savory retains much of its flavor when dried.*

SCENTED GERANIUMS
(Pelargonium species)

Scented geraniums offer a multitude of fragrant foliage possibilities. These easily grown plants also have a wide range of colors, textures, and leaf shapes. The foliage can be smooth, hairy, lobed, ruffled, finely cut, velvety, or pleated.

There are more than 50 different scented-leaved geraniums, with fragrances from "apple cider" to "strawberry." Some require an act of faith or fantasy to appreciate the connection between the name and the perceived fragrance. A few I have enjoyed include:

apple *(P. odoratissimum)*—small, green, round leaves, trailing stems good for hanging baskets, white flowers.

coconut *(P. parviflorum)*—small, deep green leaves on trailing stems, strong fragrance.

ginger *(P. torento)*—ground ginger fragrance, round, crinkled leaves with lavender blooms, upright growth.

lemon *(P. crispum)*—upright growing with small, green, crinkled leaves of strong fragrance.

nutmeg *(P. fragrans)*—good basket variety with low-growing stems, gray leaves, white blooms, and spicy scent.

peppermint *(P. tomentosum)*—large, velvety leaves with a pronounced peppermint scent, vigorous trailing stems good for containers or baskets.

rose *(P. graveolens)*—upright-growing with finely cut, strongly fragrant green leaves.

GROWING

Hardy only in frost-free areas, scented geraniums are best enjoyed as potted plants to be moved indoors in cold weather. Purchase named varieties from specialty herb growers, or obtain root cuttings from other gardeners.

Geraniums do best in a sunny location indoors, but will grow well outdoors with just a few hours' direct sun a day.

Allow plants to dry between thorough waterings. Fertilize only in the spring and summer; winter-fed plants will be leggy and floppy.

THE
MOOSEWOOD
RESTAURANT
KITCHEN
GARDEN

118

CULINARY TIPS

- *The distinctively scented fresh leaves can be used to accent bouquets, teas, potpourri, cakes, jams, biscuits, muffins, and custards. Use 1 large leaf in the bottom of a muffin tin or custard cup; 2 in the bottom of a cake tin. Add the leaves before the batter or dough.*
- *Make a rose, coconut, or ginger geranium sugar by adding 2 large, whole fresh leaves to 1 cup of sugar. Store in a closed container for 2 weeks and sift out the leaves. The sugar can be used for baking or in dessert recipes.*
- *Press scented leaves in butter or cream cheese and wrap with plastic overnight. Remove the leaves the next day and discard. Use the butter or cream cheese as a base for frostings or serve with breads, muffins, and other baked goods.*
- *Place some lightly crushed lemon geranium leaves in small finger bowls of warm water for a gracious after-dinner touch.*

SWEET CICELY
(Myrrhis odorata)

A perennial with delicate, fernlike foliage, sweet cicely has a sweet anise flavor. The 3-foot plants are topped with delicate white flower heads in early summer.

GROWING

Sow fresh seeds in the fall or purchase seedlings for spring planting. Plants should stand about 1½ feet apart.

Sweet cicely is one of the few herbs that prefers full shade and a rich, moist soil. It is hardy in zones 3 to 10 and will generously self-sow where it is happy. If this becomes a nuisance, cut off the flower heads as soon as they fade.

CULINARY TIPS

- *The young leaves, seeds, and roots will impart a licorice or anise flavor. We use the chopped leaf in delicate sauces, herb butters, fruit salads, and fruit pies, and tossed with steamed vegetables.*
- *The ground seeds can be used in baked goods instead of anise or fennel.*
- *Dried leaves lack flavor; freeze sweet cicely for winter use.*

SWEET WOODRUFF
(Galium odoratum)

A superb ground cover, sweet woodruff can create drifts of low-growing, dark green, pinwheel-shaped leaves in partially shaded or lightly wooded areas. In late spring, dainty white flowers hover above the foliage. The dried leaves have a delicious scent that reminds me of newly mown grass, pipe tobacco, and vanilla. It makes a wonderful potpourri herb.

GROWING

The 6- to 10-inch plants are perennial in zones 3 to 9. Space plants obtained by purchase, division, or cutting 1 foot apart. Woodruff is difficult to grow from seed. Its rampant growing habit can be invasive.

CULINARY TIPS

- *A traditional German May wine is made by adding sprigs of sweet woodruff to white wine and letting it steep for a day or overnight.*

TARRAGON
(Artemisia dracunculus)

One of the classic herbs of French cuisine, tarragon is an integral part of a cook's garden. A perennial, tarragon grows 2 to 3 feet tall, eventually spreading to the same width, its branching stems covered with thin green leaves.

GROWING

THE
MOOSEWOOD
RESTAURANT
KITCHEN
GARDEN

120

True French tarragon can be only grown from divisions or cuttings. Seed-grown strains are probably Russian tarragon, a poor substitute decidedly lacking in flavor. To test a plant, nibble a leaf. French tarragon has a bite that numbs the tongue. This quality is not peppery and will be unnoticed when tarragon is used in cooking.

Tarragon is hardy in zones 5 to 9. Place small plants or divisions 2 feet apart in a sunny location with rich, well-drained soil.

Northern gardeners should cover plants after the ground has frozen for better winter survival.

CULINARY TIPS

• *The flavor of tarragon has a rich fullness with a licorice/anise base. Add the fresh herb toward the end of the cooking time to preserve its bouquet.*
• *At Moosewood it is used in dressings, dips, sauces, butters, marinades, omelets, vegetable fillings, soups, stews, grains, vinegars, fish dishes, and herb breads.*
• *Make a tarragon mayonnaise with tarragon vinegar and the chopped herb (p. 248).*
• *Use whole sprigs of tarragon in slow-cooked dishes such as soups or stews. The stem can be pulled out after the leaves fall away from it.*
• *Tarragon leaves should be frozen to retain their flavor. Though dried leaves are an acceptable substitute, they lack the full-bodied aroma of fresh.*

THYME
(Thymus species)

As a diminutive, spreading ground cover or a low-growing shrub, thyme is a fragrant, ornamental presence. There are a few hundred species of thymes from throughout the world. Here's a list of a few easily obtained species we have used for culinary and/or ornamental purposes:

caraway thyme *(T. herba-barona)*—a creeping 2- to 6-inch-tall ground cover and culinary herb with caraway-scented green leaves and lavender blooms.

common thyme *(T. vulgaris)*—an attractive culinary herb with petite gray-green leaves and white or pale lavender flowers on a 10-inch woody subshrub.

lemon thyme *(T. citriodorus)*—a culinary herb with a distinct lemon fragrance and green leaves on a 10-inch-tall bushy plant. Golden-leaf-edged Aureus or silver-leaf-edged Argenteus types are also highly ornamental.

red creeping thyme *(T. praecox)*—dark green, minute foliage and prostrate stems make Coccineus a slowly spreading ornamental ground cover. Profuse tiny red flowers cover the foliage in summer. *T. praecox* Albus is a white-flowering form. Both make excellent, fragrant, sturdy herbs to place between paving stones or to edge gardens.

woolly thyme *(T. pseudolanuginosus)*—a prostrate, creeping plant with very tiny, soft, gray-green leaves. Particularly ornamental where it can languidly drape itself over rocks or cascade down from the top of a wall.

GROWING

Though hardy in zones 4 to 9, common and lemon thymes are short-lived perennials. The creeping species are more durable and long-lived.

Thymes can be started from seeds, cuttings, or divisions. Creeping plants will frequently root along their stems as they expand their territory. These "colonies" can be dug up (use a sharp spade and cut out a clump the same way you'd cut a sheet cake) and replanted elsewhere.

All thymes prefer a location where they can bask in the sun and a dryish, well-drained soil. Space plants 1 foot apart.

THE
MOOSEWOOD
RESTAURANT
KITCHEN
GARDEN

122

CULINARY TIPS

• *An all-purpose savory herb, thyme is appropriate in many dishes. Its flavor can dominate a dish, so add small amounts—1 teaspoon fresh or ½ teaspoon dried —at first, and more later if necessary. (These quantities would be for 4 servings.)*
• *Thyme suffuses its fragrance in slow cooking and can be added early on without risking flavor loss.*
• *We use thyme in chowders, stews, sauces, butters, marinades, dressings, stocks, vinegars, seasoned oils, breads, herbed croutons, bean dishes, and stuffings, and combined with nutmeg, bay leaf, and parsley.*
• *Thyme has a particular affinity for leeks and onions. Sauté in a heavy skillet with butter or oil, and cook slowly until the onions or leeks are soft and golden. Use the resulting fragrant vegetables as a soup or stew base, pizza topping, casserole addition, or part of a filling for stuffed vegetables.*
• *The petite thyme flowers make a dainty, colorful garnish. Float a few in cups of smooth, puréed soup.*
• *Use whole thyme sprigs in foods that simmer or sauté for more than a few moments. The stems can be removed after the leaves have fallen off.*
• *Thyme leaves can be frozen, but the dried herb retains most of the original flavor.*
• *Lemon or common thyme is an aromatic addition to potpourri or herbal tea mixes.*

YARROW
(Achillea species)

I have a fondness for yarrows; they are truly carefree and sturdy perennials. These drought-resistant, ornamental herbs range from the 2-foot-tall weedy common wildflower to stately 5-foot-tall varieties.

Predominantly grown today for its foliage and blooms, yarrow has an ancient history as a medicinal plant. Legend places its Latin name from Achilles' use of the herb to halt the flow of blood and heal the wounds of his fellow Greek warriors.

Common varieties include:

angel's breath (A. ptarmica)—two feet tall with profuse, small white double flowers resembling baby's-breath and with fairly mundane foliage.

coronation gold (A. filipendulina)—3 feet tall, upright stems with grayish-green feathery foliage topped by flat, yellow 3-inch wide flower heads. The visual effect has a striking quality of combined vertical and horizontal forms.

gold plate (A. filipendulina)—four to 5 feet tall with a form similar to Coronation Gold but with greener foliage and 6-inch flower heads.

red beauty and white beauty (A. millefolium)—two feet tall with lacy, finely divided, deep green foliage and red or white flower heads through the summer.

Both the *A. ptarmica* and *A. millefolium* varieties are aggressive spreaders. Take advantage of their pushy habits by using them as ground covers in a location bounded by paving, walls, deep shade, or other barriers to unlimited expansion.

All of the yarrows listed have flowers suitable for cutting and drying.

GROWING

Perennial in zones 3 to 10, yarrow plants can be obtained at most nurseries or started from seed. Plants should be divided every few years to avoid crowding. Yarrows are sun-loving and prefer a light soil of average fertility. They will not be happy in wet, heavy soils.

EDIBLE
FLOWERS

One year, when my garden was filled with nasturtiums, I brought dozens of blooms to the Restaurant to use as edible garnish. The vibrant, colorful flowers were a gorgeous accent. However, most people had to be informed that they could eat the spicy, watercress-flavored blossoms.

In the last few years, gardening books and magazines, as well as restaurants, have been promoting flower eating as if it were a new idea. In fact, written history cites the eating of blossoms as far back as the ancient Greeks and Romans. When used at the table and as ornamental plantings, most flowering edibles produce enough blooms that you can have your bouquet and eat it too.

A word of caution: Many common garden flowers are poisonous! They include: autumn crocus, azalea and rhododendron species, buttercup, clematis, daffodil and narcissus, delphinium, dicentra (bleeding heart), foxglove, hyacinth, iris, lantana, larkspur, lily-of-the-valley, lupine, oleander, poinsettia, flowering sweet-pea, and wisteria.

Pick only those flowers listed below. Begin with plants or seeds whose true identity is without question. Next, mark your edibles with metal tags or stakes (plastic fades; wood rots) to mark them clearly until you become familiar with their appearance.

Besides making positive identification, it's important to avoid picking any flowers for culinary use that have been subjected to insecticides or herbicides. To be safe, use only those flowers you've grown yourself or have obtained from a trusted supplier or friend. When in doubt, don't use.

The following listings include annuals and perennials suited to a range of garden situations. Any of the culinary herb flowers noted in the Culinary Tips in the Herbs chapter (p. 77) can be used for culinary purposes, along with the blossoms of squashes (p. 67) and bean vines (p. 21) (scarlet runner are the showiest).

Any of the flowers below can be sprinkled, in moderation, on salads or soups, or simply used to garnish the plate. Check carefully for insects and dirt, but try not to wash flowers. They bruise and tear easily, and a bedraggled flower is not very appetizing. If necessary, soak them gently in cold water, drain, and serve soon after.

THE
MOOSEWOOD
RESTAURANT
KITCHEN
GARDEN

126

ANCHUSA
(Anchusa azurea)

A short-lived perennial hardy in zones 3 to 10. Common varieties Dropmore and Loddon Royalist have sprays of purplish buds opening to intense, deep blue flowers on impressive 3- to 5-foot plants.

GROWING

Anchusa prefers a sunny location in a fertile, well-drained soil. Start from seeds or purchase small plants. Stake in windy areas. Plants become ungainly after blooming and can be cut back to the base.

CULINARY TIPS

- *The small, ¾-inch blooms will float nicely in lightly colored soups or can be frozen in ice cubes.*

CARNATIONS OR CLOVE PINKS
(*Dianthus* species)

Annual, biennial, or perennial plants with a delicious, spicy, clove-cinnamon fragrance. Look for varieties that are noted as fragrant. Some are not. Recommended: *Dianthus allwoodii alpinus, D. plumarius* (cottage pink) Spring Beauty, annual carnation (*D. caryophyllus*), fragrance or dwarf fragrance mix. All have low-growing or lax, grassy, gray-green foliage. The perennials form neat tufts for edging, between paving stones, or in rock gardens.

THE
MOOSEWOOD
RESTAURANT
KITCHEN
GARDEN

128

GROWING

Annual carnations should be started indoors early. They take up to 5 months to flower from seed. *Dianthus allwoodii* and *D. plumarius* are perennial in zones 4 to 10 and can be started from seed or obtained as divisions and plants.

Dianthus need a sandy, well-drained soil with lime added if conditions are acidic. Plants do best in full sun. Clip off faded flowers for a longer blooming season.

CULINARY TIPS

• *The clove-flavored petals can be added to custards, muffins, fruit punches and other beverages, and dessert sauces. Whole blooms are excellent garnishes.*

CHRYSANTHEMUM
(Chrysanthemum morifolium)

Chrysanthemums, or mums, are appreciated for their profuse, welcome autumn bloom when most other garden flowers are in decline. The garden mums commonly available at nurseries are *morifolium* hybrids, ranging from 1-foot-tall dwarf plants to staking varieties reaching 6 feet in height. The familiar, crisp fragrance is reminiscent of autumn and florist shops.

GROWING

Though mums are reputedly hardy in zones 4 to 10, my experience with chrysanthemums has shown them to be short-lived perennials. They can be started from seed or purchased as small plants. Divide clumps every 1 to 2 years for good growth; replant or share with friends and neighbors. Mums like a rich, well-drained soil in full sun. Plants bought at garden centers in the fall have a higher risk of winterkill, since the roots have little time to get established. If you choose to overwinter mums, mulch them heavily. Because of their shallow roots, they're easily damaged by extreme cold.

CULINARY TIPS

- *Chrysanthemums have been used in Chinese cuisine for centuries. A few brightly colored petals can garnish a stir-fry, soup, or salad.*
- *Garnish a large platter of food with the cheery, warm autumnal colors of mixed mums.*
- *The blooms are pungently flavored. Use just a few petals in food preparations.*

DAYLILIES
(Hemerocallis species)

One of the most commonly grown perennials, daylilies can be roadside weeds or choice, genetically engineered hybrids. *Hemerocallis fulva*, the orange or tawny daylily, is sometimes mistakenly called tiger lily (a very separate species). Because the plants are quick spreaders, they should not be used in regular garden beds. Grow orange daylilies where they can naturalize freely. The dense, grasslike clumps of arching green leaves effectively choke out most weeds. Gardeners with limited space may want to restrict their daylilies to hybrid varieties with more restrained growing habits or choose locations bound by permanent obstacles (house walls, paving, et cetera) for the vigorous wild species.

There are hundreds of named hybrid varieties, their colors running from the warm creams, yellows, peaches, golds, reds, and maroons to the cooler shades of pink, lavender, and purple.

GROWING

Hardy in zones 3 to 9, daylilies will tolerate full shade but flower best in partial shade to full sun. Plant divisions (purchased or from other clumps) 1 to 2 feet apart in average, well-drained soil. Divide the hybrid types after 5 to 6 years for best growth.

Individual blooms last only a day (thus its Latin name, from the Greek, meaning "beautiful for a day"), but plants may flower for 1 month or more. Though drought tolerant and low maintenance, daylilies will bloom best if not allowed to dry out before and during blooming.

THE
MOOSEWOOD
RESTAURANT
KITCHEN
GARDEN

130

CULINARY TIPS

- *The largest, unopened buds can be quickly steamed or stir-fried for a delicate vegetable with an asparaguslike flavor. These buds are dried by the Chinese and called "Golden Needles" or "Lily Buds" in many recipes. They provide a subtle taste and slight thickening effect to hot-and-sour soup and mu shu dishes.*
- *Opened flowers can be batter dipped and deep-fried, or stuffed and baked.*
- *The large, brilliant daylily flowers make elegant garnishes for platters of food. Choose a multicolored variety of blooms.*
- *Avoid picking buds or blooms from roadsides. Many localities spray herbicides to control weeds.*

HOLLYHOCK
(Alcea rosea)

Hollyhocks have an old-fashioned cottage-garden look. I prefer the traditional single-flowered types to the newer, double-flowered pom-pom varieties. The doubles are showy, but lack the grace of the singles and, being heavier, are more apt to topple in wind and rain.

GROWING

Biennial plants, hollyhocks are grown in zones 3 to 8 from seed or purchased seedlings. Grow in full sun in average, slightly alkaline soil. Plants content with their location will self-sow.

CULINARY TIPS

- *The bright petals add a mild flavor to salads. Whole flowers make appealing garnishes.*

MARIGOLDS, LEMON OR TANGERINE GEM
(Tagetes signata)

The Gem series marigolds are the only varieties suitable for culinary use. Flowers and foliage have a fresh citruslike taste more pleasing than the pungent quality of other marigolds. Plants form neat, hedgelike mounds 10 to 12 inches high with feathery foliage topped by vibrant, small, single yellow or orange blooms. Gems are small enough for containers or to edge borders and beds.

THE
MOOSEWOOD
RESTAURANT
KITCHEN
GARDEN

132

GROWING

Seeds can be sown indoors 6 to 8 weeks before the last frost, or outdoors when the soil has warmed and frosts are past. Grow 10 to 12 inches apart in average garden soil in full sun. Marigolds are profuse and long bloomers. Cutting spent flowers will encourage the production of more.

CULINARY TIPS

• *Add petals to salads, soups, sauces, marinated vegetables, and pilafs. Whole blossoms are best for garnish.*

NASTURTIUM
(Tropaeolum majus)

I remember reading about the edibility of nasturtiums long before the current flower cookery vogue. Perhaps this is due to its unique flavor, a peppery-watercress taste with a floral fragrance. Nasturtiums are not just another pretty face in the edible garnish realm. They add a desirable flavor to the foods with which they're combined. The exuberant flowers and handsome foliage are reason enough to plant this easily grown annual.

GROWING

Seeds should be planted where they are to be grown when the soil is warm and frost danger is past. Nasturtiums are difficult to transplant, and consequently not appropriate for starting indoors ahead of time. Plant in full sun, 8 inches apart, in soil of poor to moderate fertility. (Rich, fertile soil will yield bushy plants with few flowers.) Soak the husky seeds overnight in warm water for speedier germination. Whirlybird is a dwarf type that grows 8 to 10 inches tall, Jewel 12 to 16 inches. Climbing varieties include Semi-Tall Gleam at 3 feet and Fordhook Favorites at 6 feet.

CULINARY TIPS

* *Use the chopped petals in herb butters, cheese spreads, dips, sandwiches, omelets, sauces, salads, and rice pilafs.*
* *Seedpods picked while still green are frequently pickled and used as a substitute for capers.*

PANSIES
(*Viola* species)

Plantings of pansies and other members of the *Viola* family have an Alice in Wonderland quality, their perky "faces" nodding and bobbing in a gentle breeze. Children, especially, are drawn to the richly colored, whimsical blossoms. *V. wittrockiana*, commonly called pansies, are the largest of the three listed. Violas (*V. cornuta*) are smaller, and come with or without the facelike markings. Johnny-jump-ups (*V. tricolor*) are smaller still, with an abundance of yellow, blue, and purple, 1-inch-wide flowers.

THE
MOOSEWOOD
RESTAURANT
KITCHEN
GARDEN

134

GROWING

All three bloom best in the cool weather of spring, moderate summers, or mild winters. I have found the Universal Mix series to be particularly heat resistant.

Flats of pansies are usually available at nurseries and garden centers. These will give the quickest results. Plants take a few months to start from seed and require cool growing conditions. For spring or winter bloom, start seeds in late summer. Gardeners in cold climates should overwinter small plants in a protected cold frame. Seed sown indoors early to midwinter will start to bloom from late spring to early summer.

Pansies and Johnny-jump-ups are biennials or annuals. Violas are short-lived perennials. All three will self-sow; Johnny-jump-ups are particularly good for naturalizing and will pop up all over the garden, hence their common name.

Grow these *Viola* species in full sun to partial shade in a moist, fertile soil Partial shade is more appropriate for hot climates.

Plants are attractive in containers or at the front of garden beds.

CULINARY TIPS

• *All three varieties have a lightly sweet taste that reminds me of a mildly fragrant lettuce. They make amusing, charming garnishes. We like to press the blossoms into the frosting of birthday cakes.*

ROSES
(Rosa species)

Perhaps more than any other flower, the rose embodies a lush, sensual, romantic presence that is perfectly manifested in fragrance and form. It has been employed in perfumes, medicinals, food delicacies, love potions, and as a metaphor by poets through the ages.

Many modern roses have a reputation for fussiness, requiring the gardener's vigilance and a supply of pesticides to thwart pests and diseases. However, if you are an attentive gardener knowledgeable in organic pest and disease control, these roses will prove well worth growing.

Shrub roses are noted for their relative ease of cultivation compared to the named hybrid varieties. All roses need to be watered and weeded until established, but shrub roses will, in succeeding years, thrive with only moderate attention.

GROWING

The rugosa rose is one of my favorite shrub types. It is hardy to zone 2 and disease resistant, and bears multitudes of single white, pink, or deep pink blooms in the early summer and beyond. The strongly fragrant blossoms appear on thorny shrubs up to 6 feet tall that are useful for naturalized settings or the back of a border. Rugosa roses have large, vibrant orange-red fruits (hips) fall through winter. Plants are widely available at nurseries or through mail order. Space shrubs 3 to 4 feet apart (or closer for a tight hedge), in full sun, in a moderately fertile to sandy, well-drained soil.

CULINARY TIPS

- *Rose petals and buds have many uses—as garnish, in jam, syrup, potpourri, sorbet, tea, and vinegar. Clip the flowers above the bitter white heel at the junction of petal and flower center.*
- *Rose hips can be used for jams, syrup, or herbal tea. They contain 400 times more vitamin C per ounce than oranges. The English used rose hip syrup as a native vitamin C source during World War II.*

SUNFLOWER
(Helianthus annuus)

A field of sunflowers in bloom is an impressive sight, all of the heads facing the same direction, row upon row of dazzling, golden-rayed flowers. The common sunflower, growing up to 10 feet tall, is a wonderful choice for a dramatic plant. It also attracts birds to the ripening seeds. Sunspot and Zebulon are two dwarf varieties with 10-inch flowers on 2-foot-tall stalks.

A superb garden subject is the branching type of sunflower which continues to bear flowers from late summer until frost on 5- to 6-foot-tall plants. The common sunflower has one bloom that lasts about 2 weeks. Color Fashion Mixed is a recommended branching variety with flowers ranging from yellow to gold, and including brown, crimson, and mahogany.

THE
MOOSEWOOD
RESTAURANT
KITCHEN
GARDEN

136

GROWING

The sunflowers above are annuals that are seeded outdoors where they are to grow, when frost danger has passed. Thin plants to stand 2 feet apart. Plant in full sun or very light shade in average soil.

CULINARY TIPS

• *The large petals make a showy garnish. Use them as a bed for desserts or vegetable and fruit salads. Their flavor is mild and unobtrusive.*

VIOLETS
(Viola odorata)

Sweetly fragrant, petite lavender, white, and blue flowers are produced by low-growing 8-inch plants from mid- to late spring. When not in bloom, the green, heart-shaped foliage makes a handsome ground cover for partially shaded, moist locations.

GROWING

Perennial in zones 6 to 10, sweet violets can be grown from seed to bloom the following year. Plants can be purchased or obtained as divisions from an established clump.

CULINARY TIPS

- *The perfume of violets varies with type and growing conditions. However, all are useful as a garnish added to salads or floated in soups, or used in jams and vinegars.*

DESIGN

DESIGN CONSIDERATIONS

THE
MOOSEWOOD
RESTAURANT
KITCHEN
GARDEN

140

One important question to ask yourself before starting a garden is: How much time will I have to devote to this project? For a garden to become an attractive, useful addition to your home, it must be well maintained. Start with a small space that you can care for easily. If possible, locate it in a place that will accommodate future expansion. The temptation for megalomania is great, especially if you plan your garden in the dead of winter, as I do, when the landscape is bleak and barren. Seed and plant catalogs fill the mailbox every day, fueling fantasies of lush, fragrant, dazzling, and abundant Edens. Not surprisingly, most gardeners order far more seeds and plants than they can realistically take care of. I suggest that you make a list of everything you want and then cut it in half. As you are being ruthless, remember a couple of things: your garden may be small but well tended and beautiful, and you'll have time to enjoy all the other pleasures of spring and summer.

In the plans on pages 147 to 171 a wide variety of garden designs are presented including some which will need a minimum of time and effort. What your garden will become should be determined by the following factors: climate, site, pattern, plant selection, and maintenance needs.

CLIMATE

Regional differences influence planting schedules, plant selection, and maintenance. In the winter, gardeners in the mild or frost-free climates of the Pacific Coast and Deep South can grow cool-weather vegetables that are only grown in the spring or even summer in other parts of the country. Broccoli, Brussels sprouts, cauliflower, cabbage, lettuce, greens for salad or cooking, kale, onions, and spinach are all possibilities for winter growing. Asparagus and rhubarb need at least minimal winter chilling and cannot be grown in Florida and the Gulf Coast.

Each region has its own climactic character. Arrid zones need irrigation, wet areas may require more exacting soil drainage, cool climates benefit from season extenders. These subjects are covered in the Gardening Techniques chapter (p. 173).

The U.S.D.A. hardiness map (p. 278) is an important guide to use when selecting plants.

SITE

A kitchen garden should be close to the house. Easy access is a real convenience for the cook who can dash out to the patio for a sprig of thyme. A touch of grace can be provided by even the smallest doorstep garden: pots of cherry tomatoes, chives, and parsley, with nasturtiums exuberantly climbing up a drainspout. When I was growing up in New York City, all of my neighbors had tomatoes planted in the 2-foot-wide strips between their asphalt driveways. Of course, there was nowhere else to put them, but they grew very nicely, as it was a well-drained, sunny spot.

Sun is a crucial consideration. Most vegetables need at least 6 hours of sun a day. If you live in a northern locale, more than that is necessary for proper ripening. If you're planning a garden during fall or winter, it's good to remember

 Summer Sun

Winter Sun

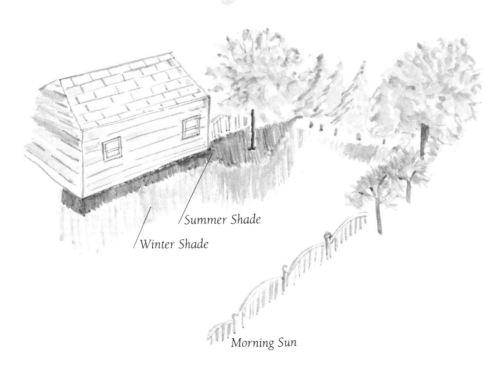

Summer Shade

Winter Shade

Morning Sun

that the sun is much lower in the sky and casts longer shadows than it will in summer. If you don't have much sun, try growing salad greens and herbs. Shade-tolerant ornamentals, such as ferns or hostas, are the only worthwhile possibility for areas that get no sun at all—under or near heavily foliaged trees and evergreens, in narrow side yards between buildings.

THE
MOOSEWOOD
RESTAURANT
KITCHEN
GARDEN

142

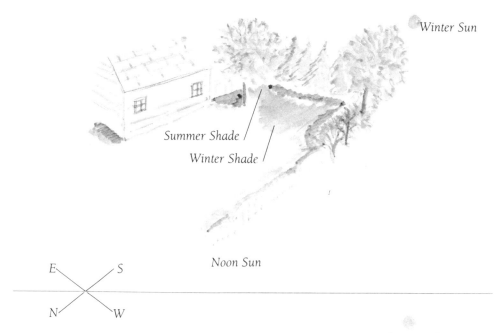

Summer Sun

Winter Sun

Summer Shade

Winter Shade

Noon Sun

E   S

N   W

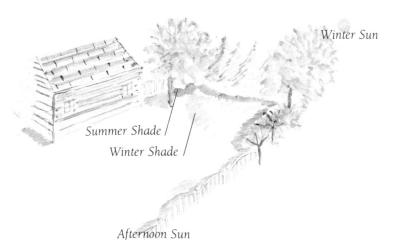

Summer Sun

Winter Sun

Summer Shade

Winter Shade

Afternoon Sun

Different sites may contain one or more of the following: varied terrain, attractive views, existing ornamental trees or plantings, a patio or sitting area, and areas to be screened for privacy.

The terrain of your garden site can be an integral aspect of the design. Steep or banked sites lend themselves to terracing. Terraced beds can be edged with annual or perennial flowers that will cascade down the walls, leaving the center of the bed open for growing herbs and vegetables. Materials to be considered for terrace walls could include masonry, railroad ties, and rot-resistant or pressure-treated timbers.

A patio or seating area surrounded by low plantings would be a good choice for any section of a yard or garden with a good view. If you plan to have corn, sunflowers, pole beans, asparagus, and other tall growers, make sure they won't obscure a vista.

Existing trees or specimen plantings will also determine the siting of your garden. You may decide to sacrifice proximity in order to save desirable trees or plantings close to the house. Ornamental specimens (flowering shrubs, trees, evergreens, perennial plants or vines) can be interplanted with vegetables and herbs to provide the longest possible season of color and interest. Avoid ornamentals with specific needs that may conflict with vegetable growing; for example, rhododendrons and azaleas require highly acidic soil. Vegetables and herbs must be sited in full sun and away from the root zones of large shrubs and trees. A progression from tree to shrub to perennial to vegetable and herb beds could take care of this concern and also create an effective privacy screen (see below). Choose semi-dwarf or dwarf fruit trees, or low-growing ornamental trees for small yards. Screens can be created with plantings alone, or by a "layered" system of plantings with fences, trellises, walls, or arbors. Grape vines, cucumbers, melons, beans, indeterminate tomatoes, and squashes can all be trained to grow up a trellised wall or fence, softening the view and creating a lush enclosure. Avoid situations where a wall or fence would block the sun from sun-loving plants.

Creating a Landscape Screen

Vegetables   Perennial Flowers   Shrubs   Fruit or Ornamental Tree

PATTERN

Traditionally, a kitchen garden was a simple rectangular plot in the yard. Today, the integration of ornamental and edible landscaping has opened up possibilities for garden patterns, freeing vegetables and herbs from their conventional boundaries. Regardless of your choice, even though a kitchen garden is utilitarian, it should harmonize aesthetically with the house and landscape.

The stylistic pattern of a garden ideally reflects two things: the personal taste and aesthetics of its creator, and the architecture of the house. Where I live, in the hills outside Ithaca, New York, personal taste covers a lot of territory ranging from tractor tires and toilets filled with geraniums to tasteful English borders lined with statuary.

Asking yourself the following questions may help in deciding on a pattern: Does the house have a formal, symmetrical appearance or is it informal and rambling? Would it be softened by curves, or enhanced by rectilinear forms? What does it need to make it a space you would enjoy spending time in? Open? Enclosed? Whimsical? Tranquil? Dynamic? The translation from desired feeling to realized design can be the most creative and personal aspect of the process. The models in this book help to illustrate the variety of patterns possible, from the formal knot garden (p. 154) to the dooryard garden entranceway (p. 156).

THE
MOOSEWOOD
RESTAURANT
KITCHEN
GARDEN

144

PLANT SELECTION

Now that you've considered how to work with your site and what overall pattern you would like to create, it's time to fill it with various forms, textures, and colors. Of course, the needs of the plants should be your first consideration. Some plants, for example, like many of us, do better with specific "buddies." I've more or less followed the companion planting recommendations (chart, p. 201), but being terribly unscientific, I've never done any control experiments to see if it really works. Others have, and claim it does work for better growth, pest control, and soil conditioning.

Tall plants should be placed where they will not block the sun from short growers. Short growers, such as lettuce, spinach, chives, alpine strawberries, carrots, and many herbs, make decorative edging plants. Lowest growers, such as creeping thymes and sweet woodruff, are best appreciated if they're close to a viewing area and planted in sufficient quantity to be noticed.

For accents, ruby chard, red-leafed lettuce, and flowers like nasturtium and calendula provide a shot of color amidst the predominately green-foliaged vegetables and herbs. I don't care for the taste of ruby chard, but it looks so glorious with the sun shining through it that I grow it and then feed it to our goats at home.

Plant selections for herb or flower borders can be placed to create different effects. The appearance of a border composed of many kinds of plants will have a pointillistic quality of varying shapes and colors. Plants that are arranged in masses, and perhaps repeated or woven through a border, can create a tapestry effect of color and form that can be natural and informal or highly staged, like the Victorian-style plantings that spell out names or dates.

In the continuing struggle to accommodate everything I would like to grow without breaking ground for more beds, I've learned to plant in progression. When planting early-maturing vegetables (peas, spinach, lettuce), leave a little more room between rows than you normally would for later additions of tomatoes, peppers, basil, squash, or melons. The latter are all mid- to late-summer maturing and will take over the space left empty by the early bloomers.

I particularly enjoy having fragrant plants near the house or sitting areas. Ironically, having hay fever has made me appreciate just how delicious the evening air can be on the summer nights when I can breathe clearly. Plants that freely release their fragrance in the air include: rosa rugosa, lavender, nicotiana, nasturtium, and thyme. Lilac, mockorange, honeysuckle, and trumpet and madonna lilies are not specifically kitchen garden material, but all are so powerfully and deliciously scented, it would be a shame to leave them out. Detailed information on these, and an infinity of other purely ornamental plants, is beyond the scope of this book, but easily available. Many herbs release their scent when brushed against, particularly basil, bee balm, geraniums, lemon balm, mint, rosemary, sage, and thyme. Creeping thyme is effectively grown between paving stones, since it's tough enough to withstand being stepped on (within reason).

MAINTENANCE

The majority of vegetables, and some herbs, are annuals and need to be replanted every year. Rhubarb, asparagus, many herbs, and fruits of all types are perennials. Place perennials where they will not be disturbed by tillers or other cultivators used to turn and break up the soil. If your garden is small and areas are turned annually with a fork or shovel, this may not be so great a concern. Nor would it be if the garden were mulched, that is, covered with a thick layer of organic materials to keep the soil loose, moist, and weed-free.

The width and type of paths between beds is influenced by such considerations as: Will you be using a wheelbarrow, garden cart, lawn mower, garden tractor, or tiller? Is there good maneuverability around the beds? Is the width of the beds such that you can cultivate from the path without stepping into a bed? It's better not to compact the soil or possibly crush some vulnerable, emerging seedling or small plant. Three to four feet is a good width for a bed that is accessible from both sides.

Gardeners who have physical difficulty working at ground level could have walled raised beds built to waist height for easier access.

Low-maintenance perennial herbs are suitable for areas that are too steep or small to mow. They are also an attractive choice for ground covers or mass plantings.

LOW-MAINTENANCE PERENNIAL HERBS

FOR SUNNY LOCATIONS

chamomile   rosemary
lady's mantle   thyme
lamb's ears   yarrow
lavender

FOR SHADIER LOCATIONS

bee balm   sweet cicely
lady's mantle   sweet woodruff

THE
MOOSEWOOD
RESTAURANT
KITCHEN
GARDEN

146

Irrigation is an important consideration for gardeners in drier climates. If you're going to have any kind of system installed in the ground, make sure you consult with a contractor before you finalize any of your designs.

In this plan, a long and narrow garden is broken up into several different spaces.

An outdoor sitting or dining area is easily accessible from the house, and is enclosed by beds for herbs, flowers, and vegetables, a grape arbor, and a play area for children. Brick raised beds for vegetables or herbs are close at hand, yet out of reach for small children. (They have the play area to dig in!) Vegetables that could be grown in the limited space of these beds include: greens for salad or cooking, bush beans, carrots, cucumbers, eggplant, garlic, herbs, onions, peppers, and tomatoes. The aggressive mints, lemon balm, sweet cicely, and daylilies can fight it out among themselves on one side of the patio.

Past the arbor, paving is flanked with lady's mantle, thyme, and chamomile. These plants will soften the edge with their sprawling habit, and also make attractive, noncompetitive, shallow-rooted underplanting for the espaliered trees.

A rounded, paved area in the back would make a nice spot for a small bench or garden seat. It's surrounded by relatively low maintenance perennial herbs selected for the season-long display of their foliage and bloom. (As an aside here, "low maintenance" is an overused term that should not imply no weeding, no watering, etc. It actually means some plants may be tougher and less fussy than others. The only thing that's *really* low maintenance is a good, thick layer of concrete.) There are many perennial plants that could satisfy these requirements; however, I'll limit the selection to herbs discussed in this book.

Some have been chosen for their silver-hued foliage—specifically, yarrow, lavender, mullein, and the artemisias. The gray tones of these plants contrast well with the full spectrum of colors presented in the foliage and blooms of the other plants, and they offer an elegant, cooling effect. Herbs have also been selected for variety in the texture and shape of the foliage: woolly-leaved mullein, needlelike lavender, finely divided lacy yarrow and artemisias, coarse, bristly sage and anchusa, pleated lady's mantle, and the delicate, minute leaves of thyme, woodruff, and chamomile.

The back wall of the garden is softened by a lilac and a clump of lovage, the latter a tall, tropical-appearing, leafy herb.

Early-spring bulbs and violets would do well planted beneath the central tree, blooming before or at the same time as the tree leafs out.

Espaliered fruit trees are placed against a side wall that will absorb heat and help fruit to ripen. The heavily pruned and shaped trees take up little room and offer a stylized architectural form, especially in the winter landscape. Having chosen "lower maintenance" plants, the gardener will have plenty of extra time to devote to pruning and training the espaliered trees! Apple and pear are the most common fruits to espalier. Henry Levthardt Nurseries, Montauk Highway, Box

666, E. Moriches, N.Y. 11940, is a source of trees suitable for espalier training. Their catalog is free, their informative handbook $1.00. A good text on the subject is *Espaliers and Vines for the Home Gardener* by Harold Perkins, Iowa State University Press, Ames, Iowa, 1979.

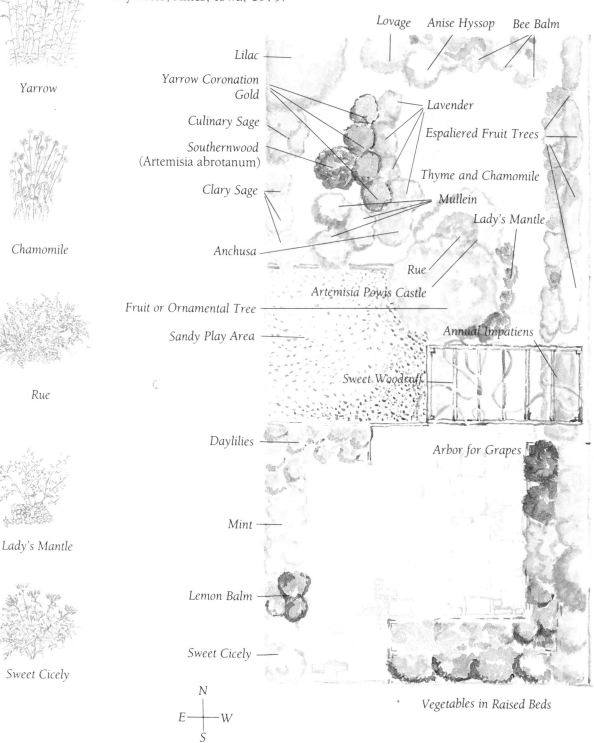

Yarrow

Chamomile

Rue

Lady's Mantle

Sweet Cicely

Lovage   Anise Hyssop   Bee Balm

Lilac

Yarrow Coronation
Gold

Culinary Sage

Southernwood
(Artemisia abrotanum)

Clary Sage

Anchusa

Lavender

Espaliered Fruit Trees

Thyme and Chamomile

Mullein

Lady's Mantle

Rue

Artemisia Powis Castle

Fruit or Ornamental Tree

Sandy Play Area

Annual Impatiens

Sweet Woodruff

Daylilies

Arbor for Grapes

Mint

Lemon Balm

Sweet Cicely

N
E —— W
S

Vegetables in Raised Beds

This plan is designed with the purpose of creating a private space using garden structures, plants, and fruit trees. (See Bibliography (p. 275) for books on fruit growing.) A central patio is surrounded by a double row of dwarf fruit trees, a lattice fence for climbing plants, hazelnut trees, a *Rosa rugosa* hedge, a double row of asparagus, an arbor for grapes and kiwifruit, pines (*Pinus koraiensis* for pine nuts!), and blueberry bushes.

The grape arbor is located on the north side of the garden, where it won't shade any plants, while the south side is screened by a *Rosa rugosa* hedge and asparagus (the foliage can be easily 5 feet tall). Mint is located at the corner of the house in its own bed, surrounded by the path. This segregation is necessary as mint is among the most invasive of plants and can bully its neighbors out of existence.

The four central beds are for annual vegetables and perennial alpine strawberries, which make a handsome edging. The edging plants—lettuces, ruby chard, nasturtiums, calendulas, and garlic—are chosen for ornamental qualities such as size, form, and texture. They are all low-growing and present a variety of color, leaf shape, and growth habit.

Herbs are located close to the house for easy access. Spring growers will make room, upon their harvest, for later replacements. Basil follows spinach, radicchio follows cauliflower, eggplant follows pak choy; peas will be harvested and ready for the vines to be removed when the tomatoes, peppers, and broccoli have grown large enough to need the space.

THE
MOOSEWOOD
RESTAURANT
KITCHEN
GARDEN

150

Grape and Kiwi Arbor

Rhubarb ——

Blueberries

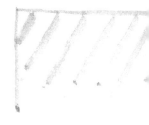

Companions that grow well together include tomatoes and basil, dill and cabbage, melon and nasturtium.

Pine Nut Trees

Dwarf Fruit Trees

Pole Beans   Cucumbers   Winter Squash   Trellised Fence

Peppers   Cauliflower Followed by Radicchio

— Garlic   — Broccoli

— Tomatoes

— Peas

Peas —
Carrots   — Beets
Parsley —   — Onions

Spinach Followed by Basil
Pak Choi Followed by Eggplant   Lettuce Followed by Calendula   Hazelnut Trees

Kale — — — Dill

Bush Melon

Ruby
Chard — — Cabbage

Nasturtium   Alpine Strawberries

Herb and
Flower Beds

Patio   Mint

House

Asparagus

Rosa rugosa Hedge

THE
MOOSEWOOD
RESTAURANT
KITCHEN
GARDEN

152

DESIGN
153

Knot gardens were very popular in the Elizabethan period of English landscape design. Herbs used for medicinal, culinary, or simply ornamental purposes were woven into geometric forms that resembled the patterns used in embroidered tapestries.

Plan a knot garden for an area that can be seen from above to best appreciate the interweaving of the variously colored and textured plants.

The formal, symmetrical quality of a knot garden suggests its use as a focal point in the center of a garden or courtyard.

Two garden possibilities are presented here, one using perennial herbs, the other annual edible flowers and culinary herbs.

The perennial herbs chosen are low-growing plants that will need to be pruned to keep the pattern neat and clear and will require winter protection in colder regions. It's a good idea to keep some backup plants in another bed to fill in any

THE
MOOSEWOOD
RESTAURANT
KITCHEN
GARDEN

154

Santolina

Germander

Knot Garden—Perennials

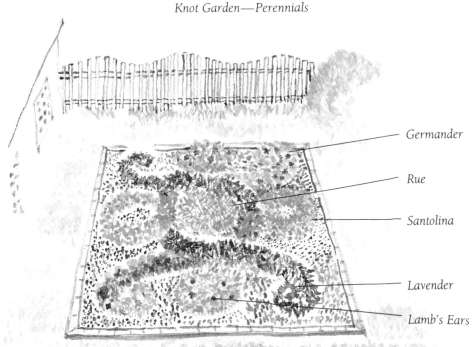

Germander

Rue

Santolina

Lavender

Lamb's Ears

gaps that may occur. I have selected plants that are fairly dense and offer a variety of textured and colored foliages: incredibly soft, gray, and floppy lamb's ears; small, bright green and pointed germander; rich, unusually blue-green rue; gray-green corallike santolina; and silvery needlelike lavender.

The annual herb-and-flower knot garden will last only a season; however, the design or plant selection can be changed from year to year. While the perennial knot garden described above is subtle and refined, the annual knot garden design is bright and vivacious. The hot colors of nasturtium and marigold flowers are set off by the brilliant purple basil, bright green parsley, and blue-green dill.

To lay out a knot garden, find the center of a square by crossing two strings from the corners to mark an *X*. From this point, you can lay out a cross (+) to determine the axes around which the design is symmetric. To create circles or curves, use a tautly held string that is measured to the length of the circle radius. Trace the curve onto the ground to use as a guide for planting. Space plants a little closer than usual for a tight, compact design.

A layer of gravel 4 to 6 inches deep to deter weeds is used as a background for the plants. For a softer effect, try shredded bark.

Edge the garden with a low border of brick, timber, or stone to contain the gravel or bark mulch.

Knot Garden—Annuals

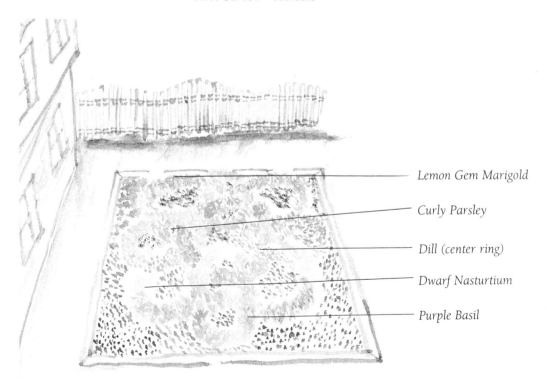

Lemon Gem Marigold

Curly Parsley

Dill (center ring)

Dwarf Nasturtium

Purple Basil

DOORYARD GARDEN

Dooryard gardens can be lush, abundantly landscaped entranceways, filled with plants that have both culinary and ornamental usefulness.

Many front yards are small squares of lawn edged with plantings. They may be more suited for a kitchen garden than, for example, a backyard with mature shade trees.

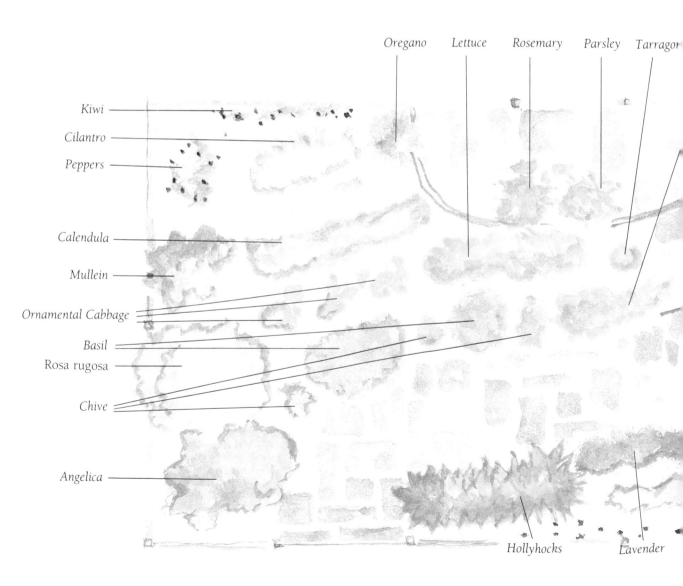

Oregano Lettuce Rosemary Parsley Tarragon

Kiwi

Cilantro

Peppers

Calendula

Mullein

Ornamental Cabbage

Basil

Rosa rugosa

Chive

Angelica

Hollyhocks Lavender

This small garden is intended for herbs, flowers, and a few vegetables.

Plantings of varying heights are used to create interest in a small space; the vertical forms of angelica, mullein, and hollyhock contrast with low, spreading plants such as dianthus, thyme, and lavender. Hardy kiwi vines and cucumbers are grown on trellises against the house. Climbing nasturtiums twine up and around a fence by the sidewalk.

Rounded green or ruby lettuce leaves, spiky chive clumps, purple basils, and fine, gray-green lavender leaves, to name a few, provide a textured pattern of various leaf shapes and colors.

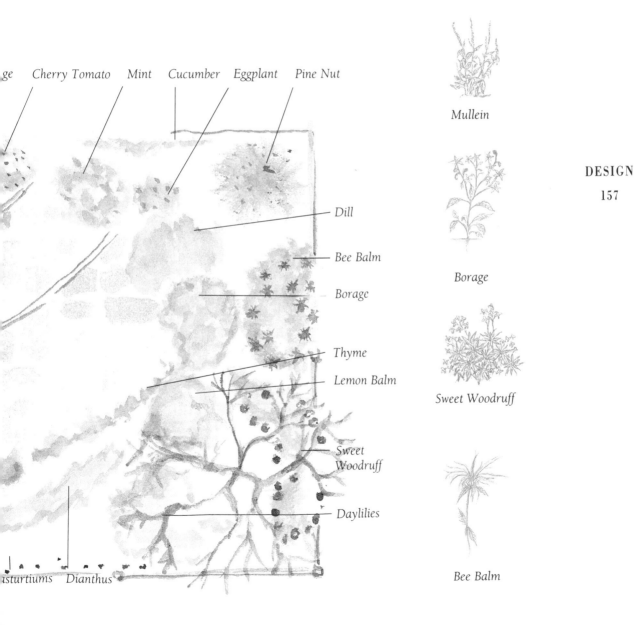

_ge_   _Cherry Tomato_   _Mint_   _Cucumber_   _Eggplant_   _Pine Nut_

— _Dill_

— _Bee Balm_

Borage

Thyme

Lemon Balm

Sweet Woodruff

— _Daylilies_

...sturtiums   _Dianthus_

Mullein

DESIGN

157

Borage

Sweet Woodruff

Bee Balm

Winter interest is added by bright orange rose hips adorning the *Rosa rugosa,* crab apples, the tall seed stalks of mullein and hollyhock, the odd yet colorful ornamental cabbages, and the evergreen foliage of the pine nut tree, thyme, lavender, and dianthus.

Tender herbs such as rosemary and parsley can be grown in pots that could be moved indoors.

All of the vegetables, and some herbs—basil, parsley, calendula, borage, dill, cilantro, and nasturtiums—are annuals that will have to be replanted yearly. The rest of the plants are perennials. This gives the opportunity for a flexible, different garden from year to year.

DESIGN

159

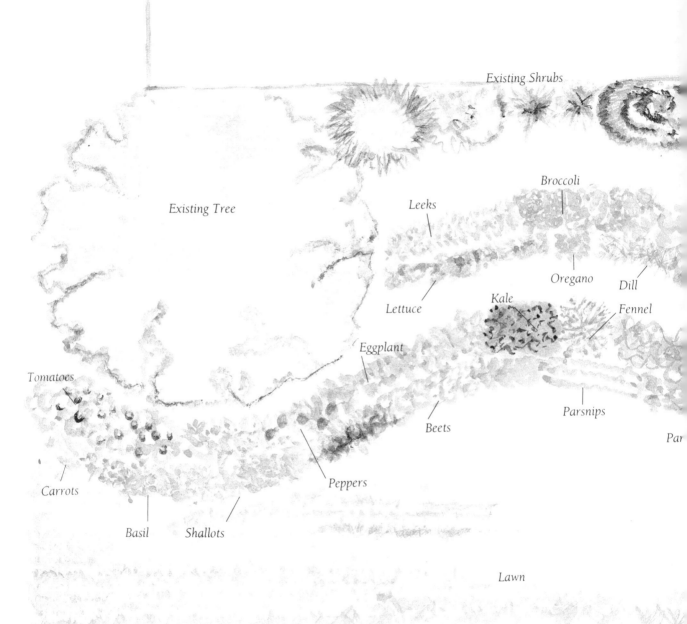

Existing Shrubs

Existing Tree

Leeks

Broccoli

Oregano

Dill

Lettuce

Kale

Fennel

Eggplant

Beets

Parsnips

Tomatoes

Peppers

Par

Carrots

Basil   Shallots

Lawn

—— Thyme

—— Tarragon

Savory

Chive   Sage   Marjoram

— Chrysanthemum

— Tah Tsoi

— Bush Beans

This kitchen garden is intended to provide a small space for growing a few favorite vegetables and herbs. The site is a front yard, a lawn space with some mature plantings of shrubs and trees. The backyard is too shady for successful vegetable crops, while the front receives plenty of sun.

Beds for vegetables and herbs snake their way across the lawn to be in full sun and away from existing plantings, specifically the sizable shrubs and trees

Thyme

Marjoram

along the right-hand side of the plan. The illustration on page 160 shows mid-summer plantings. Tall plants are located so as not to shade low growers. Plant succession, ornamental arrangement, and beneficial companions should be considered in the placement of various plants. Herbs are located near the entryway for easy access.

Beds can be maintained from either side, with enough space between them for a lawn mower to pass.

THE
MOOSEWOOD
RESTAURANT
KITCHEN
GARDEN

162

DESIGN

163

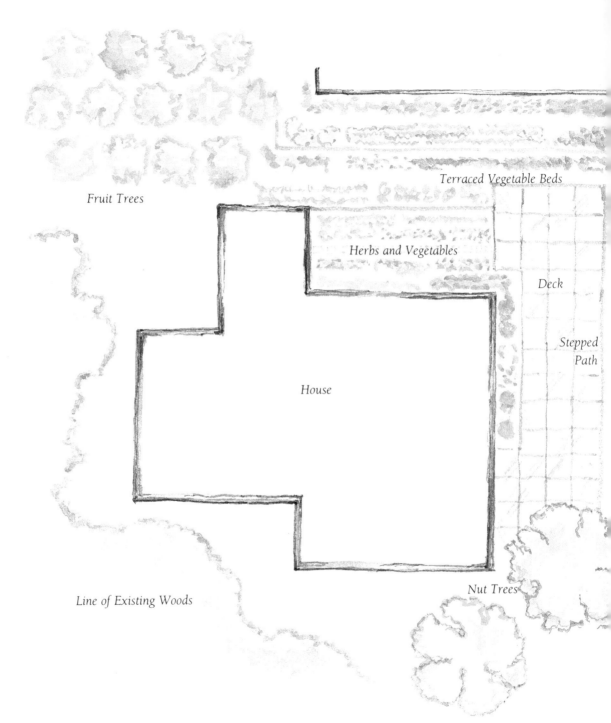

Fruit Trees

Terraced Vegetable Beds

Herbs and Vegetables

Deck

Stepped
Path

House

Line of Existing Woods

Nut Trees

A garden on a sloping site requires the consideration of specific issues: soil erosion, ease of cultivation, and aesthetic concerns of "fitting in" to a hillside. This design makes use of retaining walls and narrow terraces that follow the contours of the slope, creating beds for planting. These beds are situated and planted so as not to disturb a fine view from the decks on the south and east sides of the house.

The site offers plenty of room for people who have the desire, time, and energy to attend to an array of landscape edibles. Vegetables and herbs, fruit and nut trees, berries, grapevines, and ornamentals all have space in the site plan.

DESIGN

165

Strawberries

Herbs for Ground Cover

Raspberries

Blueberries

Pergola for Grapes and Vines

E S

N W

Lovage

Angelica

Chervil

Hyssop

This type of plan could be used as a master plan to be developed over a period of years, adding a section year by year.

A professional contractor would be needed to assure the structural integrity of walls used to retain sizable volumes of earth, which can be dangerously heavy when wet. One bed for vegetables or herbs is located in a terrace that is an integrated, structural part of the outdoor living space of the house. This would be built at the same time the foundation is laid. Terraces will involve the initial expense of clearing existing growth, providing drainage if necessary, construction, and back-filling with topsoil, compost, and/or aged manure. They can be a hand-

THE
MOOSEWOOD
RESTAURANT
KITCHEN
GARDEN

166

some, useful part of the configuration of house, hillside, and garden.

Beds below the house can be planted with space-consuming vegetables such as corn, squash, potatoes, beans, melons, asparagus, cucumbers, or a crop grown in large quantity for winter storage.

Berries and ground covers can be grown directly on the slope since they are tenacious and more or less perennial; their roots will hold the soil in place.

Grape and other vines are grown on a long, curving pergola which can be a striking landscape feature and shady spot for a hammock or two.

Fruit trees are located to the side so as not to block the view as they mature.

CONTAINER GARDENING

Container gardening is especially useful where there is no room for an in-ground garden, as in the situation below, but need not be limited to those conditions. Attractively planted containers can be colorful accents or focal points on decks, patios, stairs, and balconies, near entryways, and at windows.

During the summer, Moosewood Restaurant's outside dining area is bordered by a low wall topped with planters full of brightly colored flowers. The flower

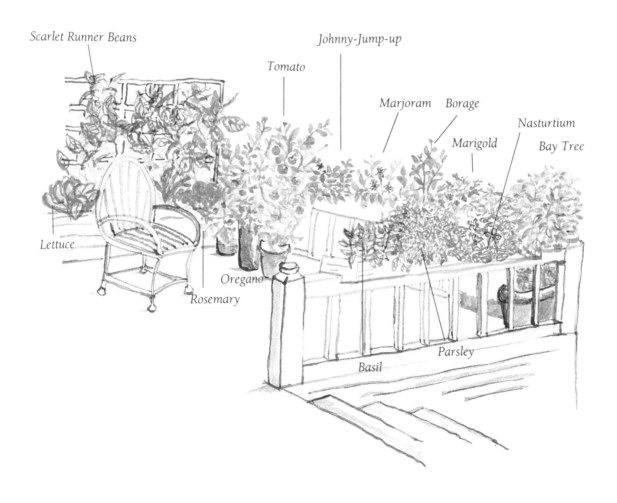

Scarlet Runner Beans

Johnny-Jump-up

Tomato

Marjoram   Borage

Nasturtium
Bay Tree

Marigold

Lettuce

Oregano

Rosemary

Parsley

Basil

boxes create a gracious visual separation between a busy street and the dining terrace. The terrace is shaded by a large canopy, limiting the planting to annual flowers that can withstand some shade.

Outdoor spaces with sufficient sun and some protection from strong winds can be suitable locations for container-planted vegetables and herbs.

Containers should be appropriately sized and rot resistant, and have adequate drainage. The range of possibilities extends from pricey imported terra-cotta to food-service 5-gallon plastic tubs. A handsome, classic choice is the simple clay pot, available in all sizes. There are also less expensive plastic and fiberglass pots made to simulate terra-cotta. Half-barrels are good for plants that need generous root space, or for mixed planting. Containers that are chosen for the beauty of their form should be discreetly matched with a plant that doesn't completely hide the pot with an abundance of flowing vegetation. Likewise, vigorous, fast-growing plants can quickly cover functional but less attractive containers. Fast growers include tomatoes, lettuce, bush cucumbers, melons, squash, nasturtiums, scented geraniums, parsley, and basil.

Choose varieties that are suited to container planting. Some catalogs key specific flowers, vegetables, and herbs that are compact enough for containers. The following list roughly divides plants into small (6- to 8-inch pots or window boxes), medium (10- to 16-inch pots), and large (24-inch pots or larger, buckets, half-barrels, and troughs). The named varieties below are good selections for containers.

SMALL

EDIBLE FLOWERS

dwarf carnations or pinks	pansies or violas
dwarf nasturtiums	mini-roses
('Whirlybird')	violets

HERBS

small-leafed basil	parsley
dwarf calendula	savory
chives	scented geraniums
marjoram	thyme
oregano	

EDIBLE FLOWERS

calendula   Gem series marigolds
dwarf chrysanthemums

HERBS

basil   mint
bay   rosemary
lemon balm   sage

VEGETABLES

alpine strawberries   salad greens
Asian vegetables   (arugula, cress,
  (tatsoi, Mei Qing Choi   corn salad)
  pak choi, mizuna)   shallots
beets (Little Ball)   basket tomatoes
carrots   (Pixie, Tiny Tim)
  (Minicor, Planet)
chili peppers
lettuce
  (Baby Oak,
  Little Gem, Lolla Rossa,
  romaine, Summer Baby
  Bibb)

THE
MOOSEWOOD
RESTAURANT
KITCHEN
GARDEN

170

Vegetables and herbs grown in containers need more than casual maintenance. Plants can dry out quickly in hot weather (especially in clay or terra-cotta) and will need to be watered often. Vegetables located close to the wall of a house may be in a substantially hotter micro-climate than those a few feet away. This could be advantageous for heat-loving plants such as eggplant or melons, but death to lettuce and other cool-weather greens. A light trellis or pergola may be useful to shade places where too much solar heat is trapped. A trellis can also double as a windbreak to lessen the drying-out or knockdown effects of wind.

LARGE

EDIBLE FLOWERS

daylilies   roses

HERBS

bay   mint

VEGETABLES

cabbage (Early Jersey   peppers (Ace, Lipstick)
  Wakefield)   bush squash (Gold Nugget
bush cucumber (Salad Bush,   winter squash)
  Spacemaster)   Swiss chard
green beans (E-Z Pick)   tomatoes (Basket King,
bush melons (Garden Baby   Super Bush)
  watermelon)

Frequent waterings and rains can leach out soil nutrients, requiring consistent fertilization of container plants. This should be at a milder strength than for plants in the ground, whose roots are surrounded by absorptive soil.

Gardeners in cold climates will need to empty ceramic or plastic containers after the first hard frosts to avoid damage from alternate freezing and thawing winter weather.

The placement of large, heavy containers on balconies or roofs should be made with the consideration of what loads the structure can handle. It may be necessary to consult with the building owner or a contractor.

The illustration on page 168 shows a balcony with an assortment of containers. Boxes have been built to fit the top railing of the balcony. Pots of various sizes and shapes are grouped together for a lush display and ease in watering. One end of the balcony has a deep planter where a double crop of lettuce and trellised beans is growing.

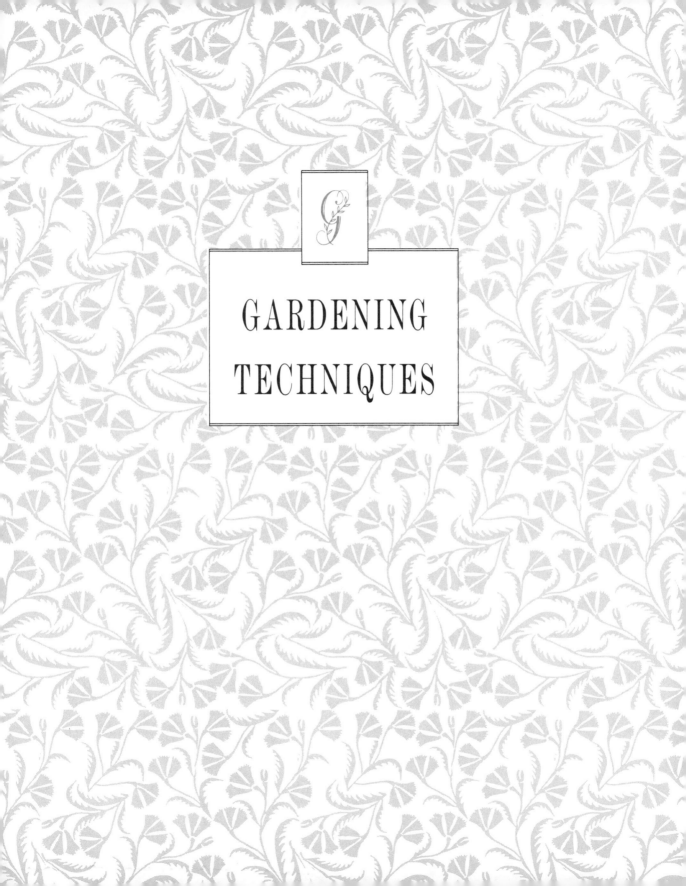

GARDENING TECHNIQUES

SOIL

My first garden was an ill-fated semi-disaster located in a spot where coal ashes, which are highly acidic and toxic to plants, had been dumped. It wasn't obvious at first glance that this wasn't an ideal site, although today I know that the scraggly grass growing there should have been a giveaway. It was the only level, non-wooded area available to me and I was eager to plant. Even with its drawbacks, this plot could have been improved with better drainage and massive amounts of soil amendments.

Soil is more than just dirt. And while improving your soil may be the most labor-intensive, least glamorous part of gardening, it's the most important. Though plants derive only 10 percent of their nutrients from the soil, that 10 percent is as crucial as water and air. Whatever attention you do or don't give your soil will surely show at harvest time.

The depth and type of soil in a chosen site give an indication of how much work will be required to create a garden. Dig a 2-foot-square hole to check for soil type, topsoil depth, and drainage.

THE
MOOSEWOOD
RESTAURANT
KITCHEN
GARDEN

174

BASIC TYPE

Soil types can be determined by a simple rule of thumb: pick up a handful of soil and try to form a ball. If it's loose and gritty, without holding any shape, it's sandy. Clay will hold together, mold to the form of your hand, and be sticky when wet. A good loam (the ideal) will hold together when moist, but have a nice, crumbly texture, like a pie crust when it is dry. Some soils will be combinations, for example, a sandy loam.

Soils that are too sandy benefit from the addition of organic matter in the form of compost, leaf mold (decayed leaves), peat moss, rotted manure, or trucked-in topsoil.

Heavy clay soils that retain too much water are improved with the addition of organic matter, sand, or grit (finely ground gravel) to provide good drainage. Most vegetables, herbs, and ornamentals need oxygen in the soil; in soggy soils, oxygen is displaced by water. The depth of the topsoil can be seen by changes in color and texture in the dug soil pit. Topsoil should be dark and crumbly, with a generous amount of humus, possibly eons worth of animal, plant, and micro-organism residues. It's interesting to note that pre-Columbian American soils averaged 4% humus as opposed to 1.5% or less now. Clearly, our methods of farming have been depleting the soil at an alarming rate. (See below for a discussion of healthy cultivation practices that help build topsoil.) Thin soils with less than 2 to 3 inches of good topsoil should be enriched with a mix of the soil amendments listed above.

DRAINAGE

Heavy clay subsoil or bedrock close to the surface may create drainage problems and overly wet soil. Fill the soil test pit with water and check to see how long it takes to drain. Drainage times of more than 8 hours indicate a need to build raised beds with plenty of soil amended with sand, compost, and organic matter, or a permanent drainage system to channel water away from the garden site.

SOIL PH AND NUTRIENT CONTENT

Your soils should be analyzed for pH and the presence of important nutritive elements. Testing for pH is an easy procedure with purchased kits; however, soil analysis for nutritive elements is difficult and not recommended for home gardeners. County Cooperative Extension agents will send your soil sample to the state service for analysis. More often than not, the results will return on a computerized printout. It may be necessary to ask your local agent to recommend organic substitutes for the synthetic fertilizers listed.

Readings of pH reflect the acidity or alkalinity of soil. Most soils range from 4.5 to 7.5, with lower numbers acidic, neutral 7.0, higher numbers alkaline. Vegetables and herbs will do well with a soil pH between 6.0 and 8.0. Specific ideal readings are given for each vegetable; however, most will tolerate a 1 point difference either way. To bring acid soils up to a higher pH, apply ground limestone in the fall at a rate of 5 pounds per 100 square feet. Ground sulfur can be applied at ½ pound per 100 square feet to lower the pH of alkaline soils. Soil additions of organic matter help vegetables tolerate some variation from their ideal pH.

The three crucial nutritive elements for good plant growth are:

nitrogen (N)—important for vigorous, sturdy green growth, a major constituent of chlorophyll. Deficiencies result in spindly, stunted plants with yellowed leaves. Excess nitrogen causes big, leafy plants with too few flowers or fruits. Organic fertilizers high in nitrogen include blood meal, cottonseed meal, sea products (fish meal and seaweed), well-rotted manures, compost, and soybean meal.

phosphorus (P)—necessary for the development of flowers and resistance to disease. Phosphorus deficiency will show with scant flowers and fruits, and small, unhealthy plants with yellow-margined leaves. Bone meal, compost, sea products, well-rotted manures, and rock phosphate are organic sources of phosphorus.

potassium or potash (K)—effects root and leaf growth, particularly for underground crops (beets, carrots, and potatoes). It also helps provide drought resistance. Yellow mottled leaves with brown edges and tips indicate potassium deficiency. Fertilizers rich in potassium include wood ashes (real wood, not synthetic fireplace logs), compost, greensand, and sea products.

Calcium, magnesium, sulfur, iron, manganese, zinc, copper, boron, molybdenum, and chlorine are trace elements needed in lesser degree for healthy growth. These should not be lacking in soil where nutrients are regularly renewed. Seaweed is an excellent source of micronutrients, as it contains minute amounts of a vast array of minerals.

Feeding healthy soil is the best way to avoid unhealthy plants. Soil microorganisms digest nutrients and alter them to a form that is usable by plants. To act effectively, these microorganisms need a regular supply of decomposing organic matter, such as compost, decaying mulches, or well-aged manure. Synthetic fertilizers give plants a quick "shot" that produces vigorous growth, but they do nothing for the long-term health of the soil. In addition, their regular use kills beneficial microorganisms and earthworms, creating nutrient-poor soil that becomes dependent on chemical boosting.

THE
MOOSEWOOD
RESTAURANT
KITCHEN
GARDEN

176

All-purpose, organic fertilizers (with balanced nutrients) are available at garden centers or through mail order. They are particularly valuable for starting new gardens, or where a compost supply is not available.

A basic guideline that I follow is to work 1 inch of compost into the top 6 to 8 inches of soil whenever a new crop is planted, spring, summer, or fall. I also supplement with rock phosphate at the rate of 4 pounds per 100 square feet, applied once every 4 to 5 years.

Not all vegetables have the same nutrient needs. Heavy feeders include: asparagus, the cabbage family, cucumbers, corn, onions, leafy greens, melons, and squash. Medium feeders are tomatoes and the legumes (peas and beans). Herbs, root crops, potatoes, sweet potatoes, and peppers are light feeders. Heavy feeders will yield best if their gluttony is satisfied by the addition of an inch or two of compost, well-aged manure, or an all-purpose, organic fertilizer at the recommended rate, midway through their growing season.

GREEN MANURES AND COVER CROPS

Green manures are crops that are planted and then turned under to decompose and thus enrich the soil. They can be used to increase the fertility of poor soil in gardens where compost or animal manures are not available. Green manures can revitalize "tired" sections of garden or improve new areas that will be planted the next season.

As a green manure, legumes are particularly effective for adding nutrients, specifically nitrogen, to the soil. These include the useful vegetables peas and beans, along with clovers, vetch, and lespedeza. Winter rye and oats can be sown in the fall to overwinter and be turned under in the spring. Buckwheat is grown in the summer to break up difficult hardpan subsoils with deep reaching roots. It should be plowed under soon after the attractive white flowers open, to avoid reseeding.

COMPOST

One of the best soil additives, compost can be made without great difficulty. It enriches, lightens the soil, and increases its ability to retain moisture. The variety of organic matter, in the form of weeds, kitchen waste, leaves, and shredded brush, added to a compost pile widens the range of elements and microorganisms available to plants in the finished compost. This material can be dug into beds, used as a potting soil for container-grown plants, or applied as a mulch.

Summer and fall are excellent times for starting a compost pile. Weeds, grass clippings, shredded or chopped brush, vegetable waste from harvested crops, and sod from newly created beds are all in good supply at this time. Other materials for the compost pile include kitchen waste (vegetable matter and eggshells only; all other waste attracts hungry rodents, dogs, and raccoons). Use manure from chickens, goats, sheep, cows, and horses only. *Never* use cat litter, since your pet's feces may contain toxoplasmosis. Add dirt or more dry material to cover the pile if any odors are offensive.

There are several composting methods, each with its defenders. My compost piles tend to be the slow, lazy type that require no athletic turning and tossing of the materials. I try to layer the drier grasses and weeds with freshly decomposing kitchen waste, fresh grass clippings, and manure (if possible) to a height of 3 feet or so. It then sits untouched until the next season, 6 months or more later.

Many garden books and articles espouse a faster method (2 weeks to a month), but this involves a bit more attention. The advantages of this quicker compost are: (1) fast decomposition allows for less leaching of nutrients by rain or snow; (2) it's ready when you need it; (3) actively decaying organic matter contains more beneficial soil microorganisms than slowly decaying compost; and (4) higher temperatures destroy many undesirable weed seeds, insect larvae, and disease germs. (They're all such good reasons, I don't know why I haven't been swayed.)

The faster composting method: Materials to be composted should be at least ⅓ fresh, green matter (weeds, grass, vegetable waste) and no more than ⅔ drier bulk (preferably shredded or chopped leaves, stems, hay, brush). Mix, but don't layer, all the materials in a bin or pile no smaller than 3 feet by 3 feet for good decomposition. Bins can be made with snow fencing or old wooden pallets. (See p. 178 for a compost bin design.) If the bin or pile is not roofed, cover with black plastic to trap and maintain heat and to protect against leaching rains. Turn the pile with a fork on the second day and every 3 days afterward. Keep the compost evenly moist, about the consistency of a damp sponge. Internal temperatures should be between 140° and 160°F. for proper decomposition. Subsequent cooler temperatures of 110°F. and crumbly compost indicate a finished product. Gardener's Supply has compost thermometers and aerators.

Compact and unobtrusive compost bins or rotating tumblers are available from mail-order sources. They will fit in even small backyards.

Newly dug gardens that need a quick boost of nutrients can benefit from a direct composting method. This warm-weather technique requires a soil temperature of 60°F. or higher to ensure proper decomposition. Dig an 8- to 10-inch-deep trench where seeds or plants will go. Place 3 to 4 inches of kitchen waste or other compost materials, ¼ cup per square foot of high nitrogen fertilizer (soy bean or cottonseed meal), and some garden dirt in the trench and chop it coarsely with a shovel. Fill in with garden soil to ground level. Seed or transplant directly above the trench as usual, immediately if desired.

THE
MOOSEWOOD
RESTAURANT
KITCHEN
GARDEN

178

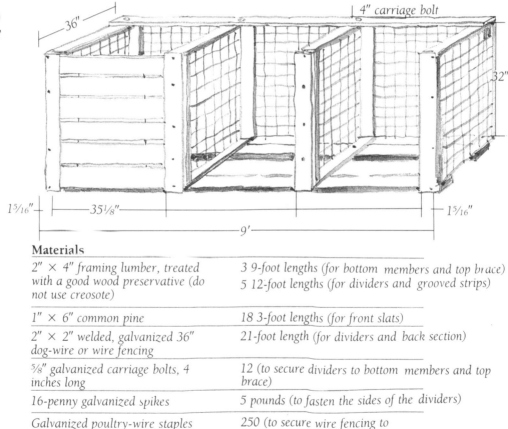

Materials

2" × 4" framing lumber, treated with a good wood preservative (do not use creosote)	3 9-foot lengths (for bottom members and top brace) 5 12-foot lengths (for dividers and grooved strips)
1" × 6" common pine	18 3-foot lengths (for front slats)
2" × 2" welded, galvanized 36" dog-wire or wire fencing	21-foot length (for dividers and back section)
⅝" galvanized carriage bolts, 4 inches long	12 (to secure dividers to bottom members and top brace)
16-penny galvanized spikes	5 pounds (to fasten the sides of the dividers)
Galvanized poultry-wire staples	250 (to secure wire fencing to dividers and back section)

MULCH

Mulch is any material placed on top of soil to inhibit weeds, retain soil moisture, keep soil cool or warm, provide nutrients, or encourage the activity of beneficial microorganisms.

Ruth Stouts' *How to Have a Green Thumb Without an Aching Back* was an early influence in my vegetable gardening career. Her method of soil building and weed control is a form of mulch mania in which there is no such thing as too much, usually in the form of rotted hay or straw. The goal is to keep a layer of mulch dense enough to block any weed growth. Some hand weeding is necessary around newly emerging seedlings, with the mulch pulled up around them as they mature. Weeds that pop up are covered with more mulch. This technique can build up a rich, deep layer of topsoil as the mulch decomposes. Mulched gardens with soil that is moist and high in organic matter will encourage earthworms. The worms' activity aerates the soil and increases water penetration. Worm "manure," or castings, are remarkably rich in nutrients.

Other mulches can be employed that are locally available through either commercial sources or the gardener's hunting and gathering efforts. These include:

- Bark chips
- Buckwheat hulls
- Cocoa bean shells
- Grass clippings
- Leaves
- Rotted manure
- Noncolored newspaper (black ink)
- Pine needles
- Sawdust
- Seaweed
- Wood chips

Bark chips, buckwheat hulls, and cocoa bean shells are attractive but expensive and so best suited for small, ornamental beds. They are available at garden centers in 25- or 50-pound bags. Grass clippings and leaves can mat and prevent water penetration. Grass clippings will decompose quickly in moist climates. Leaves work well as a winter blanket for annual vegetable beds, but may need to be weighted down with brush in windy areas. Pine needles, sawdust, and wood chips may acidify soil if used in quantity. Use them for acid-loving plants: potatoes, rhubarb, blueberries, and ornamentals such as azalea or rhododendron.

Plants mulched with materials that do not decompose quickly—newspaper, sawdust, wood or bark chips, hulls and shells—will need the addition of a nitrogen fertilizer, since the process of decomposition ties up nitrogen, making it unavailable to plants.

There are a few disadvantages, however; witchgrass and other weeds that are rhizomatous (spread by underground root stalks) can still manage to put up a good fight, even under mulch. The cool, damp conditions mulch creates can attract legions of slugs during even moderately wet seasons, and soil temperatures may be kept too cool in early spring. I like to mulch beds in late fall and early winter using rotted hay, straw, or compost. Hay should be rotted to hasten its decomposition and to destroy any weed seeds. Areas to be planted in the early spring should have the mulch pulled back a couple of weeks before planting so the soil can warm up. Mulch can be reapplied at the onset of hot, dry weather.

SEED STARTING

Gardeners who can provide the appropriate germination temperatures and conditions start many of their seeds indoors. This is often necessary in short-season areas where warm-weather crops such as tomatoes, peppers, melons, and squash will not produce unless given a head start indoors. Buying seedlings at a nursery may be the best option for those who have neither the time nor space to nurture seedlings for 2 months or more. Seed starting offers its own rewards: primal bonding with your seedlings, and personal choice of different or unusual varieties not available at nurseries.

Indoor seed starting calls for specific equipment and facilities. You must have a warm location for germination, potting mix, containers with adequate drainage, and fluorescent lights or an extremely sunny area. An indoor exposure where plants thrive in spring and summer may not provide enough light for good, strong seedlings because of the winter sun's weakness.

THE
MOOSEWOOD
RESTAURANT
KITCHEN
GARDEN

180

TEMPERATURE

Most vegetables will germinate readily in a soil temperature range of 65°F. to 80°F. Lettuce, peas, and spinach are best direct seeded outdoors and will germinate at 50°F. Eggplant, cucumbers, melons, and peppers do best at temperatures not less than 80°F. Heat mats specifically made for germination and soil heating cables buried in flats can be used to provide consistent warmth.

POTTING MIX

Potting mixes should be free of weed seeds and disease organisms, provide good moisture retention and drainage, and be of a light texture that allows for the easy pulling apart or cutting of plants with a minimum of root damage. I prefer to use commercial potting soil mixtures because they satisfy the above requirements. The use of garden soil for all or part of a potting mix requires oven sterilization in pans 3 to 4 inches deep at a temperature of 350°F. for an hour or so. This kills weed seeds and prevents the spread of soil-borne diseases.

CONTAINERS

Any container that provides good drainage can be used to start seeds: small plastic or fiber packs, plastic dairy containers with holes punched in the bottom, ceramic or plastic pots, wood or plastic flats, peat pots and strips, and Styrofoam soil cell trays. Peat pots are excellent for plants that do not like to have their roots disturbed in transplanting, like squash or melon. They can be planted as is: peel away some of the pot here and there to encourage root growth, pop in the ground, and remove any rim sticking up above the soil line. Soil cells are molded trays made up of a number of square or round cells varying in diameter from 1½ to 2½ inches. These trays fit over another tray used as a water reservoir and can be topped with a clear plastic dome to maintain moist soil and high humidity for good germination. Soil cell trays are a very efficient way to start a large quantity of seedlings, especially since they save space, last for years, and you remove seedlings simply by pushing them up through the bottom holes, virtually eliminating root, leaf, or stem damage.

SOIL BLOCKS

Soil blocks, or seed starting cubes, eliminate the need for pots or other containers, making them a good investment for both the pocketbook and the environment. They can be made at home with commercial soil block makers, which are widely available through seed and supply mail-order sources. Block makers come in large sizes (2 by 2 inches) for plants that need time to mature before being planted out, or small (11/16 by 11/16 inch) for seedlings that will be transplanted soon after germination.

To make the cubes, simply fill the block maker with thoroughly moistened potting soil, eject the blocks, and plant the seeds. Each block with its seedling can be planted directly, avoiding the messy and traumatic root separation that occurs when seedlings share a container.

SOWING SEEDS

Potting mix should be moist and spongy, but not soggy. Use warm water to avoid chilling the seeds. Allow commercial mixes to sit for a couple of hours to fully absorb added water. Scoop potting mix into containers, lightly tapping it down without packing it in.

Seed packages usually give planting information, including optimum planting time, days to harvest, plant size, germination time and percentage rate, seed depth for sowing, and specific light requirements. Seeds with a high germination rate can be sown thinly for economy, while those with lower rates may be planted 2 or 3 per individual container. Very tiny seeds (such as carrot) can be mixed with sand for easier distribution. Many seeds that are sown on the soil surface and left uncovered need light to germinate. These should be misted and kept moist with a plastic dome or cover of plastic wrap until germination occurs.

Watering is best achieved by siphoning up into the soil through the bottom drainage holes. Place seedling containers in trays of water, promptly removing them as soon as the soil appears uniformly moist. Gently probe the soil surface with your fingertip to assess the degree of moisture. Alternatively, purchase growing trays that feature mats of wicking material and water reservoirs to maintain consistent soil moisture. Avoid watering small seedlings from the top. They can be damaged by a strong stream of water, and be made more vulnerable to damping off, a fungus disease that causes the seedlings to keel over at the base of the stem.

LIGHT

Fluorescent lights are an inexpensive, easily obtained source of even, bright light for sturdy seedling growth. More expensive grow lights are not necessary for the short growing period seedlings will be indoors.

Wide temperature fluctuations and a possible lack of sufficient light intensity may make starting seeds on a windowsill impractical. Weak, pale, leggy plants that flop toward the light are not getting enough of it. Very bright sun rooms or rooms with large expanses of window and an eastern, southern, or western exposure (at least 6 hours long) could be effectively used where temperature ranges are not extreme. Southern exposure is usually the longest and so preferred.

Newly germinated plants can be grown as close as 2 to 3 inches beneath cool fluorescent lights. As plants grow, maintain a distance of 4 to 6 inches between the tops of the leaves and the light bulbs. Set a timer to ensure they receive the requisite 16 to 18 hours of light a day.

Most vegetable and herb seedlings can be raised indoors in a room temperature range of 60°F. to 75°F. Higher temperatures promote spindly, soft growth, whereas colder temperatures may stunt and delay growth. Feed with a liquid fertilizer such as fish emulsion, especially when using potting mixes that contain no nutrients.

THE
MOOSEWOOD
RESTAURANT
KITCHEN
GARDEN

182

BUYING PLANTS

When purchasing plants or seedlings, look for those that have uniform color and strong stems, and no yellowed or brown leaves or considerable insect damage. Compact and well-branched plants will be ultimately stronger and more attractive than tall, lanky ones. Check the undersides of leaves to avoid taking home any unwanted "hitchhikers." Plants in bud will adapt to transplanting more easily than those already in flower. "Hardening off" (p. 185) will be necessary for plants accustomed to greenhouse or indoor conditions.

QUITE HARDY
*seed or transplant in cool weather, when the soil is workable,
4 to 6 weeks before the last spring frost*

Asian vegetables—	daikon radish, mizuna, pak choi, tatsoi
cabbage family—	broccoli, cabbage, cauliflower, kohlrabi
onion family—	leeks, onions, scallions, shallots
pea family—	shelled, snow, sugar snap
potatoes	
salad greens—	arugula, corn salad, endive, radicchio, sorrel
spinach	

HARDY
seed in cool weather 2 weeks before the last spring frost

beets	*parsnips*
carrots	*turnips*
Swiss chard	

NOT HARDY
seed or transplant after the last spring frost (or protected earlier)

snap and shell beans	*squash, summer or winter*
corn	*tomatoes*
Chinese cabbage	

NEEDING HOT WEATHER
seed or transplant 1 week after last spring frost (or protected earlier)

cucumbers	*melons*
eggplant	*peppers*
lima beans	*sweet potatoes*

AUTUMN HARDY
seed mid- to late summer for fall crops
(6 to 8 weeks before frost in northern areas)

Asian vegetables—	Chinese cabbage, daikon radish, mizuna, pak choi, tatsoi
beets	
Brussels sprouts (need long season, start in June)	
collards and kale	
cabbage family (for Southern states and Pacific Coast)	
lettuce	
salad greens—	arugula, corn salad, endive, radicchio
spinach	
turnips	

THE
MOOSEWOOD
RESTAURANT
KITCHEN
GARDEN

184

SUCCESSION CROPS

sow through the season,
where temperatures are appropriate

Asian vegetables—	mizuna, pak choi, tatsoi
snap beans	
beets	
cabbage family	
carrots	
lettuce	
scallions	

TRANSPLANTING

Crowded seedlings can be transplanted into individual containers or thinned when 2 or more "true leaves" have developed. The initial set of leaves that appear at germination are typically 2 rounded leaves, directly opposite each other. The true leaves appear after these and are the same as the leaves of the mature plant, for example, the feathered foliage of dill.

When transplanting, hold seedlings by the sturdier leaf and not the fragile stem. Seedlings can be snipped off with a scissors to thin. Save the most robust, stocky plants for transplanting.

When garden conditions become amenable (see pp. 11–76 for appropriate planting times), seedlings need to be "hardened off," or gradually exposed to the elements. Initially allow seedlings to be exposed to 2 to 3 hours of sun and only moderate wind for the first few days. Follow this with full night and day exposure. Keep an eye on the weather; they'll have to be moved under a porch roof or other protected location if heavy rains or high winds threaten. Small plants in containers can be more easily drowned than those in the ground.

In the best of all possible worlds, seedlings and small plants would be transplanted into the garden on windless, cloudy, or soft rainy days. If you have no choice but to plant when the weather is particularly hot and dry, cover the new transplants with small berry baskets or tents of burlap or other open-weave fabrics. Water thoroughly.

PLANTING BY THE SIGNS OF THE MOON AND PLANETS

Planting by astrological signs may sound like another bit of New Age folderol. But it's actually one of the wiser things that people have been doing for millennia.

I like doing it to acknowledge the cosmic forces beyond our planet and, more practically, because it gives structure to my gardening schedule. Knowing the moon is in a propitious sign is an impetus for me to get out and plant. Being fairly unscientific, I haven't done any controlled experiments to test the efficacy of this technique, but others have and claim it to be effective. Use the astrological signs as a guide factored by such constraints as time and weather conditions. The real key to successful gardening is attentive care.

Astrological calendars and almanacs, available in bookstores, provide daily information on the signs and phases of the moon.

Moon phases go in a sequence of four quarters. The first two occur while the moon is waxing or increasing from new to full. The third and fourth occur while the moon is waning or decreasing from full back to new.

Aboveground annuals are best planted in the waxing moon. The waning moon, especially the third quarter, is best for planting perennials, biennials, and root crops. Cultivate, harvest, till, and destroy weeds and pests in the fourth quarter.

The moon will phase through all of the signs in 28 days. Here is a guide to each astrological sign:

Aries: a fire sign, barren and best for cultivating and weeding

Taurus: an earth sign, especially good for planting root crops

Gemini: an air sign, dry and best for harvesting

Cancer: a water sign, particularly fertile and excellent for planting and transplanting aboveground crops

Leo: a fire sign, dry and infertile, good for cultivation

Virgo: an earth sign, but infertile, good for cultivation

Libra: an air sign that's especially good for planting ornamentals and flowers

Scorpio: a water sign, very productive for all aboveground plants, notably vines

Sagittarius: a fire sign, good for weeding and cultivation

Capricorn: an earth sign, recommended for planting root crops

Aquarius: an air sign, dry and infertile, good for cultivation

Pisces: a water sign, plant or transplant aboveground crops

When the sun and moon are in the same sign, there is an increase in that sign's effects. Avoid planting when the moon is void, of course. This is noted on astrological calendars and occurs when the moon is "between" signs. It's not a time for decisive acts.

THE
MOOSEWOOD
RESTAURANT
KITCHEN
GARDEN

186

RAISED BEDS

Historically, kitchen gardens have been located close to houses for convenience, economy of space, and protection from grazing animals. The concept of growing vegetables in a field of long, straight rows derives from the large scale cultivation of farming and, later, commercial agriculture. The near-worldwide depletion of healthy topsoil results from certain commercial agricultural practices. For example, regularly plowing and tilling of soils accelerate the decomposition of organic matter into dust and carbon dioxide gas, which then escape into the air. Compaction by machinery or the human foot creates an impervious layer of soil that does not absorb moisture, encouraging erosion and hampering moisture as it moves to deeper soil levels.

Raised beds have many advantages. They drain fast, heat up early in the spring, and can be located in a large or small, convenient, sunny spot with whatever design configuration is pleasing. After the initial rototilling, plowing, or hand-turning of the soil, further deep disturbance should be unnecessary. Raised beds that are continually enriched with organic matter and have foot traffic limited to adjacent permanent paths lessens soil depletion, compaction, and erosion.

Limit the width of raised beds to 3 to 4 feet to allow access from either side without stepping in the bed. Topsoil dug from the paths is used to build up the height of the raised beds (below). Additional topsoil, compost, or rotted manures may be used as well. Wooden planks that evenly distribute a person's weight can be used to set across a bed for close access.

Mulch paths with straw, hay, shredded tree bark or brush, pine needles, or even newspaper covered with grass clippings. For a patterned, visually striking garden, pave paths with brick, flagstone, precast concrete, cobblestone, or gravel. Raised beds adjacent to paved paths should be edged with a barrier of weather-resistant wood, brick, or concrete to retain soil.

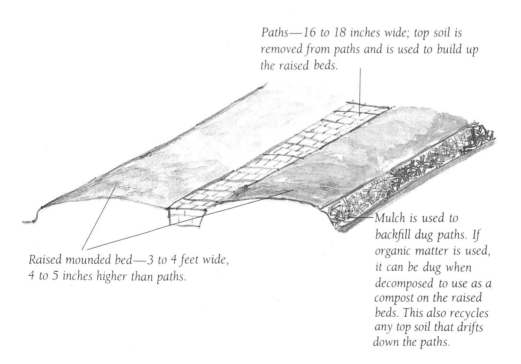

Paths—16 to 18 inches wide; top soil is removed from paths and is used to build up the raised beds.

Raised mounded bed—3 to 4 feet wide, 4 to 5 inches higher than paths.

Mulch is used to backfill dug paths. If organic matter is used, it can be dug when decomposed to use as a compost on the raised beds. This also recycles any top soil that drifts down the paths.

THE
MOOSEWOOD
RESTAURANT
KITCHEN
GARDEN

188

Gardeners who are attuned to the sensitivities of their plants know what it's like to walk past beds that are filled with weeds. The air hangs heavy with a Darwinian presence of ruthless competition and survival of the fittest. Plants are screaming "I'm choking! Weed me! Weed me!" This is the time to step in and rescue our little friends from the encroachment of the invading hordes.

Weeding is most seriously needed at the early growing stages of seedlings. Established plants tend to shade out smaller weeds which are then more easily pulled or hoed, but you should still be on the lookout.

Hand weeding is most easily accomplished when the soil is moist, after a rain or watering. It's easy to pull weeds out of an established garden with deep, light soil, a genuine reward for the years of soil-building efforts.

Cultivation with a hoe controls weeds and aerates the soil. Work only the top ½ inch of soil, cutting weeds off from their roots without damaging the underlying roots of the "good" plants. I've rarely used a hoe, preferring my hands or small tools. I suppose hoes are more efficient for large gardens and for people who prefer to stand rather than muck around in the dirt.

Organic mulches are also very effective in weed control and soil conditioning (p. 178). Rolls of commercially available biodegradable paper mulch are effective weed barriers. Because the paper "robs" nitrogen from the soil as it decomposes you'll need to provide extra fertilizer for paper-mulched plants. This is true for newspaper mulches as well. Layers of newspaper can be camouflaged with grass clippings or cut weeds.

New beds can be created without turning the soil or digging, by smothering weeds with paper, newspaper, or cardboard. Weight with stones and disguise as above. Beds will have to sit for one whole growing season to adequately destroy any sod growth or weeds. Black plastic, though unattractive, will accomplish the same job by "burning" the sod in a few weeks of hot weather.

Persistent weeds growing in nooks and crannies of paved areas or steps can be foiled with the application of boiling water. Avoid using chemical herbicides anywhere. "Sharp Shooter" is a nontoxic weed killer. Most effectively used on young weed growth, the naturally occurring fatty acids cause leaves to lose moisture.

CROP ROTATION

Crop rotation balances the give-and-take of plants and the soil.

Rotating crops accomplishes three important things:

1. It discourages soil-borne disease organisms and insects that attack specific plants.

2. It prevents the localized depletion of specific soil minerals and nutrients by one vegetable. Alternatively, it can create soils that have been nutritionally improved by a previous crop.

3. It creates deeper, aerated soils by root penetration.

Avoid planting any particular vegetable or its family members (listed below) in the same location for 3 years. It's a good idea to keep a yearly record of your garden layout to consult each year.

Vegetables are botanically classified into the following families:

Cabbage Family: broccoli, Brussels sprouts, cabbage, cauliflower, kale, mustard, pak choi, turnip

Carrot Family: carrot, celery, parsley, parsnip

Cucurbit Family: cucumber, summer and winter squash, melon

Daisy Family: lettuce

Goosefoot Family: beet, spinach, Swiss chard

Grass Family: corn

Legume Family: bean, pea

Nightshade Family: eggplant, pepper, potato, tomato

Onion Family: garlic, leeks, onion, shallot

The addition of compost and other organic matter helps to restore nutrients depleted by previous crops. This is important for "mini" gardens where crop rotation may be impractical.

IRRIGATION AND WATERING

Regional climate differences create a variety of watering needs ranging from an occasional soaking to computerized, scheduled irrigation.

A total of 1 inch per week of rainfall should be sufficient for growing most vegetables under temperate conditions. The drying effects of hot, windy weather increase a plant's need for moisture. Poke a finger into the top 2 or 3 inches of soil to gauge the depth of dry soil.

Watering is most efficient when done in the morning before the sun is strong enough to quickly evaporate moisture. Water thoroughly and redo the "finger test" to ensure that absorption has been sufficiently deep.

Sprinklers can be used to cover small or large areas, being particularly effective on lawns. Care should be taken not to flood the soil; flooding encourages fungi, soil compaction, and suffocation of plant roots. In vegetable and herb beds, sprinklers can encourage fungus diseases and rot.

Soaker hoses are part of an effective watering system for beds or borders. Made of porous or perforated rubber or vinyl, they can be buried just beneath the soil or mulch, or laid upon the ground, for the entire season. Water slowly penetrates into the surrounding soil, usually wetting a swath on either side. Advantages over sprinklers include: between 50 and 70 percent less water used (no evaporation to the air), no water damage to blooms or foliage, and less water runoff and erosion.

Soaker hoses work by gravity, so on slopes it's best to zig-zag them along parallel contours so that lower areas don't get more water than higher spots. Be sure to mark the course of buried hoses so that they won't be damaged when you're digging in the garden. Rodents, if they are a problem in your area, may chew them, and minerals in your water supply can also clog the "pores." At the start of each season, expose the entire length of the hose, then turn on the water to check for adequate water pressure, leaks or breaks, and anything else that might need repair.

THE
MOOSEWOOD
RESTAURANT
KITCHEN
GARDEN

190

STRETCHING THE SEASON

A variety of devices—both homemade and commercially available—can help you get a head start in spring and extend the growing season into fall and sometimes beyond.

black plastic—crops that need warm soil for good germination and growth (beans, corn, basil, melons, sweet potatoes, peppers, and tomatoes) benefit from a mulch of black plastic sheeting.

Lay sheets of plastic directly on the cool ground 2 weeks before the estimated sowing or planting time. Make small cuts in the plastic here and there to allow for water penetration, bury the edges, and weight down with stones.

Black plastic can be left down all season (helpful where summers are cool), but should be picked up before winter to avoid decomposition and eternally shredding bits of plastic in your garden. If you live in a warmer climate, the plastic should come up if the soil gets too hot, since roots can be damaged and beneficial life forms (such as earthworms) will move away.

floating row covers—horticultural fabrics that are light and porous provide frost, animal, and insect protection. At planting time, fabrics are draped over seedbeds or seedlings, leaving slack for the plants to push up to their ultimate height. Bury the edges with soil, or anchor securely with boards, large stones, or plastic jugs filled with water.

Temperatures can range from 10 to 15 degrees warmer under row covers on sunny days. Row covers provide frost protection down to about 27°F. Air-borne insects, such as flea and potato beetles, cabbage loopers, and flies that cause root maggots, are kept off plants. Seedlings are protected from wind, downpours, and hail, yet the covers are porous enough to admit moisture.

Row covers should be removed when daytime temperatures consistently are above 80°F., or when vegetables begin to flower and require pollination.

Unfortunately, synthetic row covers are not biodegradable; however, they usually last two to three seasons. They should be kept out of the sun when not in use, stored dry and relatively clean.

I've had good results with covering greens and lettuce in the late fall–early winter for continued harvests 4 weeks or more longer than uncovered plants.

Reemay, Kimberly Farms, and Agryl are widely available row covers. Agronet is a lighter fabric that can be used in warmer weather. Temperatures under the cover average 4 to 8 degrees higher than the air temperature. Typar is made of a heavier fabric, similar to Reemay, but with a longer life of 3 to 4 years.

hotkaps—made of waxed, translucent paper, these little hothouses are slit to allow for ventilation. Seedlings of squash, pumpkins, melons, cucumbers, and other widely spaced, heat-loving crops could be more effectively covered with individual hotkaps than with floating row covers.

plastic jugs or glass jars—plastic jugs with the bottoms cut out and glass jars can be used to cover small plants when cold weather threatens. These should be used only at night or on very cloudy days, because, in daylight, the plants would "fry" in the solar heated, unventilated jars.

slitted polyethylene tunnels—an environment 6 to 20 degrees warmer than the outside temperature (depending upon solar intensity) is created with wire hoops covered by slitted plastic sheeting. These are commercially available through many supply or seed houses. Tunnels work well for young plants that require warm conditions: peppers, tomatoes, basil, eggplant, and squash. The plastic should be removed when the weather has warmed and before plants begin to flower. This will encourage pollination and help to avoid blossom drops due to high temperatures.

INSECTS AND DISEASES

It's always frustrating to see one's efforts in the garden foiled by various pests. While there is certainly good reason to keep destructive insect populations as low as possible, it's good to realize that some insects are beneficial. Dragonflies, spiders, wasps, yellow jackets, and ladybugs will prey on insects injurious to your garden. Green lacewings, spined soldier bugs, praying mantis, and trichogramma wasps also snack on garden pests and can be ordered from the mail-order sources found on page 271.

PREVENTION

THE
MOOSEWOOD
RESTAURANT
KITCHEN
GARDEN

192

• Keep the garden clean, year round, of plant debris that can become a residence for insects.
• Practice companion planting (p. 200).
• Plant varieties resistant to insects or diseases prevalent in your region. Cooperative Extension can help with this.
• Rotate crops to inhibit the population of insects or soil-borne diseases. These pests will not prosper when their favored food is no longer in the neighborhood.
• Use row covers to protect vulnerable plants (p. 191).
• If possible, delay planting until the troublesome insect population has peaked. For example, if your spring-planted pak choi is devastated by flea beetles, plant it later in the season.

INSECTICIDE SAFETY

• Even "natural" insecticides require careful handling.
• Follow label instructions for recommended dilution rates, product warnings, or health risks.
• Wear a face mask, long sleeves, and pants. Wash exposed areas after use.
• Try to dust or spray plants on a quiet, still day. Avoid windy conditions.
• Don't mix different products.
• Wash equipment carefully after use.
• Dispose of container at a toxic-materials site.

CHARTS ON INSECTS AND DISEASES, AND PEST CONTROLS

The following charts are an abbreviated guide to common insects and diseases affecting vegetables and herbs. The Bibliography on page 275 lists sources for more extensive information.

I have limited my discussion of controls to those of simple device and botanical or biological insecticides. Rotenone, sabadilla, and pyrethrum are botanical insecticides derived from natural plant sources. Biological insecticides include life forms, such as predators (ladybugs) and beneficial bacteria (Bt—*Bacillus thuringiensis*).

Botanical insecticides decompose quickly in the presence of sun and oxygen, and their residues do not contaminate the environment. Use them only as a last resort, however, since they can kill both beneficial insects and pests, upsetting the natural balance. Synthetic chemical pesticides became popular because their effects were longer lasting and required less frequent application. Unfortunately, the residues of these toxic chemicals have been retained in our soils, water supply, and, ultimately, food sources.

COMMON INSECTS AND DISEASES

VEGETABLE—DISEASE/INSECT

Asian vegetables (Chinese cabbage, mizuna, pak choi, tatsoi)—	*see* cabbage
asparagus—	asparagus beetles, corn earworm, rust
beans—	anthracnose, aphids, corn earworms, downy mildew, Japanese beetles, spider mites, rust
beets—	flea beetles
broccoli—	*see* cabbage
Brussels sprouts—	*see* cabbage
cabbage—	aphids, cabbage worms, club root, cutworms, flea beetles, root maggots
cauliflower—	*see* cabbage
collards and kale—	*see* cabbage
corn—	corn earworms, Japanese beetles, spider mites
cucumbers—	anthracnose, aphids, corn earworms, downy mildew, spider mites, striped cucumber beetles, squash bugs
eggplant—	Colorado potato beetles, flea beetles, spider mites, tomato hornworms
kohlrabi—	*see* cabbage
lettuce and salad greens—	aphids, cutworms, slugs and snails

melons—	anthracnose, aphids, downy mildew, spider mites, squash bugs, striped cucumber beetles
okra—	aphids, corn earworms, Japanese beetles
onions—	root maggots
peas—	aphids, downy mildew
peppers—	anthracnose, aphids, blossom-end rot, Colorado potato beetles, corn earworms, damping-off, flea beetles, tomato hornworms
potatoes—	aphids, Colorado potato beetles, corn earworms, flea beetles, scab, tomato hornworms
spinach—	aphids, cutworms, slugs and snails
squash— (*summer and winter*)	corn earworms, striped cucumber beetles, squash bugs
Swiss chard—	*see* beets
tomatoes—	aphids, blossom-end rot, Colorado potato beetles, cutworms, flea beetles, tomato hornworms
turnips—	*see* cabbage

THE
MOOSEWOOD
RESTAURANT
KITCHEN
GARDEN

194

CONTROLS

bacillus thuringiensis (Bt)—a beneficial bacterium that is harmless to humans, birds, bees, and many helpful insects, but fatal to specific pests, particularly caterpillars. It's dusted or sprayed onto plants, then ingested by the attacking insect whose digestive system is quickly paralyzed, causing death in 24 hours.

diatomaceous earth—a powdery substance composed of the shells of one-celled sea plants known as diatoms. Though it feels like talcum powder to you and me, each tiny grain is sharp enough to injure or kill insects by causing dehydration through cuts. If ingested, the powder damages the pests' respiratory or digestive system.

hot pepper spray—this homemade spray can be whipped up from your own garden to serve as a general insecticide. Blend 1 cup of water with 1 cup of chopped hot peppers and steep for 1 day. Strain and add ½ cup to 1 gallon of water. Do not use on very young seedlings, and avoid getting the spray on your skin or near your eyes. A clove or two of garlic, which is reputed to repel insects, can be added with the peppers for additional clout.

Hand-picked or trapped pests can be destroyed in a container of heavily salted or soapy water.

insecticidal soap—a liquid solution derived from the salts of fatty acids, a similar process used for all soaps. Can be used on crops up until harvest; once the soap dries it is no longer harmful. Avoid contact with the spray or concentrated solution.

pyrethrum—a powder derived from the flowers of *Chrysanthemum cinerariaefolium*. Pyrethrum and pyrethins (the concentrated active compounds of the flowers) are not toxic to humans but can kill fish. The fast-acting pyrethrums are frequently combined with longer lasting rotenone.

rotenone—a powder derived from the roots of several tropical plants, rotenone should be used only when damage is extensive and the insect population high. Use rotenone only when nothing else works, since its toxicity may harm beneficial insects as well. Avoid inhaling or ingesting it. Wear a face mask when applying.

sabadilla dust—a fine powder derived from the ground seeds of a tropical lily. Avoid ingesting, inhaling, or accidentally applying to skin. Use in the evening when honeybees are at less risk of exposure.

INSECT CONTROL

INSECT	DESCRIPTION	CONTROL
Aphids	Less than ⅛ inch long, may be red, yellow, green, black, gray, or brown. They suck the juices of stems and leaves and possibly spread disease. Worst of all, a single female aphid can produce *5 billion* baby aphids in a single season. Wide variety of host plants.	• spray with a strong stream of water • insecticidal soap • ladybugs, green lacewings • pyrethrum • rotenone

INSECT	DESCRIPTION	CONTROL
Asparagus Beetles	Black with white spots, ¼ inch long. Shiny eggs deposited on stems.	• pyrethrum • rotenone
Colorado Potato Beetles	Yellow with black stripes and hard shell ⅓ inch long. Orange eggs deposited on undersides of leaves. Eggplant, pepper, potato, and tomato are common host plants.	• generous layer of clean mulch will discourage • row covers • rotenone • Bt "San Diego" strain • pyrethrum
Flea Beetles	Hop like a flea. Black, shiny, ¹⁄₁₀ inch long. Many vegetables susceptible, particularly the cabbage family.	• row covers applied at time of seeding • diatomaceous earth • pyrethrum • rotenone
Japanese Beetles	Shiny bronze body, ½ inch long with blue and green iridescent wings. Roses, beans, and corn are susceptible.	• pyrethrum • rotenone • soil treatment with milky spore disease to kill overwintering grubs • commercial traps with scented lures
Striped Cucumber Beetles	Yellow or orange with 3 black stripes, ¼ inch long. Adults eat leaves; larvae eat roots. Affect cucurbits (squash, melon, and cucumber), beans, and peas.	• row covers (remove at flower time for pollination) • trap under boards • generous layer of mulch • rotenone
Squash Bugs	Flat, brown, ½ inch long. Oval brown eggs laid on the undersides of leaves. Affect cucurbits (squash, cucumber, melon, and pumpkin).	• trap under boards • sabadilla • row covers

THE
MOOSEWOOD
RESTAURANT
KITCHEN
GARDEN

196

INSECT	DESCRIPTION	CONTROL
Cutworms	Soft, 1 to 1½ inches long, gray or brown caterpillar. Not seen in the daytime unless you happen to expose when weeding or hoeing. Seedlings cut off at ground level. Attack all vegetables, particularly young seedlings.	• expose worms by shallow cultivation around plant • protect seedlings with paper collars • trichogramma wasps • Bt • apply wood ash
Cabbage Worms (either cabbage looper or imported cabbage worm)	Green caterpillars up to 1½ inches long, can destroy crops of the cabbage family.	• Bt • handpick • row covers • rotenone • garlic infusion • trichogramma wasps
Corn Earworms	White to green, 1½-inch-long spined caterpillars. Attack bean, corn, pea, pepper, potato, squash, and tomato.	• Bt • rotenone
Tomato Hornworms	Smooth, light green caterpillars up to 4 inches long with a "horn" at one end and zig-zag stripes. Will strip leaves and eat fruits of eggplant, tomato, peppers and potato.	• handpick • trichogramma wasps, green lacewings • Bt
Root Maggots	White, ¼-inch-long larvae of flies that hibernate in the soil over winter. Destroy young plants by tunneling into roots. Affect the cabbage family, carrots, onions, and peas, especially in the spring.	• Don't apply manure within 4 to 6 weeks of planting • Diatomaceous earth or wood ash scattered on seedbeds • 3-inch tar paper squares with a slit at the center for seedlings. Lay flat on soil to keep flies from laying eggs at the base of seedlings.

INSECT	DESCRIPTION	CONTROL
Spider Mites	Tiny, almost invisible spiders that suck plant juices, causing leaves to speckle and curl. Affect indoor plants and vegetables, herbs, and ornamentals in warm, dry seasons.	• strong spray of water, particularly undersides of leaves • insecticidal soap • solution of wheat flour, buttermilk, and water sprayed on plants • rotenone • green lacewings, ladybugs
Slugs and Snails	Yellowish or gray, soft, slimy mollusks ½ to 3 inches long. Snails have a shell. Both feed at night. Can cause extensive damage and kill seedlings.	• dust with diatomaceous earth, lime, or wood ash • lay boards to trap slugs; destroy in the morning when they're full of food and sleepy • punch a hole in the side of a coffee can with a lid. Bury the can with the hole at ground level. Fill with a mixture of 1 cup water, 1 teaspoon sugar, and ¼ teaspoon baking yeast, to ground level. Remove besotted slugs and refill. • remove mulch and plant debris • cultivate top 2 to 3 inches of soil to expose slugs, hand-pick, and destroy
Whitefly	Small mothlike white insects that cluster on leaves and stems. Houseplants particularly susceptible.	• insecticidal soap • pyrethrum • yellow sticky traps for greenhouses

THE
MOOSEWOOD
RESTAURANT
KITCHEN
GARDEN

198

DISEASE	DESCRIPTION	CONTROL
Anthracnose	A fungus affecting beans, cucumbers, melons, and peppers. Dark discolored spots appear on leaves, pods, or fruits.	• rotate crops • avoid touching the wet foliage • plant resistant varieties
Blossom-end rot	Dark, pitted, rotting areas at the blossom end (opposite stem) of tomatoes and peppers. Caused by uneven watering and lack of calcium.	• keep plants evenly watered • add lime or wood ash to soil
Club root	Roots of the cabbage family are deformed and stunted by a soil fungus. Plants may not form heads; leaves yellow and drop.	• rotate crops • add wood ash and lime
Damping off	A fungus that kills young seedlings. The stem weakens and collapses at the soil line.	• use sterilized potting soil for seedlings • do not overwater or overcrowd seedlings
Powdery mildew	White splotches appear on leaves in humid weather due to fungus infection. May cause leaves to shrivel and vegetables to sunscald, ripen poorly. Affects cucurbits (melons, squashes, and cucumbers).	• dust plants with sulfur
Rust	Red or brown spores appear on leaves due to fungus growth. Leaves eventually yellow and fall off. Affects beans and asparagus.	• avoid handling or working around the wet foliage of beans or asparagus • water plants in the early morning and avoid wetting the foliage

GARDENING
TECHNIQUES

199

DISEASE	DESCRIPTION	CONTROL
Scab	A fungus causing rough dark spots on potatoes or brown sunken areas on cucumbers and squashes.	• rotate crops • plant potatoes in acidic soil with a pH of 5.0.

COMPANION PLANTING

THE
MOOSEWOOD
RESTAURANT
KITCHEN
GARDEN

200

Not all garden authorities agree on whether or not the proximity of differing species of plants affects their growth and ability to fight off insects and diseases. However, there is some scientific evidence to back up what were once considered flaky claims. Companion planting was first popularized through biodynamic gardening and the 1920s European lectures of Rudolf Steiner. Steiner's teachings promote the connection between farmer and nature and outline specific farming practices to balance "cosmic and earthly forces." Esoteric as this sounds, many of these practices are now common, often-proven organic gardening procedures, such as compost making, crop rotation, planting with the planets, and companion planting.*

Folklore and biodynamic guidelines recommend the plant combinations that follow. There are a number of reasons for felicitous companionship:
• Substances released by certain plant roots stimulate mutual growth or protection from diseases and insects.
• Companion plants make complementary nutritional demands upon the soil.
• Intercropped gardens with a variety of scents, colors, and shapes make it more difficult for insects to zero in on their favored plants than a singly cropped space. Crops varied within a single row also create interesting visual effects.

A given plant's needs for sun, space, and water must also be taken into account, as should the timing of planting. For instance, beans and corn may grow well together, but vigorous bean vines could smother newly emerging corn seedlings.

Ultimately, though, the best companion for any garden is the gardener. Check for soil moisture and insect, disease, or predator damage, and harvest potential regularly.

* For information on biodynamic farming write to: Kimberton Hills Farm, P.O. Box 550, Kimberton, PA, 19442.

BENEFICIAL COMPANIONS

VEGETABLE	VEGETABLES(v) OR HERBS(h)
asparagus	v– tomato h– basil, calendula, parsley
beans	v– cabbage family, carrot, corn, cucumber, eggplant, peas, potato, Swiss chard h– borage, lovage, marigold, nasturtium, oregano, summer savory
beets	v– bush beans, cabbage family, lettuce, onion h– garlic
cabbage family *	v– beets, cucumber, lettuce, onion, potato, spinach, Swiss chard h– chamomile, dill, garlic, hyssop, mint, nasturtium, sage, thyme
carrot	v– beans, lettuce, onion, peas, peppers, tomato h– chives, rosemary, sage, thyme
corn	v– beans, cucumber, melon, peas, potato, squash h– marigold, parsley
cucumber	v– beans, cabbage family, corn, lettuce, tomato h– marigold, parsley
eggplant	v– beans, peppers h– marigold, thyme
lettuce	v– beet, cabbage family, carrot, onion h– chive, dill, garlic, onion
melon	v– corn, pumpkin, squash h– marigold, nasturtium, oregano
onion	v– beets, cabbage family, carrot, lettuce, pepper, Swiss chard, tomato h– chamomile, dill, summer savory
peas	v– beans, carrot, corn, cucumber, turnip h– mint
peppers	v– carrot, eggplant, onion, tomato h– basil

* Members of the cabbage family: broccoli, Brussels sprouts, cabbage, cauliflower, collards, kale, kohlrabi, turnips

VEGETABLE	VEGETABLES(v) OR HERBS(h)
potato	v— beans, cabbage family, corn, eggplant, peas
	h— marigold
spinach	v— cabbage family
squash	v— corn, melon, pumpkin
	h— borage, marigold, nasturtium, oregano
tomato	v— asparagus, beans, carrot, cucumber, onion, peppers
	h— basil, bee balm, borage, calendula, chive, mint, parsley, sage, thyme
turnip	v— peas

THE
MOOSEWOOD
RESTAURANT
KITCHEN
GARDEN

202

BENEFICIAL COMPANIONS

HERB	VEGETABLES OR HERBS
basil	peppers, tomato
bee balm	tomato
borage	beans, squash, tomato
calendula	asparagus, tomato
chamomile	cabbage, onion
chive	carrot, lettuce, rose, tomato
dill	cabbage, lettuce, onion
garlic	beets, cabbage, lettuce, rose
hyssop	cabbage
lovage	lovage
marigold	beans, corn, cucumber, eggplant, melon, potato, rose, squash
mint	cabbage, tomato
oregano	beans
parsley	asparagus, corn, tomato
rosemary	beans, cabbage
sage	cabbage, carrot, tomato
summer savory	beans, onion
thyme	carrot, cabbage, eggplant, tomato

Poor companions may be detrimental to the growth of some neighbors. Happily, this is a short list. Keeping these plants a couple of rows apart shouldn't be too difficult.

POOR COMPANIONS	
VEGETABLE	**VEGETABLES OR HERBS**
beans	chive, garlic, leek, onion, shallots
beets	pole beans
cabbage family	kohlrabi, pole beans, tomato
carrot	dill
corn	tomato
cucumber	potato, sage
onions	beans, peas, sage
peas	chive, garlic, leek, onion, shallot
potato	cucumber, squash, tomato
tomato	corn, dill, kohlrabi, potato

RECIPES

You chose the perfect spot for your garden: sunny, well-drained, framing a nice view down the valley. Regionally appropriate seeds were selected and started when the moon was in a most propitious sign. Your raised beds were tilled with the richest soil, and the plants were all perfect companions, both biodynamically and aesthetically. Thinned, nurtured, watered, and fed with compost and sea nutrients, the seedlings grew, protected from frosts, hail, and insects. Now harvest is at hand; the vegetables will be picked at the peak of perfection. You can't blow it now, especially if you use the cooking techniques that follow.

VEGETABLE BASICS

THE
MOOSEWOOD
RESTAURANT
KITCHEN
GARDEN

206

Properly cooked, flavorful, and attractively presented vegetables are the happy ending to this story. Proper cooking chiefly requires attention to avoid a common, but always preventable, error: overdone, soggy, and tasteless vegetables. Pace tasks in a way that allows for your focused attention when needed, and begin with all the ingredients ready for use—chopped, peeled, minced—as the recipe calls for. At the Restaurant, we work at a brisk pace, but I still have time to admire a long cutting board filled with the assorted colors and shapes of vegetables or to be refreshed by the clean fragrance of minced herbs.

Vegetables can be loosely grouped into three general categories based on their cooking times:

hard Carrots, cauliflower, celery, green beans, onions, potatoes, sweet potatoes, turnips, winter squash.

medium hard Asparagus, broccoli, Brussels sprouts, cabbage, eggplant, fennel, leeks, mushrooms, okra, parsnips, peppers, summer squash, zucchini.

soft Greens, pak choi, peas, snow peas, scallions, shallots, spinach, tomatoes.

Cutting foods uniformly ensures they'll cook in about the same amount of time. We like to vary vegetable shapes and sizes from dish to dish. Soups work well with smaller cut or diced vegetables (one hunk of potato could almost fill a cup). Stews can be heartier, with chunkier shapes. Stir-fried dishes look attractive and cook more uniformly when foods are cut similarly. Long, slender strips of vegetables are visually suited to (and tend to clump less) in dishes featuring thin noodles.

We tend to cut vegetables by hand where appearance is important, for example, in salads or stews. We use a food processor to grate and blend or purée. Vegetables that won't be "on display," hidden in fillings or casseroles, can be cut in the processor. Hand cutting yields more pleasing, somewhat uneven food pieces, as opposed to the manufactured "perfection" of processor-sliced foods.

COOKED VEGETABLES FOR SALADS

Marinated, cooked vegetables are a standard menu item at the Restaurant. These can be prepared ahead of time, to gain in flavor as they marinate, and to free your last-minute attention for other dishes.

Salads reflect the seasons: early greens, lettuce, and asparagus in spring; scallions, new potatoes, baby carrots, and peas in early summer. The abundance of midsummer brings green beans, eggplant, peppers, zucchini, and juicy tomatoes, while endive, cabbage, broccoli and cauliflower, radicchio, and fennel are enjoyed in the fall.

Here are a few pointers:
• Be sure to remove vegetables from the heat when they're still slightly crunchy.
• Immediately plunge cooked vegetables in ice water to halt the cooking process and preserve good color. Drain well.
• Add marinade well before serving so seasonings can be absorbed. When using green vegetables (beans, peas—shelled, snap, and snow—and peppers), withhold just the lemon juice and vinegar until right before serving time, since the acidity will dull their color to an unappetizing khaki green.
• Salads that taste just right soon after a dressing is added may need more seasonings later, after the flavors have been absorbed.
• Marinated salads are best served warm or at room temperature in cool weather, chilled in hot weather. Vegetables à la Grecque (p. 218) is an interesting way of cooking foods in their marinade.

The attractive appearance of a meal is appreciated before anything is even tasted. Before I garnish a meal I've prepared, I take a walk through the garden to gather decorative edibles—sprigs of herbs and blossoms or flower petals—keeping in mind color and textural contrasts and complementary tastes. A green gazpacho is nicely set off by a garnish of bright red nasturtium; Johnny-jump-ups or violet blossoms add color to a simple salad of butter lettuces. A spring pasta salad of varying shades of green from spinach, peas, chives, asparagus, and herbed mayonnaise might need nothing to enhance the subtle harmony.

Herbs are an integral part of the Moosewood cooking style. Fresh herbs add to any food a fuller richness. It's hard to imagine a pasta primavera without fresh basil, a Russian vegetable strudel without fresh dill, a vegetable ragout without fresh tarragon, or a spicy salsa without fresh cilantro. We also use many herbs in dried form.

Some uncommon herbs, like chervil, the scented thymes, lemon or cinnamon basil, and sorrel, are available fresh only in season. Other popular fresh herbs, such as dill, cilantro, basil, and parsley, can be found year-round at large super-markets or greengrocers.

Using herbs effectively requires learning what combinations of foods and sea-sonings work well together. New cooks, excited by a garden or shelf full of herbs and spices, may naively assume that more is better. The disappointing results are often analogous to mixing together every color and coming up with a drab brown. The fresh taste of garden produce should not be overwhelmed by competing flavors.

Exercise a light hand with herbs, adding more if necessary at the completion of a dish. Cooking with just one or two herbs in a given preparation and following recipes are excellent ways to learn the basics. With a knowledge of herbs, inno-vative cooks can improvise a myriad of variations on a limited repertoire.

The following guidelines will help you maximize the culinary potential of herbs:

• Pick herbs as close to cooking time as possible for maximum flavor and fresh-ness. Leave behind enough foliage for the plant to sustain itself.

• Chop or mince herbs to release the essential oil. Food processors are effective for large quantities, or to blend herbs into a sauce or dressing. Herbs may need to be coarsely chopped before processing to avoid stringiness.

• When your recipe calls for dried herbs and you want to "convert" to fresh, the general rule for leafy herbs, such as dill or basil, is to use three to four times the quantity of fresh herbs as called for dried. Fresh sage and thyme, or the needlelike leaves of rosemary, are dry and potent, so may require no more than twice as much fresh as dried.

• Herbs that are better added at the beginning of cooking for heightened flavor include:

bay	oregano	seeds (mustard, caraway, coriander, dill,
garlic	sage	fennel, cumin)
lovage	thyme	

THE
MOOSEWOOD
RESTAURANT
KITCHEN
GARDEN

208

• Fresh herbs with essential oils that are less potent when heated should be added toward the end of cooking:

basil	chive	fennel leaf	mint
borage	cilantro	lemon balm	parsley
chervil	dill weed	marjoram	tarragon

• Some recipes call for a bouquet garni, a bundle of seasonings that is added during cooking and removed later when a delicate flavor or clean visual effect is desired. A cheesecloth bag or tea ball is filled with herb sprigs, peppercorns, cloves, allspice berries, or other seasonings and added to a simmering sauce, stew, or soup. This will be removed before serving, or as the recipe indicates.

• Allow an hour or more for herbs to infuse their essence through uncooked dressings, sauces, butters, and spreads.

• If, despite all of our warnings, you are still guilty of overseasoning, don't compost dinner until you've:

Prepared more of the original ingredients cooked to the same stage as the overseasoned food and then added to dilute the seasoning. Invite some neighbors to share the unexpected abundance.

Added bland foods that would thin out or add bulk to a dish. Try milk, cream, potatoes, rice, pasta, cooked beans, bread crumbs, or mild cheese.

Tossed in a couple of peeled raw potato chunks to be removed before serving. These will absorb some of the extra seasoning.

COOKING TECHNIQUES

The heating process can take many forms: blanching, boiling and simmering, deep-frying, grilling, roasting, sautéing, steaming, and stir-frying.

When cooking vegetables by any technique that uses medium to high heat, remove them when they are a little crunchier than desired. Their retained heat will continue the cooking process.

blanching—This is a method of boiling foods very briefly. Blanching takes the raw edge off vegetables to be used in salads or as crudités, and is a preliminary to freezing, roasting, or grilling vegetables.

The key is to provide a generous quantity of boiling water that will not quickly cool down when the vegetables are added. Use a slotted spoon or a mesh skimmer to quickly remove cooked vegetables from the water.

Foods such as bean sprouts, mushrooms, snow peas, and finely cut julienne (matchstick) vegetables may be completely cooked by blanching.

boiling and simmering—Boiling liquids have quickly moving bubbles that break on the surface. In simmering, the bubbling occurs at a more relaxed pace.

Boil vegetables in generous quantities of water. This can be a quick technique, as the water doesn't cool down much with the addition of foods. Some nutrients are absorbed by the cooking liquid, which can be used as a stock.

Sauces and stews are best cooked when allowed to gently simmer, as there is less danger of sticking or burning and more time for flavors to mingle and blend.

deep-frying—Here foods are submerged in very hot oil and cooked quickly. Deep-fried foods have a crisp succulence that is universally appealing. The goal of perfect frying is to seal the food's exterior without overcooking it before the inside is done.

It's important to have the oil reach a temperature between 350°F. and 375°F. A deep-fry or candy thermometer is a good investment. If you don't have a thermometer, you can test the temperature by dropping in a 1-inch cube of bread. It should turn a golden brown in 45 to 60 seconds. Cool oil will result in slow cooking and excessive oil absorption. Even a high oil temperature will be lowered by attempting to cook too much at one time.

Deep-frying works well for batter-dipped or dough-wrapped foods. Hard, dense vegetables used as filling should be cut into thin slices or pieces to avoid their being undercooked while the batter or wrapper is overcooked.

grilling—Cooking foods on a rack or mesh a few inches above a charcoal, gas-fueled, or similar heat source. Best used for the following vegetables: eggplant, mushrooms, onions, peppers, tomatoes, zucchini, and summer squash, as well as blanched white or sweet potatoes, carrots, and winter squash. (For instructions and recipe see p. 237.)

roasting—Oven cooking of food, frequently prepared with a marinade or basting liquid to increase flavor and prevent drying out. Roasting brings out vegetable sugars and seals in juices while creating a crisp, crunchy outer layer. It is the most time-consuming method, but it can be energy efficient if you roast vegetables when the oven is already in use. Vegetables that are blanched first will roast more quickly. Root vegetables are particularly good roasted.

sautéeing—This is similar to stir-frying in that vegetables and seasonings are cooked, uncovered, with oil or butter, but usually on a lower heat and with less vigorous stirring. Sautéeing is a good method for gently cooking vegetables while their respective flavors "marry." It can be used with any vegetable.

steaming—Foods are cooked over, but not submerged in, boiling or simmering water or stock. Properly cooked steamed vegetables are crisp and tender

THE
MOOSEWOOD
RESTAURANT
KITCHEN
GARDEN

210

with good color. Use a stainless steel steaming basket or rack that can be inserted into a pot, or a special two-piece steaming pot. Keep the water level lower than the bottom of the steamer to avoid sogginess. Allow the water to come to a boil and steam vegetables covered, for heat efficiency and better color.

Leftover noodles, rice, or other grains can be reheated in a steamer.

Save the steaming liquid from mildly flavored vegetables for a nutritious stock. Strongly flavored vegetables, such as asparagus, cabbage-family members, bitter greens, and pepper stocks, would be useful only for soups that feature these ingredients and would probably be overwhelming in anything else.

Steaming is an effective cooking method for all vegetables, with the possible exception of potatoes and sweet potatoes. Dense, hard vegetables are more quickly cooked by boiling in liquid to cover.

stir-frying—Foods are tossed and stirred continuously with a small amount of oil and seasonings over a relatively high heat. The high temperatures seal in juices and the quick cooking helps preserve vitamins and nutrients.

Stir-frying works best in a wok, where the ample surface area heats food quickly and thoroughly and the steep rounded sides facilitate stirring and tossing. A heavy deep skillet can also be used.

Since this is a fast-moving procedure that requires your full attention, it's important to have all the ingredients near the stove, lined up in the order they're to be cooked. Cooked vegetables that are crisp and juicy can be achieved by adding little or no liquid during the cooking process. While stir-frying is good for all vegetables, hard, dense ones, such as potatoes, green beans, carrots, and cauliflower, should be cut small for faster cooking without extra liquid.

SOUPS

VEGETABLE STOCK

THE
MOOSEWOOD
RESTAURANT
KITCHEN
GARDEN

212

S oups and sauces cooked with vegetable stock are noticeably more flavorful than those made with water. At Moosewood, we make stock every night for the following day's soup, using this basic recipe with the addition of optional vegetables or herbs that are leftover or close at hand. Vegetables should be cleaned, but do not need to be peeled. Avoid such strongly flavored vegetables as broccoli, cabbage, cauliflower, eggplant, peppers, or turnips.

Vegetable bouillon powders or cubes can be mixed with boiling water and used in place of stock when time is short. Natural food stores carry a good selection, many of which are salt-free.

BASIC RECIPE

2 LARGE POTATOES, ANY TYPE, THICKLY SLICED	I CELERY STALK, CHOPPED
2 TO 3 MEDIUM ONIONS, QUARTERED	I APPLE *OR* PEAR, QUARTERED
3 TO 4 MEDIUM CARROTS, THICKLY SLICED	I TO 2 BAY LEAVES
	6 PEPPERCORNS
	IO CUPS (2½ QUARTS) WATER

THESE OPTIONAL VEGETABLES OR HERBS MAY BE ADDED:

GARLIC CLOVES	PARSNIPS
LEEKS, INCLUDING TOUGH GREEN LEAVES	SCALLIONS
	SWEET POTATOES
MUSHROOMS, WHOLE OR STEMS (WILL ADD A DISTINCTIVE FLAVOR AND DARKEN THE STOCK)	TOMATOES (IN SMALL AMOUNTS ONLY, OR STOCK MAY BE TOO ACID)
	WINTER SQUASH
PARSLEY, INCLUDING STEMS	ZUCCHINI OR SUMMER SQUASH

FOR STOCK WITH AN ASIAN FLAVOR, ADD:

SLICED FRESH GINGERROOT	SOAKING WATER FROM DRIED SHIITAKE MUSHROOMS

YIELDS 2 QUARTS

Scrub and cut the unpeeled vegetables. Place in stockpot with bay leaves and peppercorns; cover with water. Bring to a boil, then simmer for 1 hour or more.

Strain the stock through a colander or cloth, pressing out the liquid from the vegetables. (The remaining solid vegetables make good compost material or can be discarded.)

The stock will keep refrigerated for 3 to 4 days, or may be frozen in 1- to 6-cup quantities.

GAZPACHO VERDE

T his refreshing, deeply green, and healthful soup is best served chilled.

GAZPACHO

8 CUPS WATER

2 LARGE BUNCHES OF FRESH SPINACH (ABOUT 8 OUNCES), WITH LARGE STEMS REMOVED, WELL RINSED AND DRAINED

½ CUP LOOSELY PACKED ARUGULA LEAVES

3 SCALLIONS, WHITE AND GREEN PARTS, ROUGHLY CHOPPED

¼ CUP FRESH LOOSELY PACKED PARSLEY LEAVES

¼ CUP FRESH LOOSELY PACKED DILL LEAVES

8 FRESH NASTURTIUM LEAVES *OR* 2 TABLESPOONS MINCED FRESH GARDEN CRESS LEAVES

I CUCUMBER, ROUGHLY CHOPPED

2 TABLESPOONS EXTRA VIRGIN OLIVE OIL

I TO 2 GARLIC CLOVES, MINCED OR PRESSED

3 TABLESPOONS FRESH LIME JUICE

3 CUPS VEGETABLE STOCK (P. 212)

½ TEASPOON SALT

FRESHLY GROUND BLACK PEPPER TO TASTE

I SCALLION, WHITE AND GREEN PARTS, FINELY CHOPPED

½ CUCUMBER, SEEDED IF MATURE, FINELY DICED

GARNISH (USE ONE)

THINLY SLICED LIME

NASTURTIUM OR CHIVE BLOSSOMS

CHERRY TOMATO HALVES

CROUTONS

SERVES 4 TO 6

Bring the water to a boil. Add the spinach, arugula, and 3 scallions. Cook until the spinach just begins to wilt, not more than 1 minute or so. Drain.

In a food processor or blender, purée until smooth the remaining greens, the 1 cucumber, olive oil, garlic, lime juice, vegetable stock, salt, and pepper.

Add the chopped scallion and diced cucumber to the blended soup. Chill and serve with one of the recommended garnishes.

PORTUGUESE KALE SOUP

A hearty, colorful soup to warm fall and winter meals. The sun-dried tomatoes add a nice piquancy and chewy texture.

½ CUP DRIED WHITE BEANS (NAVY, PEA, OR GREAT NORTHERN)
2½ CUPS WATER *OR* VEGETABLE STOCK (P. 212)
2 WHOLE GARLIC CLOVES, PEELED
2 BAY LEAVES

3 TABLESPOONS OLIVE OIL
½ TEASPOON GROUND FENNEL SEED
1 GARLIC CLOVE, MINCED OR PRESSED
1½ CUPS CHOPPED ONION
1 MEDIUM POTATO, CHOPPED (ABOUT 1 CUP)
1 SMALL CARROT, CHOPPED (ABOUT ½ CUP)
1 SMALL PARSNIP, CHOPPED (ABOUT ½ CUP)

1½ CUPS CHOPPED FRESH OR CANNED TOMATOES
6 CUPS VEGETABLE STOCK (P. 212)
2 BAY LEAVES
1 TABLESPOON CHOPPED FRESH OREGANO (1 TEASPOON DRIED)
12 SUN-DRIED TOMATOES (ABOUT ½ CUP), PACKED IN OIL OR DRY PACKED
4 CUPS LOOSELY PACKED CHOPPED KALE
PINCH OF SAFFRON (OPTIONAL)
SALT AND FRESHLY GROUND BLACK PEPPER TO TASTE

THE
MOOSEWOOD
RESTAURANT
KITCHEN
GARDEN

214

SERVES 4 TO 6

Cook the beans in the water or stock with the whole garlic cloves and 2 bay leaves. The beans should be tender in 1½ to 2 hours.

While the beans are cooking, prepare the other ingredients.

Heat the olive oil in a soup pot, adding the fennel seed and minced or pressed garlic. Sauté for 1 minute, then add the onion, and sauté for 2 minutes. Add the potato, carrot, and parsnip. Sauté an additional minute before adding the chopped tomatoes, vegetable stock, 2 bay leaves, and oregano. Simmer for 10 more minutes.

If using oil-packed sun-dried tomatoes, drain. Dry-packed tomatoes should be soaked in boiling water for 2 minutes, then drained. Chop the dried tomatoes coarsely and add, with the kale and the drained cooked beans, to the ingredients in the soup pot.

Simmer for about 10 minutes, until the vegetables are tender and the flavors have mingled. Add the saffron, if desired, and salt and pepper to taste.

Serve with Gougère (p. 234) or Cheddar-Herb Bread (p. 263).

SALADS

NORTH AFRICAN ROASTED VEGETABLE SALAD

R oasting eggplant, peppers, and tomatoes gives them a sweet juiciness. The simple marinade is highlighted by the aromatic flavors of garlic, olive oil, and rosemary. We like to serve this as part of a combination plate with hummus, stuffed grape leaves, and pita bread. On its own, it can be an appetizer, dip, or sandwich filling with pita bread.

I LARGE EGGPLANT. 8 INCHES LONG OR SO

2 PEPPERS. I RED AND I GREEN IF POSSIBLE

2 FIRM, NOT OVERRIPE. TOMATOES

2 TABLESPOONS OLIVE OIL

2 TABLESPOONS FRESH LEMON JUICE

2 GARLIC CLOVES. MINCED OR PRESSED

1½ TABLESPOONS MINCED ONION

2 TABLESPOONS CHOPPED FRESH PARSLEY

I TO 1½ TEASPOONS CHOPPED FRESH ROSEMARY (½ TO ¾ TEASPOON DRIED)

SALT AND FRESHLY GROUND BLACK PEPPER *OR* CAYENNE PEPPER TO TASTE

SERVES 6 TO 8 AS AN APPETIZER, SIDE DISH, OR PITA-BREAD FILLING

Preheat the oven to 400°F.

Prick the eggplant four to five times with the tines of a fork.

On an unoiled cookie sheet bake the peppers for 35 minutes, and the eggplant for 35 to 50 minutes, turning the vegetables every 10 minutes or so. About 25 minutes into the cooking time, add the tomatoes and cook for about 10 minutes or until softened. The eggplant and peppers are done when they're tender and look somewhat collapsed.

While still hot, place the peppers in a brown paper bag. This will facilitate peeling later.

Allow the other vegetables to cool to the touch.

Scoop the eggplant pulp from the skin. Though it will be mushy, chop any long strands of pulp. The pepper skin should rub off easily after 10 minutes in the paper bag. Chop the roasted peppers into ½-by-½-inch pieces. Peel the tomatoes if desired, and cut in half to remove the seeds and juice (reserve for other uses). Chop the pulp into pieces roughly ½ by ½ inch.

Mix the roasted vegetables with all the remaining ingredients. If the salad is to be served within 2 to 3 hours, use the greater amount of rosemary. Since the intensity of rosemary increases with time, 1 teaspoon or less will be plenty if the salad is refrigerated overnight before serving.

SUMMER TOMATO AND BREAD SALAD

THE
MOOSEWOOD
RESTAURANT
KITCHEN
GARDEN

216

Simple and refreshing, this is one of our favorite salads for high summer, when tomatoes are juicy and ripe. You won't have to dip your bread to soak up the flavorful juices; it's already in there.

4 MEDIUM FRESH TOMATOES, CUT INTO ½-INCH-THICK SLICES, THEN ½-INCH CUBES (ABOUT 3½ CUPS)

1 MEDIUM CUCUMBER, PEELED AND SEEDED, CUT INTO ½-INCH CUBES (ABOUT 1½ CUPS)

2 TABLESPOONS CHOPPED FRESH BASIL

2 TABLESPOONS CHOPPED FRESH PARSLEY

1 TABLESPOON CHOPPED FRESH OREGANO

⅓ CUP CHOPPED RED ONION OR SCALLION

2 GARLIC CLOVES, MINCED OR PRESSED

¼ CUP OLIVE OIL (EXTRA VIRGIN IS NICE)

2 TABLESPOONS OPAL BASIL VINEGAR (P. 242) OR RED-WINE VINEGAR

SALT AND FRESHLY GROUND BLACK PEPPER TO TASTE

2 HEAPING CUPS STALE ITALIAN, FRENCH, OR SOURDOUGH BREAD (½-INCH CUBES), LIGHTLY TOASTED UNTIL GOLDEN

SERVES 6 OR MORE

Combine all the ingredients except the bread cubes and marinate at room temperature for 30 minutes. The opal basil vinegar adds a brilliant ruby color and enhances the basil flavor.

At serving time, toss on the bread cubes.

You can make this a substantial one-dish meal with the addition of fresh mozzarella cheese, cubed (see note), artichoke hearts (canned or frozen), and roasted red or green peppers

Fresh mozzarella is more delicate in both flavor and texture than the variety sold in the dairy department of most supermarkets. It is packed in water to retain its creamy texture and should be used as soon as possible after purchasing. It is available in cheese and Italian specialty stores, and some well-stocked supermarkets.

MIDDLE EASTERN BEAN SALAD

L emon basil and aromatic spices combine to give this marinade an unusual, sweet but citrusy flavor. Fresh shelled peas were in season when I first made this salad. You can substitute other fresh vegetables, such as green beans, snap peas, or peppers, all cut into small pieces.

MARINADE

¼ CUP CHOPPED FRESH LEMON
  BASIL
¼ CUP FRESH LEMON JUICE
½ TABLESPOON GRATED FRESH
  GINGERROOT
¼ TEASPOON GROUND CINNAMON

½ TEASPOON GROUND CORIANDER
  SEED
⅓ CUP VEGETABLE OIL

3 CUPS COOKED BEANS (I CUP DRIED;
  WHITE BEANS, GARBANZOS, OR
  KIDNEYS ARE GOOD; SEE NOTE)

VEGETABLES

½ CUP PEARL ONIONS *OR* ¼ CUP
  FINELY CHOPPED RED ONION

⅓ CUP GREEN PEAS

GARNISH (USE ONE)

CHERRY TOMATOES

ROASTED RED PEPPER STRIPS

SERVES 4 TO 6

Combine all the marinade ingredients, then toss with the cooked beans.

Blanch the pearl onions in boiling water for a moment to facilitate peeling. The red onion is added raw. Cook the peeled pearl onions, using the blanching water, for 3 to 4 minutes. Add the green peas and cook briefly, 2 to 3 minutes, until tender. Drain well and add to the bean salad, with salt and pepper to taste.

Allow the salad to marinate a couple of hours. Refrigerate if desired.

Garnish with halved cherry tomatoes or roasted red pepper strips.

NOTE *If using dried beans, cook 1 cup dried beans in water. Alternatively, use drained, canned beans.*

VEGETABLES À LA GRECQUE

S immered in an herbed broth, these vegetables fully absorb the seasonings for a richly flavored dish.

MARINADE

4 CUPS VEGETABLE STOCK (P. 212)

¾ CUP OLIVE OIL (PART OR ALL EXTRA VIRGIN)

I CUP DRY WHITE WINE

I TABLESPOON TARRAGON VINEGAR

½ CUP FRESH LEMON JUICE

3 GARLIC CLOVES, COARSELY CHOPPED

¼ CUP FRESH PARSLEY LEAVES

I SPRIG OF FRESH THYME (½ TEASPOON DRIED)

I½ TABLESPOONS CHOPPED FRESH DILL (I½ TEASPOONS DRIED)

I TEASPOON SALT

I2 PEPPERCORNS

VEGETABLES

I CARROT, CUT INTO STICKS 2 INCHES LONG BY ¼ INCH SQUARE

I LEEK, WHITE PART ONLY, CUT INTO STICKS 2 INCHES LONG BY ½ INCH THICK

I RED PEPPER, CUT INTO ¼-INCH-THICK STRIPS

I YELLOW SQUASH, CUT INTO STICKS 2 INCHES LONG BY ¼ INCH SQUARE

¼ POUND GREEN BEANS, STEM ENDS CUT OFF

I FENNEL *(FINOCCHIO)* BULB, CUT INTO ¼-INCH-THICK SLICES

SERVES 4 TO 6

THE
MOOSEWOOD
RESTAURANT
KITCHEN
GARDEN

218

Combine all the marinade ingredients in a stainless steel or enameled saucepan. Heat the marinade, letting it gently simmer partially covered for ¾ hour to 1 hour. Strain and discard the solid ingredients. Return the marinade to the cooking pot.

Bring the marinade to a gentle boil again. Cook each type of vegetable separately in the simmering liquid until just tender, then remove with a strainer or slotted spoon and place in a casserole or deep dish.

Pour some of the marinade over the vegetables, just to cover. Though the flavor will intensify after 3 to 4 hours, the vegetables are ready to eat right after cooking.

Remove the vegetables from the marinade and artfully arrange on a serving platter. Serve at room temperature, or chilled for hot-weather salads.

VIETNAMESE RICE NOODLE AND VEGETABLE SALAD

I nspired by a dish that I had in a San Francisco Vietnamese restaurant, this soup/salad impressed me with the clean, unencumbered taste of its fresh herbs and greens. We make our version as a refreshing summer salad.

Spring Rolls add a savory crispness that harmonizes well with the slippery, soft noodles.

SWEET AND SOUR DRESSING

1 CUP WELL-FLAVORED VEGETABLE STOCK (P. 212)
¼ CUP SOY SAUCE
¼ CUP PLUS 2 TABLESPOONS FRESH LIME JUICE
3 TABLESPOONS BROWN SUGAR
PINCH OF CAYENNE PEPPER OR A FEW DROPS OF TABASCO SAUCE OR SOME FRESH HOT PEPPER SLIVERS

DIP ADDITIONS

1 TABLESPOON CHOPPED FRESH CILANTRO
2 GARLIC CLOVES, MINCED OR PRESSED

VEGETABLES AND HERBS

⅓ CUP LOOSELY PACKED, TORN FRESH BASIL LEAVES
⅓ CUP LOOSELY PACKED, TORN FRESH MINT LEAVES
1½ CUPS GRATED OR SHREDDED CARROT
1 MEDIUM CUCUMBER, CUT INTO MATCHSTICKS (IF USING A STORE-BOUGHT, WAXED CUCUMBER, FIRST PEEL AND REMOVE THE LARGE SEEDS) (ABOUT 1½ CUPS)
4 TO 6 LEAVES OF A CRISP LEAF LETTUCE (ROMAINE, BUTTERCRUNCH, CANASTA), TORN OR CUT INTO SHREDS
½ CUP CHOPPED SCALLION

RICE NOODLES

¾ POUND RICE STICK NOODLES, ABOUT ⅛ INCH WIDE (NOT THE VERMICELLI TYPE)
3 QUARTS BOILING WATER

GARNISH

6 COOKED SHRIMPS PER PERSON
FRESH HOT PEPPER SLIVERS
LIME WEDGES
SPRING ROLLS (P. 221), 1 PER PERSON, CUT INTO BITE-SIZE PIECES

Make the dressing by combining the stock, soy sauce, lime juice, brown sugar, and cayenne, Tabasco sauce, or hot pepper. If using spring rolls as a garnish, divide the dressing into two equal portions. Make a dip for the spring rolls by adding the cilantro and garlic to one. If not serving spring rolls, just add the cilantro and garlic to the dressing.

Divide all the vegetables and herbs equally into 4 or 6 (however many diners there will be) shallow, wide pasta or soup bowls.

Put the rice noodles in a pot and cover with the boiling water. Boil for 1 to 2 minutes, or until tender; then drain. Place equal amounts of noodles in each bowl. Pour the sweet and sour dressing over the noodles, herbs, and vegetables, then toss with chopsticks. Add the desired garnishes and serve at once.

THE
MOOSEWOOD
RESTAURANT
KITCHEN
GARDEN

220

OTHER DISHES

SPRING ROLLS

A popular appetizer with a fairly simple shredded vegetable filling.

1½ CUPS SHREDDED PAK CHOI *OR*
CHINESE CABBAGE
1 RED *OR* GREEN PEPPER, SHREDDED
(ABOUT 1 CUP)
1 LARGE CARROT, SHREDDED
(ABOUT 1 CUP)
¾ CUP CHOPPED SCALLION
2 CUPS MUNG BEAN SPROUTS
1 TABLESPOON VEGETABLE OIL
1 TABLESPOON GRATED FRESH
GINGERROOT

2 GARLIC CLOVES, MINCED OR
PRESSED
2 TABLESPOONS SOY SAUCE

1½ TO 4 CUPS VEGETABLE OIL FOR
DEEP FRYING
8 SPRING ROLL WRAPPERS (SEE
NOTE)
1 EGG, BEATEN

YIELDS 8 SPRING ROLLS

Prepare the vegetables and have all the ingredients close to the stove. You'll be quickly stir-frying the vegetables until just barely wilted, not cooked to completion.

Heat the 1 tablespoon of vegetable oil in a very hot wok or large skillet, then add the ginger and garlic and stir-fry a moment. Add the vegetables to the wok in sequence, stir-frying continuously. Start with the pak choi or cabbage, followed in 1 minute by the pepper, then 30 seconds later the carrot, and after an additional 30 seconds the scallion and mung bean sprouts. Add the soy sauce. Remove from the heat.

Scoop the vegetables into a strainer or colander and allow them to drain. Wipe the wok or skillet clean and add the oil for deep-frying. Use 1½ cups for cooking

NOTE *Spring roll wrappers are thinner and more delicate than egg roll skins. I recommend Oriental Mascot brand. They're 8 inches square, made of wheat, and available frozen in Asian food stores. Other egg roll wrappers can be used in a pinch.*

the spring rolls 1 at a time or 4 cups of oil to do 2 at a time. Heat the oil slowly while you assemble the spring rolls.

Arrange the spring roll wrappers so that their corners form diamond shapes. Spoon 2 to 3 tablespoons of filling onto the lower third of the wrapper. Roll the filled wrapper up from the bottom corner to cover the filling. Fold in the side corners as if they were envelope flaps, making them even with the bottom rolled section. Continue rolling upward, sealing the top corner of the diamond by dipping your finger in the beaten egg and moistening the remaining edges. Roll and gently press the surfaces together.

Deep-fry in the hot oil, about 375°F., for about 5 minutes each, or until the rolls are crispy and golden. (See p. 210 for deep-frying instructions.)

Serve with Vietnamese Rice Noodle and Vegetable Salad (p. 219), or as an appetizer.

THE
MOOSEWOOD
RESTAURANT
KITCHEN
GARDEN

222

VEGETABLE "PASTA"

For this recipe, vegetables are cut into long, thin strips to resemble spaghetti. This makes a visually appealing side dish, tossed with fettucine or linguini, or can provide a "nest" for broiled or grilled fish.

1 LARGE CARROT	RINSED CAREFULLY, TOUGH GREENS
1 RED *OR* GREEN PEPPER	REMOVED
1 MEDIUM ZUCCHINI	1 CELERY STALK
1 LARGE LEEK, SPLIT IN HALF AND	1 LARGE PARSNIP

SERVES 4

Cut each vegetable into lengthwise slices, 4 to 5 inches long, ⅛ to ¼ inch thick. Then cut these slices into sticks, about ⅛ to ¼ inch square by 4 to 5 inches long. Use 2 of any vegetable if they're small.

Boil a gallon (8 cups) of water. A large volume of water will cook the vegetables quickly without cooling down each time a new batch is added. Blanch each vegetable separately. It will only take a couple of minutes for the harder ones (carrot, celery, and parsnip) and a minute for the softer ones (zucchini, leek, and pepper). They should be crisp but tender.

Remove each vegetable with a strainer or slotted spoon and place on a covered platter to keep warm. If you're cooking a large quantity, use a 200°F. oven to keep the vegetables warm until serving time.

Top with a simple Herb Butter (p. 254), Shallot-Herb Butter Sauce (p. 241), Red Pepper Sauce (p. 240), or a light tomato sauce.

Alternatively, toss with pasta, butter, and grated Parmesan cheese.

POLENTA WITH ROASTED GARLIC

R oasting garlic gives it a creamy texture and a nutty sweetness with the familiar but mellowed garlic flavor. Here, it's spread on crusty slices of broiled polenta, a cornmeal preparation popular in Northern Italy. Serve as an appetizer or a side dish.

3 CUPS WATER

1 CUP YELLOW CORNMEAL

1 TEASPOON SALT

2 HEADS OF GARLIC, LEFT WHOLE,
  BUT WITH THE OUTERMOST PAPERY
  SKIN REMOVED

OLIVE OIL

⅓ CUP GRATED PARMESAN CHEESE
  (OPTIONAL)

SERVES 4 TO 6

Prepare the polenta the night before it's to be served, or in the morning for an evening meal. Bring the water to a boil in a heavy saucepan. Add the cornmeal slowly, stirring all the while with a wooden spoon or whisk. Add the salt. Cook over very low heat, stirring often, for 20 to 30 minutes, until the polenta begins to pull away from the sides of the saucepan. Pour the polenta into an oiled baking dish approximately 10 by 14 inches. The polenta should be about ½ inch deep. Let cool, then refrigerate, covered, for at least 4 hours.

Preheat the oven to 425°F.

Rub the garlic heads with olive oil and bake covered for 25 minutes, then uncovered 20 minutes. Brush with additional oil two or three times during baking.

Remove the garlic and set the oven on broil. Cut the polenta into serving-size portions and place on a lightly oiled cookie sheet. Top with Parmesan cheese if desired. Broil until heated through and somewhat crusty on top, about 5 minutes.

To serve the garlic, pierce each clove, squeeze onto the polenta, and spread with a knife.

CRISP-FRIED TOFU AND GREENS

T ofu that has been frozen and thawed can better absorb the seasonings of a marinade than tofu in its standard, creamy form. Here, crisp, firm tofu is paired with stir-fried greens in a classically seasoned sauce.

MARINADE

⅓ CUP SOY SAUCE

¼ CUP RICE VINEGAR

1 TABLESPOON FINELY GRATED FRESH GINGERROOT

2 GARLIC CLOVES, MINCED OR PRESSED

PINCH OF CAYENNE PEPPER

THE
MOOSEWOOD
RESTAURANT
KITCHEN
GARDEN

224

2 CAKES OF TOFU, FROZEN OVERNIGHT (SEE NOTE)

SAUCE MIX

3 TABLESPOONS SOY SAUCE

¼ CUP RICE WINE *OR* DRY SHERRY *OR* SAKE

½ CUP WATER *OR* VEGETABLE STOCK (P. 212)

1 TEASPOON CORNSTARCH

2 TEASPOONS RICE VINEGAR

2 TEASPOONS HONEY *OR* BROWN SUGAR

½ CUP CORNMEAL *OR* CORNSTARCH

VEGETABLE OIL FOR FRYING

VEGETABLES

3 TABLESPOONS VEGETABLE OIL

3 GARLIC CLOVES, MINCED OR PRESSED

1 CUP THINLY SLICED ONION

6 CUPS COARSELY CHOPPED PAK CHOI, TATSOI, SWISS CHARD, KALE, CHINESE CABBAGE

(YOU MAY USE ONLY ONE VARIETY OR A MIXTURE), *OR* 9 CUPS SPINACH *OR* 9 CUPS MUSTARD GREENS (THESE WILL GREATLY REDUCE IN VOLUME)

GARNISH (USE ONE)

CHOPPED SCALLION

MUNG BEAN SPROUTS

NOTE   *Tofu will thaw in 24 hours in the refrigerator, or in 8 hours at room temperature. Gently squeeze as much liquid from the thawed tofu as possible without tearing or breaking. Cut the tofu blocks, first crosswise into ½-inch-thick slices, then diagonally, to make 4 triangles.*

Combine all the marinade ingredients and mix well. Arrange the tofu triangles one layer deep in a dish, cover with the marinade, and let sit for at least 10 minutes to absorb the flavors.

For the sauce mix, combine all the ingredients in a small bowl. In a separate bowl, thoroughly mix the water and 1 teaspoon cornstarch.

Dredge the marinated tofu pieces in the cornmeal or cornstarch. Cornstarch is the more authentic coating, but cornmeal gives a crunchier texture. Fry the coated tofu over a medium-high heat in a skillet with ⅛ to ¼ inch of oil. They'll take 3 to 4 minutes on each side and should be golden. Drain, and keep warm in a 200°F. oven.

Add any leftover marinade to the sauce mix.

Heat the 3 tablespoons of vegetable oil in a wok or large skillet. Stir-fry the garlic and onion until the onion is nearly tender. Add the greens and continue stir-frying over a fairly high heat until they are just wilted but not mushy. Add the sauce mix and the cornstarch mix and stir-fry a moment or two until the sauce is slightly thickened. Add the reserved fried tofu.

Garnish with chopped scallion or mung bean sprouts.

RED, WHITE, AND GREEN PHYLLO PIZZAS

R ich with a variety of herbs, vegetables, and cheeses, phyllo pizzas are a popular lunch entrée at the Restaurant. Using packaged phyllo pastry saves the time of preparing a yeast dough for the crust.

We make large sheets of this pizza with a variety of toppings. Feel free to make just one kind. Doing all three at once is an ambitious effort for special occasions or when you have kitchen helpers.

RED TOPPING

½ CUP LOOSELY PACKED SUN-DRIED
   TOMATOES (DRY PACKED)
2 MEDIUM FRESH TOMATOES, SLICED
¼ CUP CHOPPED FRESH OREGANO
   LEAVES (2 TABLESPOONS DRIED)

2 GARLIC CLOVES, MINCED OR
   PRESSED
1 TABLESPOON OLIVE OIL
1 CUP GRATED MOZZARELLA CHEESE
½ CUP GRATED PARMESAN CHEESE

WHITE TOPPING

- 2 MEDIUM SPANISH ONIONS, THINLY SLICED (ABOUT 2½ CUPS)
- 3 GARLIC CLOVES, MINCED OR PRESSED
- 1 TEASPOON FRESH THYME LEAVES (½ TEASPOON DRIED)
- 2 TABLESPOONS VEGETABLE OIL OR OLIVE OIL
- ½ CUP CREAM CHEESE
- ½ CUP GRATED SMOKED MOZZARELLA OR SMOKED SWISS CHEESE
- ½ CUP GRATED SHARP CHEDDAR CHEESE

GREEN TOPPING

- 10 OUNCES FRESH SPINACH (2 TO 3 BUNCHES), STEMMED, WELL RINSED, AND DRAINED
- ¼ CUP CHOPPED SCALLIONS, GREEN AND WHITE PARTS
- ¼ CUP CHOPPED FRESH PARSLEY
- ¼ CUP CHOPPED FRESH BASIL (1½ TABLESPOONS DRIED)
- 1 CUP GRATED FETA CHEESE
- ½ CUP COTTAGE CHEESE

CRUST FOR THE 12-BY-18-INCH SHEET

- ½ CUP VEGETABLE OIL OR OLIVE OIL OR A COMBINATION OF THE TWO
- 1 1-POUND BOX OF PHYLLO PASTRY

CRUST FOR EACH 9- OR 10-INCH PIE

- 3 TABLESPOONS OIL AS ABOVE
- ⅓ OF A 1-POUND BOX OF PHYLLO PASTRY

THE
MOOSEWOOD
RESTAURANT
KITCHEN
GARDEN

226

YIELDS 1 12-BY-18-INCH SHEET OR 3 9- OR 10-INCH PIES

For the red topping, soak the sun-dried tomatoes in 1 cup of warm water. Set aside until ready to assemble the pizza (20 minutes minimum). Drain and chop coarsely. Gently toss the fresh tomato slices with the oregano, garlic, and olive oil. Have the cheeses ready for assembly.

Prepare the white topping. In a heavy skillet over low heat, gently cook the onions, garlic, and thyme in 2 tablespoons of oil until lightly browned, about 20 minutes. Cut the cream cheese into small bits, add to the hot onions, garlic, and thyme. Mix until smooth. Reserve the grated cheeses for assembly.

For the green topping, blanch the cleaned spinach in boiling water until just wilted, about 2 to 3 minutes. Drain, press out the excess water, chop, and mix with the remaining topping ingredients.

To assemble, use all 3 toppings on a 12-by-18-inch baking sheet, or each topping separately in a 9- or 10-inch pie plate.

Preheat the oven to 400°F.

Lightly brush each pie plate or the baking sheet with oil. Lay 2 sheets of phyllo so they just reach the edge of the baking sheet without hanging over. Fold the overhang back into the pie plate. Brush with oil. Cover any gaps with the next 2 sheets of phyllo dough, then brush with oil. Repeat this process until you have a "base" of phyllo about 12 sheets deep. It won't matter if some sections are thicker where there's an overlap. Leave a ½-inch-wide outer margin of pastry uncovered when spooning on the topping.

If using the baking sheet, each topping will fill one-third of the surface, yielding an Italian-flag: red, white, and green from left to right.

Red: Sprinkle the drained, chopped sun-dried tomatoes on the pastry. Top with half of the mozzarella and Parmesan, then the fresh-tomato mixture, followed by the remaining cheese.

White: Spoon the onion and garlic mixture onto the pastry and top with the grated cheese.

Green: Spoon the spinach mixture onto the pastry.

Bake for 20 to 30 minutes, until the pastry is lightly browned and the toppings are bubbly and melted.

MAMA FLORA'S BAKED LEEKS

F lora Marranca is a neighbor of mine and a former, but not forgotten, cook at Moosewood. This is a delicious saucy side dish of her invention.

3 GOOD-SIZED LEEKS, 1 TO 2 INCHES IN DIAMETER. (USE MORE IF THE LEEKS ARE TOO SMALL TO YIELD ABOUT 1 POUND AFTER THE TOUGH UPPER GREENS ARE REMOVED.)

2 TABLESPOONS VEGETABLE OIL (OLIVE OIL IS NICE)

8 4-INCH-LONG SPRIGS OF FRESH DILL (1 TABLESPOON DRIED)

3 GARLIC CLOVES, HALVED

2 TEASPOONS MISO

1 TEASPOON SOY SAUCE

½ CUP WATER

SERVES 4

Preheat the oven to 350°F.

Cut and split the leeks in half and carefully rinse to remove any dirt lodged between the layers. Choose a baking dish that will accommodate the leeks in 2 layers, about 10 by 16 inches. Put the 2 tablespoons of oil into the dish and coat the leeks, using your hands or a pastry brush. Tuck in the dill and garlic cloves here and there throughout.

Dissolve the miso, soy sauce, and water in a small bowl. Pour over the leeks.

Bake covered for 25 minutes. Uncover and stir to prevent sticking and scorching, and bake uncovered for an additional 20 minutes. Add small quantities of water if the leeks are in danger of drying out; they should be lightly sauced.

VARIATIONS   *Use 2- to 3-inch-long, thin slices of carrot, fennel, onion, parsnip, potato, or turnip, or combinations of them, instead of the leeks.*

FETTUCINE WITH CHEVRE, SPINACH, AND HERBS

T his recipe is a collaboration between me and my partner David Deutsch. At our house, the Double Dave Goat Ranch and Gardens, David H. grows the vegetables and herbs, while David D. tends the goats.

THE
MOOSEWOOD
RESTAURANT
KITCHEN
GARDEN

228

SPINACH-HERB MIXTURE

2 TABLESPOONS VEGETABLE OIL

⅔ CUP CHOPPED SCALLION

I POUND FRESH SPINACH, WASHED,
  WITH THE LARGE STEMS REMOVED
  AND BIG LEAVES TORN INTO PIECES

⅓ CUP VEGETABLE STOCK (P. 212) *OR*
  WATER

⅓ CUP CHOPPED FRESH PARSLEY

⅓ CUP CHOPPED FRESH DILL
  (I TABLESPOON DRIED)

12 OUNCES DRIED FETTUCINE *OR*
  ABOUT I POUND FRESH

4 TABLESPOONS BUTTER, CUT INTO
  SMALL PIECES

12 OUNCES CHEVRE (FRESH GOAT
  CHEESE, NOT AGED), CRUMBLED OR
  DICED INTO SMALL PIECES

TOPPINGS

½ CUP CHOPPED, TOASTED
  HAZELNUTS

I FRESH TOMATO, DICED

SERVES 4 AS AN ENTRÉE OR 6 TO 8 AS AN APPETIZER

Boil 1½ gallons of salted water in a large pot to cook the pasta.

Heat the oil in a pan large enough to hold all the spinach. Sauté the scallion for 30 seconds, then add the spinach and stock or water. When the spinach is wilted, add the parsley and dill, and remove from the heat.

Warm a large heatproof serving bowl and individual dishes in a 200°F oven, or with hot water. This will keep the pasta from cooling down too fast.

Cook the fettucine, then drain, and quickly pour into the large serving bowl. Toss it first with the butter and chevre, then add the spinach-herb mixture. Serve immediately, garnishing the individual servings with either the hazelnuts or diced tomato, or both.

VARIATIONS *Substitute 1 cup shelled green peas or 1½ cups sugar snap peas cut in 1-inch lengths for the spinach. Add the herbs when the peas are just tender; ⅓ cup chopped fresh basil or chervil may be substituted for the dill.*

MEXICAN STUFFED ONION WITH FRESH SALSA

ONIONS

2 SPANISH ONIONS, ABOUT 3 INCHES
  IN DIAMETER

I BAY LEAF
6 WHOLE CLOVES

FILLING

I GARLIC CLOVE, MINCED OR PRESSED
2 TABLESPOONS VEGETABLE OIL
¼ TEASPOON GROUND ALLSPICE
I TEASPOON CHOPPED FRESH
  OREGANO (½ TEASPOON DRIED)

⅔ CUP CORN, FRESH OR FROZEN
A DROP OR TWO OF TABASCO SAUCE
I CUP GRATED MONTEREY JACK
  CHEESE

FRESH SALSA

2 TOMATOES, FINELY CHOPPED
3 TABLESPOONS CHOPPED SCALLION
I½ TABLESPOONS CHOPPED FRESH
  CHILI PEPPER (MORE OR LESS TO
  TASTE)
I TABLESPOON CHOPPED FRESH
  CILANTRO

2 TABLESPOONS FRESH LIME JUICE
I TABLESPOON OLIVE OIL
I TEASPOON FINELY GRATED FRESH
  GINGERROOT
¼ TEASPOON GROUND CUMIN SEED
SALT TO TASTE

SERVES 4 AS A SIDE DISH OR APPETIZER

About an hour beforehand, prepare the Fresh Salsa (see below).

To prepare the onions: peel the onions, leaving them whole with the root ends intact. Boil the onions in enough water to cover with the bay leaf and cloves for 12 minutes. Drain, and let cool while preparing the filling. Reserve the cooking liquid for a stock to use in other recipes.

To make the filling: sauté the garlic in 2 tablespoons of oil for a moment, then add the allspice, oregano, corn, and Tabasco sauce. Sauté for an additional minute or two and remove from the heat. Combine with the grated cheese.

Preheat the oven to 350°F.

Cut each onion in half crosswise, through the widest part. Scoop out at least half of each, leaving a wall about ½ inch thick. Use the scooped-out onion for another dish, or add it to a stockpot. Fill each onion half with the corn and cheese filling. Bake covered in a lightly greased dish for 30 minutes. Uncover and bake an additional 10 to 15 minutes, until the onions are tender. Serve with the Fresh Salsa.

Combine all the ingredients in a medium-sized, nonreactive bowl. Set aside for an hour or so to allow the flavors to mingle.

This salsa is good with chips and as a spicy condiment for other dishes. It will keep refrigerated for about 1 week.

SQUASH-APPLE CHEDDAR GRATIN

T his is a homey casserole that will warm the chilly evenings of fall and winter. Apples with a bit of tartness, such as Granny Smiths, bring out the sweetness of sautéed onions and squash.

THE
MOOSEWOOD
RESTAURANT
KITCHEN
GARDEN

230

2 CUPS SLICED ONION

1 TEASPOON FRESH THYME LEAVES
(½ TEASPOON DRIED)

2 TABLESPOONS VEGETABLE OIL

2½ CUPS THINLY SLICED APPLES

1 TABLESPOON UNBLEACHED WHITE
FLOUR

1½ CUPS GRATED CHEDDAR CHEESE

2 TABLESPOONS BREAD CRUMBS

3 CUPS COOKED, LIGHTLY MASHED
WINTER SQUASH (SEE NOTE)

SALT AND FRESHLY GROUND BLACK
PEPPER TO TASTE

SERVES 4 TO 6

Gently sauté the onion and thyme in the oil for about 20 minutes, or until the onion is soft and golden. Meanwhile, toss the apple slices with the flour; and in a separate bowl, the cheddar cheese with the bread crumbs.

Preheat the oven to 350°F.

Oil a casserole or baking dish approximately 8 by 8 by 3 inches and layer the ingredients as follows: the squash, with a sprinkling of salt and pepper if desired; the sautéed onions; the apple slices and a bit more salt and pepper; the cheddar–bread crumb mixture.

Bake covered for 30 minutes, then uncovered for 15 minutes. The apples should be tender, and the topping bubbly and golden.

NOTE   *Squash will be easier to peel and handle if it's cooked in advance and allowed to cool.*

CREPES

repes are an elegant, simple dish for a starter course, brunch, light dinner, or dessert. They are a popular entrée at the benefit brunches we host at Moosewood throughout the year.

Cooked crepes and fillings can be made in advance and filled at the last minute for easy preparation. Crepe batter will keep in the refrigerator for a day or two. Cooked crepes will keep for three days under refrigeration, or a couple of months in the freezer.

A crepe can be a wrapper for any number of vegetable fillings. Leftover vegetables that are still presentable can be combined with cheese or a cheese sauce, and, voilà, an elegant brunch or dinner.

CREPE BATTER

3 EGGS

1½ CUPS MILK

1 CUP PLUS 2 TABLESPOONS WHOLE WHEAT PASTRY FLOUR *OR*

UNBLEACHED WHITE FLOUR

¼ TEASPOON SALT

3 TABLESPOONS BUTTER, MELTED

ZUCCHINI-LEEK-CHEESE FILLING

2 MEDIUM LEEKS, TENDER GREEN AND WHITE PARTS CAREFULLY RINSED, CUT INTO STRIPS ¼ BY 1½ INCHES

2 TABLESPOONS VEGETABLE OIL

2 MEDIUM ZUCCHINI, CUT INTO STRIPS ¼ BY 1½ INCHES

½ TEASPOON FRESH THYME LEAVES (¼ TEASPOON DRIED)

GENEROUS PINCH OF FRESHLY GRATED NUTMEG

SALT AND FRESHLY GROUND BLACK PEPPER TO TASTE

¾ POUND FONTINA CHEESE, GRATED (ABOUT 2½ CUPS)

YIELDS 11 CREPES USING AN 8-INCH-DIAMETER PAN

To make the crepes: blend the eggs, milk, flour, and salt in a blender or food processor, or whisk in a bowl until just smooth. Whisk the melted butter into the batter right before cooking.

Heat a skillet, crepe pan, or omelet pan on medium-high heat. A heavy, well-seasoned cast iron skillet works well. When the pan is hot, brush it with a very thin film of vegetable oil. This should be sufficient for cooking all the crepes, but if sticking should occur, brush the pan before each crepe.

For an 8-inch pan, use ¼ cup of batter. For a smaller pan, use less. There should be just enough batter to thinly coat the pan bottom. Tilt the pan to distribute the batter and cook a moment or two until the edges are light brown and lacy, and the crepe is no longer runny. Flip it with a spatula and cook the second side just a moment, until it's speckled light brown. Remove with a spatula to a platter and continue cooking crepes until all the batter is gone.

Preheat the oven to 325°F.

To make the filling: sauté the leeks in the oil for a couple of minutes, until they begin to soften. Add the zucchini, thyme, nutmeg, and salt and pepper. Cook over medium heat until the vegetables are just tender, about 5 minutes. Remove from the heat.

Fill each crepe with about 3 tablespoons of grated cheese and an equal amount of cooked vegetables. Either roll the crepe up with the filling, or place the filling in a strip down the center and fold the sides over.

Bake the filled crepes in a buttered casserole dish for 10 to 15 minutes, loosely covered with waxed paper to keep them from drying out.

THE
MOOSEWOOD
RESTAURANT
KITCHEN
GARDEN

232

SAVORY FILLING VARIATIONS

Vegetables for the filling variations should be sautéed, steamed, or blanched until just tender. Bake only to warm through and melt the cheeses, if any.

Asparagus spears and Parmesan cheese

Sautéed spinach and mushrooms with toasted walnuts

Cauliflower, scallions, and cheddar cheese

Sautéed broccoli and tofu seasoned with gingerroot and soy sauce

Green beans, pearl onions, and Gorgonzola cheese

Sautéed eggplant, zucchini, peppers, garlic, and fresh basil, topped with a tomato sauce

DESSERT CREPE VARIATIONS *Dessert or brunch crepes can be filled with lightly sweetened fruits (use all-fruit preserves, maple syrup, or honey) and will not need further cooking.*

Sautéed apples with raisins, walnuts, and cinnamon, topped with vanilla yogurt

Fresh berries with whole- or skim-milk ricotta cheese

Fresh, diced peaches with crème fraîche or sour cream and grated nutmeg

Bananas or diced cantaloupe with cottage cheese

FRAGRANT BULGUR PILAF

B ulgur wheat is a nutty-flavored processed grain that is an interesting, tasty alternative to rice. This pilaf can be made with dried herbs, but is far superior with fresh or even frozen.

¾ CUP DICED ONION

½ CUP DICED CARROT

½ CUP DICED RED *OR* GREEN PEPPER

2 TABLESPOONS OLIVE OIL

1½ CUPS BULGUR

3 CUPS VEGETABLE STOCK (P. 212) *OR* WATER

¼ CUP TOASTED, GROUND NUTS (OPTIONAL)

¼ CUP CHOPPED FRESH PARSLEY

¼ CUP CHOPPED FRESH BASIL (1 TABLESPOON DRIED)

3 TABLESPOONS CHOPPED FRESH SPEARMINT (1½ TABLESPOONS DRIED)

2 TABLESPOONS CHOPPED FRESH LOVAGE *OR* CELERY LEAF

1 TEASPOON SOY SAUCE

¼ TEASPOON SALT

FRESHLY GROUND BLACK PEPPER TO TASTE

1 CUP CRUMBLED FETA CHEESE (OPTIONAL)

SERVES 6 PLUS

Preheat the oven to 300°F.

In an ovenproof skillet large enough to contain all the ingredients, sauté the onion, carrot, and pepper in the oil. When the onion and carrot have just softened, add the bulgur and sauté for a minute or two, stirring constantly to prevent scorching. Add all the rest of the ingredients and bring to a boil. Cover and bake for 20 minutes, until all the liquid is absorbed.

Serve topped with crumbled feta cheese if desired.

GOUGÈRE

A crisp, crusty, toasty cheese puff. Admittedly, this recipe does not highlight any vegetables, but it is a wonderful accompaniment to soups and salads.

1 CUP WATER

6 TABLESPOONS BUTTER

1 CUP UNBLEACHED WHITE *OR* WHOLE
 WHEAT PASTRY FLOUR

4 EGGS

1 CUP GRATED GRUYÈRE *OR* SHARP
 CHEDDAR CHEESE

OPTIONAL ADDITIONS

2 TABLESPOONS CHOPPED PIMIENTO

2 TABLESPOONS CHOPPED FRESH
 TARRAGON

2 TABLESPOONS CHOPPED FRESH OR
 CANNED CHILI PEPPER

THE
MOOSEWOOD
RESTAURANT
KITCHEN
GARDEN

234

SERVES 4

Preheat the oven to 425°F. Lightly oil a baking sheet.

Heat the water and butter in a saucepan until boiling, then add the flour all at once. Mix quickly with a spoon; the batter will form a ball. Remove from the heat and beat in the eggs, one at a time, until the mixture is relatively smooth. Stir in most of the cheese, reserving 2 to 3 tablespoons for the top.

Using a sturdy, large spoon, arrange small mounds of the batter on the baking sheet to form a ring about 12 inches across. Sprinkle the reserved cheese and the optional additions, if any, on top.

Bake for 40 to 45 minutes, until the puff is golden and set (it shouldn't jiggle). Serve at once; gougère is at its best fresh from the oven.

The rich, buttery quality of gougère is a nice complement to zesty Vegetables à la Grecque (p. 218).

Bob Love serves roasted garlic (p. 223) in the center of the gougère. They both take about the same amount of time to bake.

SESAME BAKED TOFU WITH SNOW PEAS AND ALMONDS

BAKED TOFU

1 12-OUNCE CAKE OF PRESSED TOFU

1½ TABLESPOONS SESAME OIL

⅓ CUP WHOLE ALMONDS, TOASTED IN
  350°F. OVEN FOR 5 MINUTES

2 CUPS SNOW PEAS, BLANCHED IN

2 TABLESPOONS SOY SAUCE

BOILING WATER FOR 30 SECONDS
AND DRAINED

DRESSING

1½ TABLESPOONS VEGETABLE OIL

2 TEASPOONS SESAME OIL

2 TABLESPOONS RICE VINEGAR

2 TEASPOONS GRATED FRESH
  GINGERROOT

½ TEASPOON GROUND CORIANDER
  SEED

1 TEASPOON HONEY OR BROWN
  SUGAR

¼ TEASPOON SALT

GARNISH

½ CUP THINLY SLICED SCALLION

SERVES 4 AS AN APPETIZER OR 2 AS A SIDE DISH

Preheat the oven to 350°F.

Cut the tofu into 1-inch-square cubes and arrange in a single layer in a baking dish. Mix the sesame oil and soy sauce together, pour over the tofu, and bake for 30 minutes.

At the same time, set a timer for 5 minutes and toast the almonds in the oven on a separate baking sheet. Remove the almonds to cool, and turn the tofu with a heatproof rubber spatula (to prevent breaking the cubes) so that all the surfaces can get browned and crispy. Do this twice more before baking is completed. Set aside the tofu and let cool.

Combine all the dressing ingredients and toss gently with the tofu, snow peas, and almonds. Garnish with the sliced scallion and serve at once, or chill a couple of hours. The snow peas will retain the brightest green color if the dish is served soon after the dressing is applied.

VARIATIONS *Asparagus, broccoli, green beans, or red and green peppers can be used in place of the snow peas. Cut the vegetables into bite-size pieces; you will need approximately 2 cups. Blanch or steam them so they are tender yet crisp.*

VEGETABLE LASAGNA

T his lasagna relies more upon the flavors of the fresh vegetables and herbs than a traditional, higher-calorie lasagna. It's also quicker to prepare, since the sauce is barely cooked.

THE
MOOSEWOOD
RESTAURANT
KITCHEN
GARDEN

236

1 1-POUND BOX OF LASAGNA NOODLES
4½ CUPS CHOPPED FRESH TOMATOES
1 MEDIUM RED ONION, FINELY DICED
 (ABOUT ⅔ CUP)
5 GARLIC CLOVES, MINCED OR
 PRESSED
3 TABLESPOONS OLIVE OIL
2 TEASPOONS GROUND FENNEL SEED
2 CUPS CHOPPED LEEKS (WHITE AND
 TENDER GREEN PARTS, CAREFULLY
 RINSED) OR ONION
3 CUPS GREEN BEANS, CUT INTO
 1½-INCH LENGTHS
3 MEDIUM RED OR GREEN PEPPERS,
 SLICED

SALT AND FRESHLY GROUND BLACK
 PEPPER TO TASTE
3 MEDIUM ZUCCHINI, CUT INTO STICKS
 1½ INCHES LONG BY ½ INCH THICK
¼ CUP COARSELY CHOPPED FRESH
 PARSLEY
¼ CUP COARSELY CHOPPED FRESH
 BASIL (½ TABLESPOON DRIED)
¼ CUP COARSELY CHOPPED FRESH
 OREGANO (½ TABLESPOON DRIED)
3½ CUPS GRATED MOZZARELLA
 CHEESE
2 CUPS FRESHLY GRATED PARMESAN
 CHEESE

SERVES 6 TO 8

Cook the lasagna noodles in a generous amount of boiling water until they are firm but tender. Rinse in cold water to prevent sticking, drain, and set aside.

Combine the tomatoes, red onion, and 3 of the garlic cloves in a saucepan. Set aside.

In a separate pot, sauté the remaining 2 garlic cloves in the olive oil for 1 minute. Add the fennel seed and leeks or onion. Sauté for 2 minutes before adding the green beans. Add 3 tablespoons of water, cover, and simmer for 5 minutes, more or less depending upon the tenderness of the beans. Add the peppers and a pinch of salt and black pepper, cover, and simmer, stirring occasionally, for 3 minutes. Add the zucchini, cover, and simmer for 1 minute.

In the first saucepan, bring the tomatoes to a boil and simmer to heat the sauce through, about 2 minutes. Add the parsley, basil, and oregano, then remove from the heat.

Preheat the oven to 350°F. Lightly oil an 11-by-14-inch baking dish.

Layer the ingredients as follows: half of the tomato sauce, a layer of noodles, half of the vegetables, a third of the cheeses, a layer of noodles, the rest of the vegetables, a third of the cheeses, a layer of noodles, the remaining tomato sauce and cheeses. It may not be necessary to use all the noodles.

Bake tightly covered for 50 minutes, then uncovered for 5 to 10 minutes, until the top is golden. Allow to sit for 10 to 15 minutes for ease of serving.

GRILLED VEGETABLES

Smoky flavored, crisp on the outside and juicy within, grilled vegetables are a highlight of summer meals. This is a treat that I've enjoyed at home, as the Restaurant has no grill. Try roasting vegetables (p. 211) in the oven, regardless of the season, for a similar dish.

HERBED VINAIGRETTE MARINADE

¼ CUP VEGETABLE OIL

¼ CUP OLIVE OIL

¼ CUP BALSAMIC VINEGAR

3 GARLIC CLOVES, MINCED OR
  PRESSED

3 TABLESPOONS CHOPPED FRESH
  HERBS (CHOOSE FROM BASIL,
  TARRAGON, CHERVIL, OREGANO,
  PARSLEY, THYME, OR ROSEMARY.)

YIELDS ABOUT 1 CUP

SPICY GINGER-CITRUS MARINADE

½ CUP VEGETABLE OIL

JUICE OF 1 LIME

JUICE OF ½ LEMON

1 TEASPOON CHOPPED FRESH
  CILANTRO

1½ TEASPOONS GRATED FRESH
  GINGERROOT

1 TEASPOON MINCED FRESH HOT
  PEPPER *OR* 3 TO 4 SQUIRTS
  TABASCO SAUCE

YIELDS ABOUT 1 CUP

Cut the vegetables so that the pieces are large enough not to fall through the grill. Special grill baskets designed to hold smaller foods are also available.

The following work well if marinated for 1 to 2 hours before cooking:

Zucchini or summer squash. Cut diagonally across the length into ½-inch-thick slices.

Scallions. Peel the outer layer, cut off the roots, and leave whole.

Onions. Peel baby onions and leave whole. Slice larger, peeled onions from the top to the bottom in ¼-inch-thick slices, leaving some of the root end attached to keep slices intact.

Mushrooms. If larger than 3 inches across, slice in half or into thirds; otherwise leave whole.

Some vegetables will get soggy on the grill if they marinate too long. The following should be generously brushed with marinade just 10 to 15 minutes before grilling:

Eggplant. Cut diagonally or lengthwise into ½-inch-thick slices. Thin Asian or "baby" eggplants can be cut in half lengthwise.

Green or firm red tomatoes. Cut into ½-inch-thick slices.

Sweet potatoes. Parboil until just tender; cut into 1-inch-thick slices.

Potatoes. Use whole new potatoes (about 1 to 2 inches in diameter) that have been parboiled until just tender.

Winter squash (smaller varieties such as acorn or delicata). Cut crosswise into 1-inch-thick slices and parboil until barely tender.

Greens. Individual leaves of kale, quarter heads of radicchio, or small fennel bulbs, whole or cut in ½-inch-thick slices.

Have platters of vegetables and tongs on a table close to the grill. Vegetables will be crisper if salted *after* grilling.

The charcoal should be at the gray-ash stage for grilling to begin. Adjust the grill so the heat is in a medium range. You can test this by holding your hand at grill level. If you can wait for 5 seconds before you have to move it, it's just right.

Place sprigs of thyme, rosemary, savory, oregano, sage, or marjoram on top of the hot coals to add their smoky essence to the grilled food.

Most vegetables will need 2 to 3 minutes per side. They should be just slightly blackened on the outside, yet tender on the inside. Cooking times may vary depending upon the height of the grill and intensity of the fire.

THE
MOOSEWOOD
RESTAURANT
KITCHEN
GARDEN

238

TIMBALES

 timbale is a savory custard, sort of a quiche without a crust, that can be prepared simply with a variety of vegetables.

VEGETABLE (CHOOSE ONE)

1½ CUPS GREEN PEAS

2 CUPS COOKED, DRAINED, AND
FINELY CHOPPED SPINACH *OR* SWISS
CHARD (2 10-OUNCE PACKAGES)

2 CUPS SNAP PEAS *OR* GREEN BEANS
OR ASPARAGUS, CUT INTO ½-INCH
LENGTHS

2 CUPS CUT CORN

1½ CUPS DICED RED AND GREEN
PEPPER

2 CUPS MASHED SWEET POTATO

2 CUPS BROCCOLI *OR* CAULIFLOWER,
CUT INTO SMALL FLORETS

⅓ CUP MINCED ONION

2 TABLESPOONS BUTTER

4 EGGS, LIGHTLY BEATEN

1½ CUPS MILK

½ CUP GRATED CHEDDAR CHEESE *OR*
SWISS CHEESE

¼ TEASPOON EACH SALT AND
FRESHLY GROUND BLACK PEPPER

A COUPLE OF PINCHES OF FRESHLY
GRATED NUTMEG

SERVES 6 FOR BRUNCH, AS A LIGHT MEAL, OR AS PART OF A LARGER DINNER

Fresh corn cut from the cob can be used as is. Sweet potato should be peeled, fully cooked, and mashed. All other vegetables should be cooked until just barely tender.

Preheat the oven to 350°F.

Sauté the onion in 1 tablespoon of butter until softened. With the second tablespoon of butter, lightly coat 6 6-ounce ceramic or Pyrex ramekins (ovenproof custard cups).

Combine the vegetable of choice with the sautéed onion, eggs, milk, cheese, salt, pepper, and nutmeg. Spoon into the 6 custard cups and place these in a larger ovenproof pan filled with 1 inch of hot water.

Bake for 20 to 35 minutes, until the custard is set. A knife inserted in the center of a cup should come out clean.

Allow to cool for a few minutes. Unmold by gently running a knife along the inner edge of the baking cup, then invert onto a plate. Serve as is or surround with Red Pepper Sauce (p. 240) or Fresh Salsa (p. 229).

SAUCES, BUTTERS, AND CONDIMENTS

RED PEPPER SAUCE

THE
MOOSEWOOD
RESTAURANT
KITCHEN
GARDEN

240

A zesty sauce, featuring the smoky sweetness of roasted red peppers.

½ CUP DRY RED WINE

⅓ CUP CHOPPED SCALLION, WHITE
PART ONLY

¼ TO ⅓ CUP HERB VINEGAR
(TARRAGON, BASIL, DILL)

½ MEDIUM TOMATO, DICED

4 MEDIUM RED PEPPERS, ROASTED
(P. 215)

⅓ CUP PINE NUTS (PIGNOLIA) *OR*
GROUND ALMONDS

SALT AND FRESHLY GROUND BLACK
PEPPER TO TASTE

YIELDS 3 CUPS

Simmer the wine, scallion, and ¼ cup herb vinegar in a nonreactive saucepan until the mixture is reduced by almost half, to about ½ cup. Soften the diced tomato by simmering a moment or two in the reduced sauce base. In a blender or food processor, purée the cooked ingredients with the peppers and nuts until smooth. Season to taste with salt and pepper, adding more herb vinegar if desired.

Serve with Crepes (p. 231), Timbales (p. 239), pasta, or grilled or broiled fish.

SHALLOT-HERB BUTTER SAUCE

A creamy, tangy sauce that brightens steamed vegetables and grilled or broiled fish.

3 TABLESPOONS FINELY CHOPPED
SHALLOT
4 TEASPOONS HERB *OR* WINE *OR*
FRUIT VINEGAR
3 TABLESPOONS WATER
¾ CUP BUTTER (1½ QUARTER-POUND
STICKS), CUT INTO ½-INCH PIECES
1 TEASPOON MINCED FRESH
TARRAGON (½ TEASPOON DRIED)

1 TABLESPOON FINELY CHOPPED
FRESH PARSLEY
1 TEASPOON FINELY CHOPPED FRESH
CHIVES *OR* SCALLION GREENS
1 TABLESPOON FRESH LEMON JUICE
SALT AND FRESHLY GROUND BLACK
PEPPER TO TASTE

YIELDS ALMOST 1 CUP

Combine the shallot, vinegar, and water in a small saucepan and simmer until the volume is reduced by half or most of the liquid has evaporated. This should take about 10 minutes.

Reduce the heat to very low and whisk in the butter, a few pieces at a time. The butter should melt, but not separate. Low heat and continued whisking will result in a creamy, opaque sauce. Remove the pan from the heat when there are no butter lumps remaining; add the herbs, lemon juice, and salt and pepper to taste.

The sauce can be slowly reheated in a double boiler or on a flame tamer or "waffle."

Serve small amounts of this rich herb butter on individual servings at the table. It makes a nice topping for Vegetable "Pasta" (p. 222).

VARIATIONS *Instead of tarragon, try one of these herbs: chervil, cilantro, dill, basil, fennel, lemon balm, lemon basil, sorrel, thyme, or marjoram.*

Add a pinch of saffron or paprika for a golden hue and rich flavor.

HERB VINEGARS AND HERB-INFUSED OIL

erb vinegars and herb-infused oils offer cooks a convenient way of incorporating the rich essence of summer herbs all year round. Spiking a marinated vegetable salad in January with a splash of basil vinegar or rosemary oil adds a taste dimension that dried herbs can't achieve.

Dressings, marinades, and mayonnaise prepared with herb vinegars will be more deeply flavored. Add a splash to steamed vegetables, herb butters, soups, sauces, and stews. The sharp tanginess of herb vinegars also allows you to cook with less or no salt.

THE
MOOSEWOOD
RESTAURANT
KITCHEN
GARDEN

242

vinegars Making homemade herb vinegar is a simple, rewarding task. Jars of vinegar make nice gifts from the garden.

First choose the appropriate vinegar for the herbs. I especially like the flavor of apple cider vinegar and white- and red-wine vinegars. Distilled white vinegar and rice vinegar are acceptable as well. Distilled white vinegar provides a clear, uncolored base for brightly colored herbs or flowers such as purple basil leaves, and the blooms of chives, nasturtiums, violets, roses, and carnations.

For the most intense flavor, pick herbs when the plants are beginning to bloom. Strip the leaves from the heavier stems. Remove and discard the bitter green or white petal base from flower blossoms.

Stuff a clean glass jar with fresh, dry, clean herbs or flowers. Fill with vinegar. Cover and let sit in the sun, outdoors or at the brightest window, for 4 to 6 weeks. Residents of very hot, sunny climates (like the American Southwest) may want to place the vinegar in a partially shaded spot for a shorter time. Pour the steeped vinegar through a paper coffee filter into a nonreactive pot (stainless steel, enamel, or heatproof ceramic or glass) and discard the herbs or flowers; they've given their all. Gently heat until the vinegar just starts to simmer. Do not boil. Pour into hot, sterilized jars and cap to seal. Store in a dark place away from heat, where it will keep for about 1 year.

Some favorite herb-vinegar combinations are:
* chervil, shallots, and white-wine vinegar
* dill, chives, and apple cider vinegar
* cilantro, chives, and rice vinegar
* purple basil, garlic, and white vinegar
* oregano or marjoram and red-wine vinegar
* tarragon, shallots, and apple cider vinegar

Use 1 to 2 whole, peeled cloves of garlic, a few peppercorns, a small whole, peeled shallot, or a fresh chili pepper for each pint of vinegar, if desired.

infused oils Herb-infused oils have such a concentrated flavor, only a small amount is needed to enhance seasoning. At Moosewood we use them for sautéing and in marinades, vinaigrette dressings, mayonnaise, sauces, grain or bean salads, tossed with pasta, and drizzled directly on salads or cooked vegetables. When steaming, broiling, or grilling, just a bit of infused oil—as a marinade or final garnish—can impart a rich taste to low-fat meals.

Mild oils that will not compete with the herb flavor are the best choices: canola, corn, light olive, safflower, or soy. For 1 cup of oil use ½ cup of chopped fresh herb. Let stand at room temperature for 4 to 5 days to infuse the oil with the herb's essence. The herbs will settle to the bottom. Carefully ladle or decant the clear oil into clean jars; discard the spent herbs. Tightly cap, and store refrigerated for up to 6 months.

Basil, cilantro, dill, lemon balm, marjoram, mint, oregano, rosemary, sage, tarragon, and thyme have been our favorite fresh herbs to use.

MOOSEWOOD RESTAURANT HOUSE DRESSING

O ver the years our house dressing has evolved as many subtle variations on a theme created by Linda Dickinson. This creamy green dressing changes somewhat from meal to meal and season to season, since each cook has a slightly different interpretation. Here's mine:

¼ CUP LOOSELY PACKED FRESH PARSLEY LEAVES

¼ CUP LOOSELY PACKED FRESH BASIL LEAVES (1½ TEASPOONS DRIED)

3 TABLESPOONS COARSELY CHOPPED SCALLION GREENS

½ TEASPOON FRESH LEMON THYME LEAVES (¼ TEASPOON DRIED)

¼ TEASPOON FRESHLY GROUND BLACK PEPPER

1 TEASPOON DIJON MUSTARD

½ CUP MILK

3 TABLESPOONS CIDER VINEGAR

3 TABLESPOONS WATER (OR PART APPLE JUICE FOR SWEETER DRESSING)

1 CUP VEGETABLE OIL (CAN BE PART OLIVE)

YIELDS 2 CUPS

In a blender, whirl all the ingredients, except the oil, for 1 minute. While the blender is running, slowly add the oil. Blend only until the dressing is thick and creamy.

The herbs can be varied to suit your taste, but maintain the proportions of liquid to oil for a creamy consistency.

Will keep refrigerated for up to 1 week.

VINAIGRETTE DRESSINGS

Zesty vinaigrettes enliven salads. Be versatile and vary the types of oils and vinegars. Try an Herb Vinegar (p. 242), red- or white-wine, rice, cider, and balsamic vinegars. Olive oil (extra virgin is rich and flavorful), peanut oil, soy oil, and corn oil are also recommended. Fresh or frozen herbs will yield superior dressings to dried.

Regardless of the recipe, the procedure for all vinaigrette dressings is the same. Combine the ingredients in a jar or bottle that can be tightly sealed. The dressing ingredients will separate on standing, so shake well before using.

Vinaigrettes will keep refrigerated for several weeks.

THE
MOOSEWOOD
RESTAURANT
KITCHEN
GARDEN

244

RASPBERRY VINAIGRETTE

e like to serve this dressing with a simple green salad featuring tender, buttery Boston lettuce. It is lightly fruity with a subtle raspberry flavor.

⅓ CUP RASPBERRY VINEGAR

⅔ CUP MILD VEGETABLE OIL

2 TEASPOONS DIJON MUSTARD

1 TEASPOON FRESH THYME
  (½ TEASPOON DRIED)

1 TEASPOON CHOPPED FRESH
  MARJORAM (½ TEASPOON DRIED)

SALT AND FRESHLY GROUND BLACK
  PEPPER TO TASTE

YIELDS 1 CUP

BASIL-SHALLOT VINAIGRETTE

Wonderful on ripe sliced tomatoes.

½ CUP OLIVE OIL (ALL OR PART
 EXTRA VIRGIN)
¼ CUP FRESH LEMON JUICE
¼ CUP MINCED SHALLOT (SCALLION
 CAN SUBSTITUTE)

¼ CUP CHOPPED FRESH BASIL
 LEAVES (1 TABLESPOON DRIED)
SALT AND FRESHLY GROUND BLACK
 PEPPER TO TASTE

YIELDS 1¼ CUPS

TARRAGON VINAIGRETTE

Good with mixed green salads or as a dressing for a marinated cooked vegetable salad.

⅔ CUP PEANUT OIL
¼ CUP WHITE-WINE VINEGAR
1 TEASPOON DRY MUSTARD
1 TABLESPOON CHOPPED FRESH
 CHIVES

1 GARLIC CLOVE, MINCED OR PRESSED
1½ TABLESPOONS CHOPPED FRESH
 TARRAGON
SALT AND FRESHLY GROUND BLACK
 PEPPER TO TASTE

YIELDS 1 CUP

DILL–RED ONION VINAIGRETTE

We especially like this as a marinade for potato and other cooked vegetable salads.

½ CUP VEGETABLE OIL
¼ CUP RED-WINE VINEGAR
¼ CUP MINCED RED ONION
1½ TABLESPOONS CHOPPED FRESH
 DILL

1 TABLESPOON CHOPPED FRESH
 PARSLEY
1 TEASPOON DIJON MUSTARD
SALT AND FRESHLY GROUND BLACK
 PEPPER TO TASTE

YIELDS 1 CUP

CREAMY DRESSINGS

GOLDEN SESAME

Carrot adds a gentle sweetness to the rich, creamy tahini in this tangy dressing.

THE
MOOSEWOOD
RESTAURANT
KITCHEN
GARDEN

246

½ CUP GRATED RAW CARROT

¼ CUP FRESH LEMON JUICE

2 TABLESPOONS CHOPPED SCALLION
(WHITE PART ONLY)

⅓ CUP WATER

1 TEASPOON DIJON MUSTARD

¼ TEASPOON SALT

½ CUP TAHINI

YIELDS 1⅔ CUPS

Purée the carrot, lemon juice, scallion, water, mustard, and salt in a food processor or blender until smooth. Slowly add the tahini while continuing to blend. The dressing will thicken as it sits.

Keeps refrigerated for up to 10 days.

CREAMY PARMESAN

Good with romaine lettuce, croutons, cucumbers, tomato wedges, and hard-boiled eggs.

½ CUP FRESHLY GRATED GOOD-
QUALITY PARMESAN CHEESE

2 GARLIC CLOVES, BLANCHED (SEE
NOTE) AND MINCED OR PRESSED

¼ CUP MILK

2 TABLESPOONS FRESH LEMON JUICE
OR WHITE-WINE VINEGAR OR HERB
VINEGAR (P. 242)

1 TABLESPOON CHOPPED FRESH
PARSLEY

1 TABLESPOON CHOPPED FRESH
BASIL OR OREGANO OR MARJORAM
(1 TEASPOON DRIED)

½ CUP VEGETABLE OIL (ALL OR PART
OLIVE)

SALT AND FRESHLY GROUND BLACK
PEPPER TO TASTE

YIELDS 1¼ CUPS

Purée the Parmesan cheese, garlic, milk, and lemon juice or vinegar until smooth. Add the herbs and continue to blend, slowly drizzling in the oil.

Keeps refrigerated for up to 1 week. Reblend if separation occurs.

NOTE *Blanched garlic has a milder, nuttier flavor than raw. To blanch, drop the garlic cloves in boiling water for 1 minute. Drain and use. Raw garlic can be used for a more robust flavor.*

CREAMY YOGURT SAUCE

T angy, flavorful, and low in fat, this sauce can be used as a dip, or a dressing for greens, pasta, or cooked vegetable salads.

½ CUP PLAIN LOW-FAT YOGURT (WE USE AN ALL-DAIRY, NO ADDITIVE TYPE)

2 TABLESPOONS FRESH LEMON JUICE

3 TABLESPOONS OLIVE OIL

I TEASPOON DIJON MUSTARD

I TABLESPOON CHOPPED FRESH PARSLEY

I TABLESPOON CHOPPED FRESH CHERVIL OR DILL

2 TEASPOONS CHOPPED FRESH BASIL

SALT AND FRESHLY GROUND BLACK PEPPER TO TASTE

YIELDS ¾ CUP

Combine all the ingredients in a small bowl and mix until smooth. Serve immediately, or refrigerate, covered, until needed. Use within 1 week.

Minted Cucumber-Yogurt Dip (p. 258), makes a refreshing salad dressing as well.

Thin Herbed Mayonnaise (p. 248) with an equal volume of yogurt to make a rich, creamy dressing for cooked vegetables or leafy greens. Adjust seasonings if necessary.

HERBED MAYONNAISE AND MAYONNAISE ALTERNATIVES

THE
MOOSEWOOD
RESTAURANT
KITCHEN
GARDEN

248

Due to the increase in salmonella-related, food-borne illnesses, it is wise to avoid using recipes that call for uncooked eggs. Since the traditional recipes for mayonnaise fall into this category, I am offering some suggestions for enhancing store-bought mayonnaise, as well as a recipe for a cooked egg variety, and a few eggless alternatives.

You can customize commercial mayonnaise with the addition of fresh herbs or herbal vinegars.

To each cup of mayonnaise, add 2 to 3 tablespoons of chopped fresh herbs. Basil, chervil, chives, dill, nasturtium blossoms, sorrel, or tarragon are delicious alone or in various combinations.

The addition of herb vinegars makes a tangy, assertively flavored dressing. Add 1 to 2 tablespoons of vinegar per cup of mayonnaise.

For a Mediterranean sauce, or aioli, add 1 to 2 cloves of pressed or minced raw garlic and 2 tablespoons of a fragrant, extra virgin olive oil to each cup of mayonnaise.

The addition of a tablespoon of curry powder or a pinch of saffron dissolved in a tablespoon of warm water will add fragrance, warmth, and color.

COOKED MAYONNAISE

This rich, golden-hued dressing utilizes cooked egg yolks, and should satisfy the most ardent fans of homemade mayonnaise. The spreadable consistency makes it a good candidate for sandwiches as well as a thick dressing for salads. The basic recipe may be "dressed up" using the suggestions for commercial mayonnaise above.

4 EGG YOLKS

1 TABLESPOON CORNSTARCH

¼ CUP VEGETABLE OIL, ALL OR PART
  OLIVE OIL

2 TABLESPOONS FRESH LEMON JUICE
  OR HERB VINEGAR (P. 242)

½ CUP HOT WATER

½ TEASPOON DIJON MUSTARD

SALT AND FRESHLY GROUND BLACK
  PEPPER TO TASTE

YIELDS 1 CUP

Combine the egg yolks and cornstarch in a small saucepan. Slowly whisk in the oil, followed by the lemon juice and water. Cook over low heat, whisking constantly, until the mixture thickens. Remove from the heat and add the mustard, salt and pepper, and any additional seasonings desired. Transfer the mayonnaise to a bowl, cover tightly, and refrigerate immediately. It will keep refrigerated for up to 1 week.

TARATOUR

Laura Branca originated a version of this rich, creamy sauce at Moosewood Restaurant. We use it on steamed and raw vegetables, on baked fish, or in pita sandwiches. It makes a luscious dip for crudités and steamed artichokes.

¾ CUP LIGHTLY TOASTED ALMONDS
  (SEE NOTE)

1 CUP FINE FRENCH OR ITALIAN
  BREAD CRUMBS

JUICE OF 1 LEMON

½ TEASPOON DIJON MUSTARD

2 GARLIC CLOVES, MINCED OR
  PRESSED

½ CUP OLIVE OIL

1 CUP WATER

2 TABLESPOONS CHOPPED FRESH
  PARSLEY

2 TABLESPOONS CHOPPED FRESH
  CHERVIL, CHIVES, DILL, FENNEL,
  MARJORAM, OR MINT (OPTIONAL)

SALT AND FRESHLY GROUND BLACK
  PEPPER TO TASTE

Combine the almonds, bread crumbs, lemon juice, mustard, garlic, olive oil, and ½ cup of the water in a blender or food processor. (If using a blender, coarsely chop the almonds before blending.) Blend or process until smooth. Add the parsley and remaining ½ cup of water. Blend until smooth. Add salt and pepper to taste and stir in the desired herbs if any. Serve immediately, or store, covered, in the refrigerator for up to 1 week.

NOTE *To toast almonds, bake in a 350°F. oven for 5 minutes.*

ROUILLE

THE
MOOSEWOOD
RESTAURANT
KITCHEN
GARDEN

250

T raditionally used as a spicy garnish for the Provençal seafood stew Bouillabaisse, rouille makes a zesty dressing or dip for steamed vegetables, grilled or poached fish, hard-boiled egg, and potato and other cooked vegetable salads. Use as much Tabasco sauce as suits your personal taste.

⅔ CUP CHOPPED ROASTED RED PEPPER OR PIMIENTO (P. 215 OR PURCHASED IN JARS)

½ CUP FRENCH OR ITALIAN BREAD CRUMBS, BRIEFLY SOAKED IN WATER TO COVER, THEN DRAINED AND SQUEEZED DRY

2 GARLIC CLOVES, MINCED OR PRESSED

¼ CUP WATER *OR* VEGETABLE STOCK (P. 212)

¾ CUP OLIVE OIL

1 TABLESPOON CHOPPED FRESH PARSLEY

A FEW DROPS OF TABASCO SAUCE

SALT AND FRESHLY GROUND BLACK PEPPER TO TASTE

YIELDS 2 CUPS

In a blender or processor, purée until smooth, everything except the parsley, Tabasco, and salt and pepper. Stir in the parsley and seasonings to taste. Serve immediately, or store, covered, in the refrigerator for up to 1 week.

HERB PESTOS

In Italian, the word *pesto* means "pounded," a reference to the pre–food processor method of making pesto with a mortar and pestle. Pesto Genovese, the classic basil preparation, is the most well known pesto, but not the only one. The recipes below share Pesto Genovese's rich, concentrated quality but utilize different herbs, nuts, and seasonings. Our cookbook, *Sundays at Moosewood Restaurant,* offers other pesto ideas and recipes.

When fresh herbs are plentiful, make extra batches to freeze in small jars.

These highly flavored mixtures should be served in moderation (just a spoonful or two for each bowl of pasta), to complement, not overwhelm, the foods they accompany.

All pestos are made in the same way. Place all the ingredients, except the oil, in a food processor or blender. Mix until everything is well chopped, then slowly add the oil in a thin stream to form a fairly smooth paste. If using a blender, it may be necessary to prechop the herbs and nuts by hand.

Pesto will keep refrigerated for a couple of weeks. Keep in an airtight container and cover with a thin layer of oil, if desired, to prevent discoloring.

PESTO GENOVESE

We toss this pesto with pasta and top with additional Parmesan cheese and chopped fresh tomatoes. It's a wonderful enrichment as a final garnish for soups and added to cheese fillings for lasagna or stuffed vegetables. Fill mushroom caps with pesto and toasted bread crumbs, then briefly bake for a savory hors d'oeuvre. Top grilled or broiled fish with a dollop of pesto.

3 CUPS LOOSELY PACKED FRESH
  BASIL LEAVES
⅓ CUP PINE NUTS (PIGNOLIA)
½ CUP FRESHLY GRATED PARMESAN
  CHEESE

3 GARLIC CLOVES, COARSLEY
  CHOPPED
½ CUP OLIVE OIL
SALT AND FRESHLY GROUND BLACK
  PEPPER TO TASTE

YIELDS 2 CUPS

CILANTRO PESTO

A spicy and tangy pesto that we serve in dollops to top beans, enchiladas, burritos, tostadas, huevos rancheros, and baked or grilled fish. It makes a zesty dip when added to avocadoes mashed with a squeeze of lemon juice. Use ⅔ cup cilantro pesto for 3 small avocadoes.

1 CUP LOOSELY PACKED FRESH CILANTRO LEAVES

1 CUP LOOSELY PACKED FRESH PARSLEY LEAVES

⅓ CUP WHOLE ALMONDS

1 SMALL FRESH CHILI (JALAPEÑO ARE GOOD), COARSELY CHOPPED

2 GARLIC CLOVES, COARSELY CHOPPED

2 TABLESPOONS FRESH LIME JUICE

¼ CUP VEGETABLE OIL

SALT AND FRESHLY GROUND BLACK PEPPER TO TASTE

YIELDS 1 CUP

THE
MOOSEWOOD
RESTAURANT
KITCHEN
GARDEN

252

DILL PESTO

A rich, mellow blend that is nice by the spoonful to garnish potato or cucumber soups. We use it as a filling for thin, rolled fish fillets. Spread on crackers, canapés, or rye bread for sandwiches. Add it to mayonnaise-based salads for additional flavor.

1 CUP LOOSELY PACKED FRESH DILL LEAVES

½ CUP COARSELY CHOPPED FRESH CHIVES

½ CUP GRATED SHARP CHEDDAR CHEESE

½ CUP COARSELY CHOPPED WALNUTS

¼ CUP VEGETABLE OIL

SALT AND FRESHLY GROUND BLACK PEPPER TO TASTE

YIELDS 1 CUP

TARRAGON PESTO

T his pesto has the full, aromatic flavor of tarragon. I like to serve this at home on grilled fish steaks. Toss a few tablespoons with steamed vegetables or a grain pilaf, or use as a garnish for a light tomato soup. Add a little to a cream or cheese sauce.

1 CUP LOOSELY PACKED FRESH
  PARSLEY LEAVES
½ CUP LOOSELY PACKED FRESH
  TARRAGON LEAVES
¼ CUP COARSELY CHOPPED SCALLION
  OR 3 TABLESPOONS CHOPPED
  SHALLOT

⅓ CUP PINE NUTS (PIGNOLIA)
½ CUP FRESHLY GRATED PARMESAN
  CHEESE
1½ TEASPOONS FRESH LEMON JUICE
¼ CUP VEGETABLE OIL
SALT AND FRESHLY GROUND BLACK
  PEPPER TO TASTE

YIELDS 1 CUP

HAZELNUT PESTO

L emon and hazelnuts are wonderfully fragrant and combine here in a rich yet delicate pesto. For an elegant side dish, toss with a small-shaped pasta or steamed vegetables. Use as a spread for fresh biscuits, rolls, or French bread.

1½ CUPS LOOSELY PACKED FRESH
  PARSLEY LEAVES
½ CUP LOOSELY PACKED FRESH
  CHERVIL LEAVES (IF UNAVAILABLE,
  USE MORE PARSLEY)
1 TABLESPOON FRESH LEMON THYME
  LEAVES
½ CUP TOASTED, SKINNED
  HAZELNUTS (SEE NOTE)

1 TABLESPOON FRESH LEMON JUICE
½ TEASPOON GRATED LEMON PEEL
  (FROM ABOUT ½ LEMON)
¼ CUP VEGETABLE OIL
SALT AND FRESHLY GROUND BLACK
  PEPPER TO TASTE

YIELDS 1 CUP

NOTE *Hazelnuts have a finer flavor if skinned. Bake on a cookie sheet at 325°F. for 10 minutes. Cool for a few minutes, then rub with a small towel to remove the skins.*

HERB BUTTERS

Butter that is used as a spread, as an enrichment, or for sautéing can be easily enhanced with fresh herbs.

Toss toasted bread cubes with herb butter for savory croutons. Bread crumbs toasted in herb butter make a superb topping for steamed vegetables, casseroles, and simple pasta with grated Parmesan cheese.

Herb butter can be prepared in the summer and kept frozen in small packages for winter use. It will keep refrigerated for up to 1 month, and frozen for up to 6 months.

Herb-Infused Oils (p. 242) provide a good alternative to people who are avoiding butter in their diet.

Allow the butter to soften for ease of preparation. Cream in the remaining ingredients. For full flavor, use the butter after the herbs have imparted their essence, about an hour or so.

THE
MOOSEWOOD
RESTAURANT
KITCHEN
GARDEN

254

TARRAGON-DIJON BUTTER

D ijon and lemon provide a sharpness that will accent mildly flavored foods.

¼ POUND (1 STICK) SOFTENED
   BUTTER
1 TABLESPOON FINELY CHOPPED
FRESH TARRAGON

1 TABLESPOON FINELY CHOPPED
   FRESH PARSLEY
2 TEASPOONS FRESH LEMON JUICE
1 TEASPOON DIJON MUSTARD

DILL-CHIVE BUTTER

We like to toss new potatoes with this herb butter. It's also good with steamed members of the cabbage family: broccoli, Brussels sprouts, cauliflower, cabbage, and kohlrabi.

¼ POUND (1 STICK) SOFTENED
  BUTTER
2 TABLESPOONS FINELY CHOPPED
  FRESH DILL

1 TABLESPOON FINELY CHOPPED
  FRESH CHIVES
1 TEASPOON PREPARED HORSERADISH

BASIL-GARLIC BUTTER

A robust butter for garlic bread, croutons, or steamed zucchini, or simply tossed with egg noodles.

¼ POUND (1 STICK) SOFTENED
  BUTTER
2 TABLESPOONS FINELY CHOPPED
  FRESH BASIL
1 TEASPOON FINELY CHOPPED FRESH
  OREGANO

½ TEASPOON FINELY CHOPPED FRESH
  THYME
1 LARGE GARLIC CLOVE, MINCED OR
  PRESSED

FINES HERBES BUTTER

A classic combination used in French cuisine. Toss with steamed vegetables or use to top broiled or baked fish.

¼ POUND (1 STICK) SOFTENED
  BUTTER

2 TEASPOONS EACH OF FINELY
  CHOPPED FRESH CHIVES, PARSLEY,
  TARRAGON, AND CHERVIL

MINT BUTTER

T ry this delicately fragrant herb butter with breakfast breads, muffins, and peas or carrots.

¼ POUND (1 STICK) SOFTENED
  BUTTER
2 TABLESPOONS FINELY CHOPPED
  FRESH SPEARMINT
1 TABLESPOON FINELY CHOPPED
  FENNEL LEAF

1 TABLESPOON FINELY CHOPPED
  FRESH PARSLEY
½ TEASPOON FINELY CHOPPED FRESH
  LEMON THYME
1 TEASPOON FRESH LEMON JUICE

SAGE BUTTER

**THE
MOOSEWOOD
RESTAURANT
KITCHEN
GARDEN**

256

T his hearty blend goes well with bread cubes for stuffings or croutons, baked winter squash, bean and potato dishes, cornbread, or crusty loaves.

¼ POUND (1 STICK) SOFTENED
  BUTTER
2 TABLESPOONS FINELY CHOPPED
  FRESH SAGE

1 TEASPOON FINELY CHOPPED FRESH
  MARJORAM
½ TEASPOON FINELY CHOPPED FRESH
  THYME

DIPS

Toss out that tired onion soup mix! Fresh herbs make perky, easily prepared, delicious dips. Use raw vegetables, crackers, chips, and toasted pita bread wedges for dipping.

CLASSIC CHIP DIP

Cool and tangy, yogurt makes this a lighter dip than those made of all sour cream.

I CUP SOUR CREAM

I CUP PLAIN YOGURT

3 TABLESPOONS CHOPPED FRESH
  DILL

3 TABLESPOONS CHOPPED FRESH
  PARSLEY

⅓ CUP CHOPPED SCALLION *OR*
  FRESH CHIVES

2 TEASPOONS PREPARED
  HORSERADISH (OPTIONAL)

SALT AND FRESHLY GROUND BLACK
  PEPPER TO TASTE

YIELDS ABOUT 2½ CUPS

Combine all the ingredients. Vary this classic by substituting some of the herb combinations listed in the Herbed Cheese Spreads (p. 259) for the dill and parsley. Keeps refrigerated for at least 1 week.

MISO-TAHINI DIP

Rich and savory, this dip also makes a good spread for rice cakes and can be added to stir-fried dishes to enrich the sauce.

3 TABLESPOONS MILD, LIGHT MISO

¾ CUP COOL WATER

¾ CUP TAHINI

I TEASPOON FINELY GRATED FRESH
  GINGERROOT

2 TABLESPOONS CHOPPED SCALLION

YIELDS ABOUT 1¾ CUPS

Mix the miso and water until smooth. Add the tahini and mix until smooth. It should have the consistency of sour cream; add 1 or 2 additional tablespoons of water, if necessary, and the ginger and scallion. Will keep refrigerated for several weeks.

DIP OR SAUCE FOR FRESH FRUIT

This could also be used as a topping for pancakes, French toast, or fruit-filled Crepes (p. 231).

¾ CUP SOUR CREAM

¾ CUP PLAIN YOGURT

2 TABLESPOONS CHOPPED FRESH
LEMON BALM

I TABLESPOON CHOPPED FRESH MINT

2 TABLESPOONS HONEY OR MAPLE
SYRUP OR BROWN SUGAR

½ TEASPOON GROUND CINNAMON

PINCH OF FRESHLY GRATED NUTMEG

YIELDS ALMOST 2 CUPS

Combine all the ingredients. Will keep refrigerated for at least 1 week.

MINTED CUCUMBER-YOGURT DIP

This refreshing dip could also double as a low-calorie salad dressing if you use low-fat yogurt. Use less lemon juice to reduce tartness.

I CUP PLAIN YOGURT

½ CUCUMBER, PEELED, SEEDED, AND
GRATED (ABOUT ½ CUP)

2 TABLESPOONS FRESH LEMON JUICE

I TABLESPOON OLIVE OIL

1½ TABLESPOONS CHOPPED FRESH
MINT

I TABLESPOON CHOPPED FRESH
CILANTRO

2 TABLESPOONS CHOPPED FRESH
CHIVES OR SCALLION

SALT AND FRESHLY GROUND BLACK
PEPPER TO TASTE

YIELDS ABOUT 2 CUPS

Combine all the ingredients. Allow the flavors to meld for at least 30 minutes before serving. Will keep refrigerated for up to 4 days.

THE
MOOSEWOOD
RESTAURANT
KITCHEN
GARDEN

258

HERBED CHEESE SPREADS

Cheese spreads are familiar as appetizers with bread or crackers. Try these assorted, lively spreads as fillings for sandwiches, omelets, crepes, or stuffed vegetables.

There are countless possible combinations of herbs; here are a few that we think work well. Use smaller quantities of stronger herbs, such as cilantro, rosemary, sage, and thyme.

- dill and chervil
- basil and tarragon
- mint and chives
- lemon balm and chervil
- thyme and lemon basil

- cilantro and chilies
- rosemary and shallot
- marjoram and sage
- summer savory and chives
- fennel leaf and parsley

BASIC CHEESE SPREAD

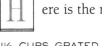ere is the master recipe followed by four delicious variations.

1½ CUPS GRATED FIRM CHEESE
(CHEDDAR, MONTEREY JACK, SWISS,
JARLSBERG, GOUDA)
⅔ CUP CREAM CHEESE *OR* COTTAGE
CHEESE (REGULAR OR LOW-FAT)
¼ CUP OR LESS CHOPPED FRESH
HERBS

2 TO 3 TABLESPOONS ADDITIONAL
SEASONINGS: CHOPPED VEGETABLES,
CHILIES, NUTS, GARLIC, OR EDIBLE
FLOWER BLOSSOMS

YIELDS ABOUT 2½ CUPS

Allow the grated cheese to soften at room temperature for easier mixing. Use a food processor or stationary or hand-held mixer to whip the cheeses together until smooth and well blended. Add the remaining ingredients.

SPICY MONTEREY JACK SPREAD

1½ CUPS GRATED MONTEREY JACK CHEESE

⅔ CUP COTTAGE CHEESE *OR* CREAM CHEESE

2 TABLESPOONS CHOPPED FRESH CHILIES

1 TABLESPOON CHOPPED FRESH CILANTRO

1 TABLESPOON CHOPPED FRESH PARSLEY

½ TEASPOON GROUND CORIANDER SEED

YIELDS ABOUT 2 CUPS

Proceed as for Basic Cheese Spread (p. 259).

THE
MOOSEWOOD
RESTAURANT
KITCHEN
GARDEN

260

HERBED CHEVRE SPREAD

1¼ CUPS FRESH CHEVRE (MILD GOAT CHEESE) *OR* FETA CHEESE

½ CUP LOW-FAT RICOTTA CHEESE

¼ CUP CHOPPED FRESH PARSLEY

2 TABLESPOONS CHOPPED FRESH BASIL

2 TABLESPOONS CHOPPED FRESH TARRAGON

2 GARLIC CLOVES, MINCED OR PRESSED

½ CUP GROUND, TOASTED NUTS (OPTIONAL)

FRESHLY GROUND BLACK PEPPER TO TASTE

YIELDS ABOUT 2½ CUPS

Cream the chevre and ricotta until light and fluffy. Add the remaining ingredients. If the chevre or feta is particularly salty, increase the quantity of ricotta.

VARIATIONS *Try some of the combinations listed on page 259.*

BLUE CHEESE SPREAD

I CUP CRUMBLED BLUE CHEESE

I CUP SOUR CREAM

3 GARLIC CLOVES, MINCED OR
PRESSED

2 TABLESPOONS CHOPPED FRESH
PARSLEY

2 TABLESPOONS CHOPPED FRESH
DILL (I TEASPOON DRIED)

I TABLESPOON CHOPPED FRESH
MARJORAM (I TEASPOON DRIED)

YIELDS ABOUT 2¼ CUPS

Reserve ¼ cup of the crumbled blue cheese. Combine all the other ingredients and cream until well blended. Gently stir in the reserved blue cheese.

CHEDDAR-SAGE-THYME SPREAD

1½ CUPS GRATED SHARP CHEDDAR
CHEESE, SOFTENED

⅔ CUP COTTAGE CHEESE OR CREAM
CHEESE

2 TEASPOONS CHOPPED FRESH SAGE
(I TEASPOON DRIED)

I TEASPOON FRESH THYME LEAVES
(½ TEASPOON DRIED)

2 TABLESPOONS CHOPPED PIMIENTO

YIELDS ABOUT 2¼ CUPS

Combine all the ingredients and cream until well blended.

BREADS

SWEET POTATO MUFFINS

 weet potato gives a moist, lightly sweet presence to these relatively low fat, spiced muffins.

**THE
MOOSEWOOD
RESTAURANT
KITCHEN
GARDEN**

262

2 EGG WHITES
¼ CUP APPLE JUICE *OR* ORANGE
  JUICE CONCENTRATE
2 TABLESPOONS VEGETABLE OIL
½ CUP MILK (CAN BE SKIM)
1 CUP MASHED, COOKED SWEET
  POTATO (COOKED PUMPKIN, WINTER
  SQUASH, OR CARROT COULD
  SUBSTITUTE)
⅓ CUP DATES *OR* RAISINS *OR*
  CHOPPED, PITTED PRUNES MIXED

WITH 1 TEASPOON UNBLEACHED
WHITE FLOUR
1 TABLESPOON BAKING POWDER
¼ TEASPOON GROUND NUTMEG
½ TEASPOON GROUND CINNAMON
½ TEASPOON GROUND GINGER
¼ TEASPOON SALT
1¾ CUPS FLOUR (½ WHOLE WHEAT
  PASTRY FLOUR AND ½ UNBLEACHED
  WHITE FLOUR)

YIELDS 12 MUFFINS

Preheat the oven to 375°F. Lightly oil a 12-muffin tin.

Combine the wet ingredients, including the sweet potato and dried fruit. In a separate bowl, sift the baking powder, spices, and salt into the flour. Add these to the wet ingredients, mixing until just blended. Divide the batter into 12 muffin cups. These are dense muffins, so the batter will fill the muffin cups higher than other batters.

Bake for 30 to 35 minutes or until the muffins separate from the pan and bounce back when lightly tapped.

CHEDDAR-HERB BREAD

The addition of savory herbs and cheddar cheese gives this bread a distinctive accent. The cheese flavor is particularly enhanced when the bread is toasted.

- 1 EGG, LIGHTLY BEATEN
- 1 CUP MILK, SCALDED AND COOLED TO LUKEWARM
- 1 TABLESPOON HONEY *OR* SUGAR
- 2 TABLESPOONS VEGETABLE OIL
- 1 PACKAGE DRY YEAST (1 TABLESPOON)
- 2 TABLESPOONS CHOPPED FRESH HERBS (ONE OF THE FOLLOWING: SAGE, DILL, BASIL, OR TARRAGON)
- 2 TABLESPOONS CHOPPED SCALLION
- 1 TEASPOON SALT
- ½ TEASPOON FRESHLY GROUND BLACK PEPPER
- 1 CUP WHOLE WHEAT FLOUR
- 2 TO 2½ CUPS UNBLEACHED WHITE FLOUR
- 1 CUP GRATED SHARP CHEDDAR CHEESE (ABOUT 4 OUNCES)
- 1 TABLESPOON DILL *OR* POPPY *OR* SESAME SEED

YIELDS 1 LOAF

Combine the egg, milk, honey or sugar, 1 tablespoon oil, yeast, herbs, scallion, salt, and pepper. Add the flours, about ½ cup at a time, stirring well after each addition. Use as much of the flour as you need to make a dough stiff enough to knead.

Turn the dough onto a lightly floured surface and knead in the cheddar cheese. Knead the dough for about 10 minutes; it should be smooth and elastic.

Place the dough in an oiled bowl, flipping it over to grease the top. Cover with a towel and let rise in a warm place for about 1 hour, or until doubled in bulk.

Punch down the dough and put it in a lightly oiled loaf pan, 9½ by 5½ inches. Cover, and let rise again until doubled in bulk, about 1 hour.

Preheat the oven to 375°F.

Brush the top of the bread with 1 tablespoon oil and sprinkle with the seeds.

Bake for 45 to 50 minutes, or until the crust is golden and the bread makes a hollow sound when tapped. Cool on a rack.

DESSERTS

FRESH RASPBERRY SORBET

THE
MOOSEWOOD
RESTAURANT
KITCHEN
GARDEN

264

A very quick, vividly colored, and irresistible dessert with pronounced fruit flavor. It requires no special equipment and little or no sweetener besides fruit and fruit concentrates.

ABOUT 2 CUPS FRESH RASPBERRIES (I 12-OUNCE PACKAGE OF FROZEN)

⅓ CUP UNSWEETENED FROZEN JUICE CONCENTRATE (I USED A READY-MIXED BLEND OF CHERRY, GRAPE, AND APPLE.)

I TO 2 TABLESPOONS SUGAR *OR* MILD HONEY, IF BERRIES ARE VERY TART, OR FOR A SWEET TOOTH

I TEASPOON ROSE WATER (OPTIONAL)

I TABLESPOON LIQUEUR (AMARETTO OR COINTREAU), OPTIONAL

SERVES 4 (SMALL SERVINGS)

Freeze the fresh berries on a tray until hard. Place the frozen berries in a blender with the other ingredients. Blend until smooth but not soupy. Serve immediately, garnished with pale rose petals.

Any leftover thawed sorbet can be used as a dessert sauce or ice cream topping.

VARIATION *Strawberries could be substituted for the raspberries. Slice the berries in half or into thirds before freezing.*

PUMPKIN CAKE

Pumpkin and honey have an affinity; the flavors harmonize without overwhelming each other. Use either the small pumpkins specifically noted as "pie pumpkins" or winter squash; both will make a moist, rich cake.

CAKE

- 1¼ CUPS HONEY
- 4 EGGS
- 1 CUP MILD VEGETABLE OIL
- 2 CUPS COOKED, MASHED PUMPKIN OR WINTER SQUASH
- 2½ CUPS UNBLEACHED WHITE FLOUR (UP TO 1 CUP OF WHICH COULD BE WHOLE WHEAT PASTRY FLOUR)
- 1½ TEASPOONS BAKING SODA
- 1½ TEASPOONS BAKING POWDER
- 1 TEASPOON SALT
- 2 TEASPOONS GROUND CINNAMON
- ½ TEASPOON GROUND NUTMEG
- 1 CUP CHOPPED WALNUTS

FROSTING

- 8 OUNCES SOFTENED CREAM CHEESE
- ¼ CUP PURE MAPLE SYRUP

YIELDS 3 9-INCH LAYERS

Preheat the oven to 325°F. Lightly oil 3 9-inch cake pans.

Cream the honey, eggs, oil, and pumpkin or squash. In a separate bowl, sift together the dry ingredients and then add to the wet mixture, stirring until smooth. Fold in the nuts. Pour the batter into the prepared cake pans. Bake for 25 to 30 minutes, or until the cake is done. Cool the layers on a rack.

Whip the softened cream cheese with the maple syrup until light and fluffy. When the cake has cooled, spread the frosting between the layers and on the top and sides.

BLUEBERRY-LEMON TART

ncooked berries in the filling and a creamy, fragrant lemon custard topping make this tart the very essence of freshness.

9-INCH PIE SHELL

1½ CUPS UNBLEACHED WHITE FLOUR

3 TABLESPOONS SUGAR

½ CUP BUTTER

2 EGG YOLKS

½ TEASPOON VANILLA EXTRACT

2 TABLESPOONS COLD WATER

Preheat the oven to 400°F.

Combine the flour and sugar. Using a pastry blender or two knives, cut in the butter until the mixture resembles coarse meal (pieces of butter no larger than baby peas). Stir in the egg yolks, vanilla, and cold water. Either roll out the dough or pat it into a pie plate. Prick the dough with fork tines and bake for 10 minutes, or until lightly browned. Cool on a rack before filling.

BLUEBERRY FILLING

4 CUPS FRESH BLUEBERRIES

⅓ TO ½ CUP SUGAR (DEPENDING UPON THE TARTNESS OF THE

BERRIES AND YOUR SWEET TOOTH) SIFTED WITH 2 TABLESPOONS CORNSTARCH

Place 2 cups of the berries in a saucepan over medium heat. Set aside the remaining 2 cups of berries. With the back of a spoon, smash a few of the berries, and after a couple of minutes, add the sugar-cornstarch mixture. Cook, stirring for 1 to 2 minutes until the juices are extracted and the mixture bubbles and simmers. Remove from the heat and chill for at least 2 hours.

LEMON CUSTARD

2 EGG YOLKS, LIGHTLY BEATEN

¼ CUP PLUS 1 TABLESPOON SUGAR

2½ TABLESPOONS UNBLEACHED WHITE FLOUR

1 CUP MILK

2 TEASPOONS FRESH LEMON JUICE

1 TEASPOON GRATED LEMON RIND

Combine the egg yolks, sugar, and flour in a saucepan, stirring to blend. Slowly whisk in the milk. Simmer over low heat or in a double boiler, carefully stirring, until the sauce thickens. It will be ready when it just begins to bubble; do not let

THE
MOOSEWOOD
RESTAURANT
KITCHEN
GARDEN

266

it boil vigorously. Remove from the heat and whisk in the lemon juice and rind. Chill, covered, for at least 2 hours.

To assemble the tart, fold the 2 cups of uncooked blueberries into the chilled berry mixture. Pour into the cooled pie shell and serve, or allow to chill further. Top each serving with the chilled lemon custard and an edible flower garnish.

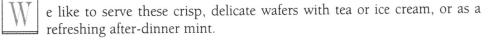

PEPPERMINT BUTTER WAFERS

W e like to serve these crisp, delicate wafers with tea or ice cream, or as a refreshing after-dinner mint.

½ CUP SWEET (UNSALTED) BUTTER
¼ CUP FINELY CHOPPED FRESH
  PEPPERMINT LEAVES
½ CUP SUGAR

I EGG, LIGHTLY BEATEN
PINCH OF SALT
¾ CUP UNBLEACHED WHITE *OR*
  WHOLE WHEAT PASTRY FLOUR

YIELDS ABOUT 2 DOZEN COOKIES

Preheat the oven to 375°F.

Cream the butter with the fresh mint, then let stand at room temperature for 1 hour to suffuse the butter with mint flavor. Cream the sugar into the butter and mint. Add the beaten egg and mix until well blended. Add the salt and flour, and mix just until the batter is smooth.

Drop teaspoonfuls of the batter onto a lightly oiled cookie sheet, 2 inches apart. The batter will spread and flatten as it bakes. Bake for 10 to 15 minutes in the center of the oven, until the wafers are light brown at the edges.

If desired, place a small piece of semisweet chocolate in the center of each unbaked cookie for a classic mint-chocolate combination.

NOTE *We've found double-layered, insulated cookie sheets good for avoiding unevenly baked or burnt cookies.*

ALL-FRUIT PRESERVES OR JAMS

Naturally sweet preserves can be made using fresh fruit and fruit juice concentrates. Strawberries, raspberries, blackberries, blueberries, and grapes go well with white grape juice concentrate; peaches and apricots with apple juice concentrate; sweet cherries and plums with cherry juice concentrate. Tart fruits may require the addition of a mild, light honey or sugar for better flavor.

THE
MOOSEWOOD
RESTAURANT
KITCHEN
GARDEN

268

I QUART FRESH, RIPE FRUIT
(STRAWBERRIES, RASPBERRIES,
BLUEBERRIES, BLACKBERRIES,
PEACHES, APRICOTS, SWEET
CHERRIES, GRAPES, OR PLUMS)
I CUP UNSWEETENED FROZEN FRUIT
JUICE CONCENTRATE (UNDILUTED)

I CUP LOW-METHOXYL PECTIN
SOLUTION (SEE NOTE I)
4 TEASPOONS CALCIUM SOLUTION
(SEE NOTE 2)
LIGHT, MILD HONEY, SUGAR, OR
FRESH LEMON JUICE TO TASTE
(OPTIONAL)

YIELDS 1½ QUARTS

Cut, peel, and pit the fruit if necessary. There should be about 4 cups of fruit. Gently heat the fruit and juice concentrate together. Add the pectin solution and stir to dissolve. When the mixture is near boiling, add 4 teaspoons of the calcium solution. Taste-test for additional sweetener (honey or sugar) or 1 to 2 teaspoons of lemon juice. Bring to a boil, pour into canning jars, and process for 10 minutes in a boiling water bath, or allow to cool and then freeze.

Serve as a spread, or add to cakes, crepes, or other dessert fillings.

The recipe can be halved, doubled, or tripled.

NOTE I *This pectin is the only type that will gel with little or no sugar. Pomona's Universal Pectin is one widely available brand. Prepare the solution by placing 1 quart of very hot tap water in the blender. Turn it to low speed and add 4 tablespoons of pectin all at once. Whirl at high speed in a blender for several minutes to dissolve all the pectin. The mixture will thicken, but gel more upon cooling. It can be kept refrigerated for several weeks.*

NOTE 2 *Calcium phosphate comes in a small packet with the pectin. It allows the pectin to gel without the sugar or acid used in standard jams. Add ⅛ teaspoon calcium phosphate to ¼ cup water and stir well to make a calcium solution. Stir again vigorously when ready to use.*

HERBAL TEA MIXES

We serve herbal teas for their taste and ability to soothe, like chamomile, or stimulate, like peppermint. The mints continue to be our most popular teas.

Gardeners can expand their tea repertoire to reflect the full range of aromatic flavors in the kitchen garden:

basil	lemon balm
bee balm	lemon basil
borage	lemon thyme
chamomile	various mints
fennel	rose hips
lady's mantle	rosemary
lavender	garden sage

Spices and herbs from tropical or frost-free areas give additional possibilities:

cardamom	gingerroot
cinnamon	jasmine flowers
citrus peel	lemon grass
cloves	lemon verbena

When making tea with garden-grown herbs, use the fresh or dried leaf. The exceptions are chamomile and lavender (bud and flower), fennel (seed), and rose hip (fruit). Generally, 1 heaping tablespoon of dried herbs (or 2 of fresh) is sufficient for each generous cup or mug of boiling water.

Selections from either or both lists above combine to create the following tea blends that are good either hot or iced. These proportions are for dried herbs and spices.

1 cup apple mint	1 cup spearmint
½ cup rose hips	¼ cup garden sage
1 tablespoon orange peel	½ cup lemon balm
1 teaspoon ground cinnamon	
1 cup lemon basil	1 cup bergamot mint
2 tablespoons lemon thyme	1 tablespoon ground fennel seed
1 cup lemon verbena	1 tablespoon ground ginger
½ cup chamomile	1 cup peppermint
½ cup peppermint	1 cup lemon grass
½ cup lemon verbena	½ cup rose hips

1 cup spearmint
¼ cup borage
½ cup lemon grass

½ cup basil
1 cup lemon balm
2 tablespoons ground cloves
1 tablespoon lemon peel

Be energy efficient! Make sun teas by placing herbs and cool water in a covered glass jar for a few hours in a sunny spot.

NOTE *NEVER make tea from any plant that you cannot identify with certainty as being one of the above.*

THE
MOOSEWOOD
RESTAURANT
KITCHEN
GARDEN

270

MAIL-ORDER SOURCES

SEEDS, NURSERIES, AND SUPPLIES

ABUNDANT LIFE SEED FOUNDATION
P.O. Box 772
Port Townsend, WA 98368

A nonprofit corporation specializing in open-pollinated and heirloom vegetable and herb seeds as well as plants of the North Pacific rim. Catalog $1.00.

BEAR CREEK NURSERY
P.O. Box 411
Northport, WA 99157

Hardy, drought-resistant fruit, nut, and other edible landscape shrubs and trees. Catalog for two first-class postage stamps.

BLUESTONE PERENNIALS
7223 Middle Ridge Road
Madison, OH 44057

Reasonably priced young flowering perennial and herb plants sold in packs of 3 or more. Catalog free.

BOUNTIFUL GARDENS
19550 Walker Road
Willits, CA 95490

Part of an organic gardening research project, Bountiful Gardens offers open-pollinated and heirloom vegetable and herb seeds, as well as green manure seeds, beneficial insects, organic fertilizers, and other gardening supplies. Catalog free.

W. ATLEE BURPEE CO.
300 Park Avenue
Warminster, PA 18974

Venerable catalog featuring flower, vegetable, and herb seeds, plus nursery stock, supplies, and beneficial insects. Many new introductions. Catalog free.

COMPANION PLANTS
7247 North Coolville Ridge Road
Athens, OH 45701

Listings of more than 500 potted herb plants. Catalog $2.00.

THE COOK'S GARDEN
P.O. Box 65
Londonderry, VT 05148

Excellent selection of culinary vegetable and herb seeds, with a particularly wide array of lettuces and other salad greens. Catalog $1.00.

CROWNSVILLE NURSERY
P.O. Box 797
Crownsville, MD 21032

Perennials, herbs, and shrubs with a large selection of daylilies. Refundable $2.00 catalog.

FEDCO SEEDS
52 Mayflower Hill Drive
Waterville, ME 04901

A cooperative offering seeds for vegetables, flowers, and herbs that do well in cool climates. It's best to order as a group of households; seeds are quite inexpensive with volume discounts. Catalog free.

FOX HILL FARM
444 West Michigan Avenue
Parma, MI 49269

Large selection of herb plants with many varieties of culinary herbs. Price list free; catalog $1.00.

GARDENER'S SUPPLY
128 Intervale Road,
Burlington, VT 05401

Tools, garden supplies, season extenders, beneficial insects, organic fertilizers, furniture, and more. Catalog free.

GARDENS ALIVE!
Highway 48
P.O. Box 149
Sunman, IN 47041

Biological and botanical pest controls, beneficial insects, organic fertilizers, and garden supplies. Discount for members. Catalog free.

HARRIS SEEDS
60 Saginaw Drive
Rochester, NY 14623

Large selection of vegetable, flower, and herb seeds. Many varieties specifically bred for good results in the Northeast and Midwest. Catalog free.

J. L. HUDSON, SEEDSMAN
P.O. Box 1058
Redwood City, CA 94064

Features seeds from open-pollinated vegetables and ornamentals. Plants from all over the planet, some rare and endangered species. Catalog $1.00.

JOHNNY'S SELECTED SEEDS
299 Foss Hill Road
Albion, ME 04910

An excellent source of vegetable, herb, and flower seeds for Northern gardeners. Many new introductions are bred at Johnny's. Helpful catalog with good cultural information, garden supplies, and soil test kits. Catalog free.

LOGEE'S GREENHOUSES
North Street
Danielson, CT 06239

Potted herb plants and a vast array of ornamentals for indoor culture.

MEADOWBROOK HERB GARDEN
Route 138
Wyoming, RI 02898

Wide selection of seeds for culinary, ornamental, or medicinal herbs. Catalog $1.00.

J. E. MILLER NURSERIES
5060 West Lake Road
Canandaigua, NY 14424
    Large selection of fruit and nut trees, or-
namentals, and berry plants. Catalog free.

N. Y. STATE FRUIT TESTING COOPERATIVE
ASSOCIATION
West North Street
Geneva, NY 14456
    New unnamed varieties of fruit along
with popular time-tested selections. Mem-
bership $5.00. Catalog free.

NICHOLS GARDEN NURSERY
1190 North Pacific Highway
Albany, OR 97321
    Seeds for vegetables, flowers, potato and
garlic varieties. Plants and seeds of many
herbs. Catalog free.

NOLIN RIVER NUT TREE NURSERY
797 Port Wooden Road
Upton, KY 42784
    Grafted trees for quicker crops and
named varieties. Catalog free.

PARK SEED CO.
Box 31
Greenwood, SC 29647
    Seeds for vegetables and flowers plus
nursery stock. Good selection for Southern
gardeners. Catalog free.

RAINTREE NURSERY
391 Butts Road
Morton, WA 98356
    Disease-resistant fruit and nut trees plus
other landscape edibles for organic growers. Catalog free.

REDWOOD CITY SEED CO.
P.O. Box 361
Redwood City, CA 94064

Good selection of Native American corn,
beans, and peppers as well as vegetables
and herbs. Catalog $1.00.

RONNIGER'S SEED POTATOES
Star Route
Moyie Springs, ID 83845
    Wide selection of heirloom and new po-
tato varieties. Catalog $1.00.

SEED SAVERS EXCHANGE
R.R. 3, Box 239
Decorah, IA 52101
    Nonprofit seed exchange network of
many nonhybrid and heirloom varieties
not commercially available. Annual mem-
bership $15.00.

SEEDS BLUM
Idaho City Stage
Boise, ID 83706
    Seeds for open-pollinated and heirloom
varieties. Wide selection of potatoes and
edible ornamentals. Catalog $3.00.

SHEPHERD'S GARDEN SEEDS
30 Irene Street
Torrington, CT 06790
    Vegetable, herb, and flower seeds featur-
ing gourmet varieties; many of European
origin not widely available in the United
States. Catalog $1.50.

SMITH AND HAWKEN
25 Corte Madera
Mill Valley, CA 94941
    Garden supplies, tools, furniture, cloth-
ing, ornamentals, bulbs, and more. Catalog
free.

SONOMA ANTIQUE APPLE NURSERY
4395 Westside Road
Healdsburg, CA 95448
    Apple and other fruit trees organically

grown from varieties that have proven themselves for generations. Refundable $1.00 catalog.

SOUTHERN EXPOSURE SEED EXCHANGE
P.O. Box 158
North Garden, VA 22959
   Open-pollinated and heirloom varieties adapted to the Southeast and Gulf Coast. Catalog $3.00.

STARK BROS. NURSERIES
Highway 54 West
Louisiana, MO 63353
   New and proven fruit, nut, berry, and ornamental plants and trees. Catalog free.

STOKES SEEDS
P.O. Box 548
Buffalo, NY 14240
   Wide assortment of vegetable, flower, and herb seeds for commercial and home growers. In-house varieties and generous cultural information are featured in free catalog.

TERRITORIAL SEED CO.
P.O. Box 157
Cottage Grove, OR 97424
   Flower, herb, and vegetable seeds suited to the maritime Pacific Northwest. Catalog free.

THE TOMATO SEED COMPANY, INC.
P.O. Box 323
Metuchen, NJ 08840
   Hundreds of tomatoes of all kinds and sizes. Catalog free.

TSANG AND MA
P.O. Box 294
Belmont, CA 94002
   Asian kitchen garden specialty vegetables. Catalog free.

VERMONT BEAN SEED CO.
Garden Lane
Fair Haven, VT 05743
   Heirloom and new varieties of beans. Vegetable, flower, and herb seeds as well. Catalog free.

WELL-SWEEP HERB FARM
317 Mt. Bethel Road
Port Murray, NJ 07865
   Large selection of potted herb plants cataloged according to use and hardiness. Catalog $2.00.

WHITE FLOWER FARM
Litchfield, CT 06759
   Informative catalog lists many perennials, herbs, shrubs, and vines. Refundable $5.00 catalog.

GILBERT WILD & SON
P.O. Box 338
Sarcoxie, MI 64862
   Over 2,000 varieties of daylilies, along with many peony varieties. Refundable $2.00 catalog.

WILTON'S ORGANIC CERTIFIED POTATOES
P.O. Box 28
Aspen, CO 81612
   Organically grown seed potatoes. Free price list.

BIBLIOGRAPHY

GENERAL GARDENING BOOKS

Brookes, John. *The Garden Book*. New York: Crown, 1984. Comprehensive, detailed information on garden design.

Bubel, Nancy. *The Seed Starter's Handbook*. Emmaus, Pennsylvania: Rodale Press, 1988. How to start a wide variety of plants from seed.

Creasy, Rosalind. *The Complete Book of Edible Landscaping*. San Francisco: Sierra Club Books, 1982. An excellent source of information on the design and selection of landscape material. Includes information on vegetable, herb, and fruit growing.

Druse, Ken. *The Natural Garden*. New York: Clarkson N. Potter, 1989. Text with beautiful photographs to illustrate gardens that work with the natural assets of a site.

Editors of Mother Earth News. *The Healthy Garden Handbook*. New York: Fireside/Simon and Schuster, 1989. Wealth of information for organic gardening.

Johnson, Hugh. *Principles of Gardening*. New York: Simon and Schuster, 1979. Well-written and -illustrated survey of gardens past and present.

Kourik, Robert. *Designing and Maintaining Your Edible Landscape Naturally*. Santa Rosa, California: Metamorphic Press, 1986. Techniques and detailed information on all aspects of gardening.

Kraft, Ken and Pat. *Fruits for the Home Garden*. New York: William Morrow, 1968. Information on berry plants and fruiting trees or vines.

Lima, Patrick. *The Harrowsmith Perennial Garden*. Camden East, Ontario: Camden House, 1987. Informative text and attractive photos of perennial flower gardens.

Sheldon, Elisabeth. *A Proper Garden*. Harrisburg, Pennsylvania: Stackpole Books, 1989. Delightfully written, well-informed text on perennial flowers.

Smith, Miranda and Anna Carr. *Rodale's Garden Insect, Disease and Weed Identification Guide*. Emmaus, Pennsylvania: Rodale Press, 1988. Comprehensive book on plant protection.

HERBS

Adams, James. *Landscaping with Herbs*. Portland, Oregon: Timber Press, 1987. Detailed information on common and unusual herbs.

Kowalchik, Claire and William Hylton, editors. *Rodale's Illustrated Encyclopedia of Herbs*. Emmaus, Pennsylvania: Rodale Press, 1987. Thorough discussion of the history, use, and cultivation of over 150 herbs.

Lima, Patrick. *Harrowsmith Illustrated Book of Herbs*. Camden East, Ontario: Camden House, 1986. Herb lore, usage, and garden information.

Tolley, Emelie and Chris Mead. *Herbs: Gardens, Decorations and Recipes*. New York: Clarkson N. Potter, 1985. Beautifully photographed.

VEGETABLES

Ball, Jeff. *Jeff Ball's 60 Minute Garden*. Emmaus, Pennsylvania: Rodale Press, 1985. Good source book for beginning gardeners. It includes an efficient system for building raised beds, trellises, and growing tunnels.

———*Rodale's Garden Problem Solver*. Emmaus, Pennsylvania: Rodale Press, 1988. Environment-friendly controls for vegetable, herb, and fruit growing.

Coleman, Eliot. *The New Organic Grower*. Colchester, Vermont: Chelsea Green, 1989. Techniques for every step of gardening. An excellent, thorough guide for market and home gardeners.

Jabs, Carolyn. *The Heirloom Gardener*. San Francisco: Sierra Club Books, 1984. Information and history on seed saving including sources of heirloom vegetables.

Jeavons, John. *How to Grow More Vegetables*. Berkeley, California: Ten Speed Press, 1982. Extensive guide to the Biodynamic/French Intensive Method of vegetable growing; a technique that achieves maximum yields from minimum space.

Ogden, Shepherd and Ellen. *The Cook's Garden*. Emmaus, Pennsylvania: Rodale Press, 1989. A market gardener's primer for all aspects of culinary gardening. The Ogdens have a seed company (see Mail-Order Sources p. 271) and here discuss many of their recommended varieties.

Organic Gardening Magazine Staff. *Encyclopedia of Organic Gardening*. Emmaus, Pennsylvania: Rodale Press, 1978. A classic compendium that I have used for many years.

Riotte, Louise. *Carrots Love Tomatoes, Secrets of Companion Planting*. Pownal, Vermont: Garden Way, 1981. Nicely written, helpful guide to companion planting.

GARDEN TO KITCHEN

Creasy, Rosalind. *Cooking from the Garden*. San Francisco: Sierra Club Books, 1988. Thorough compendium of information including discussions with renowned cooks and gardeners.

Greene, Janet, Ruth Hertzberg, and Beatrice Vaughan. *Putting Food By*. New York: Stephen Greene Press, % Viking Penguin, 1988. Helpful guide to preserving, canning, freezing, and storage of garden produce.

Katzen, Mollie. *The Moosewood Cookbook*. Berkeley, California: Ten Speed Press, 1977. Vegetarian recipes from a time-honored classic.

Moosewood Collective. *New Recipes from Moosewood Restaurant*. Berkeley, California: Ten Speed Press, 1987. Two hundred original recipes explore a cornucopia of garden produce.

————*Sundays at Moosewood Restaurant*. New York: Fireside/Simon and Schuster, 1990. Each of eighteen chapters explores a different cuisine from around the world. Traditional and original recipes provide a wealth of ideas for using garden vegetables and herbs.

Scaravelli, Paola and Jon Cohen. *Cooking from an Italian Garden*. New York: Holt, Rinehart and Winston, 1984. Home-style Italian recipes featuring vegetables.

Smith, Leona Woodring. *Forgotten Art of Flower Cookery*. New York: Harper and Row, 1973. Historical information and novel recipes using edible flowers.

Stoner, Carol Hupping, editor. *Stocking Up*. New York: Fireside/Simon and Schuster, 1990 reprint. Definitive guide to vegetable and fruit selection and harvest, plus freezing, canning, pickling, drying, juicing, preserving, and storage.

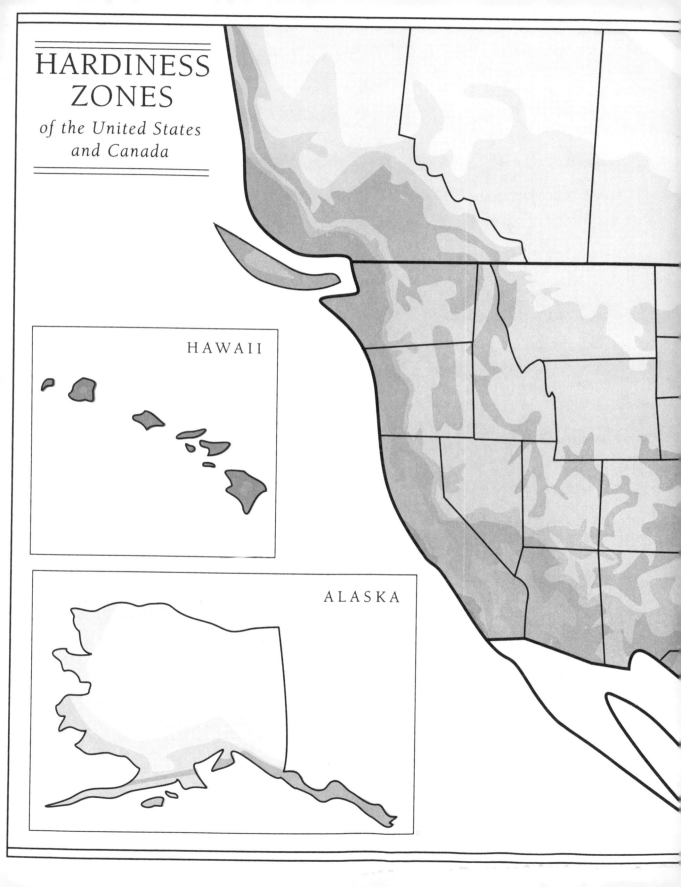

HARDINESS
ZONES
of the United States
and Canada

HAWAII

ALASKA

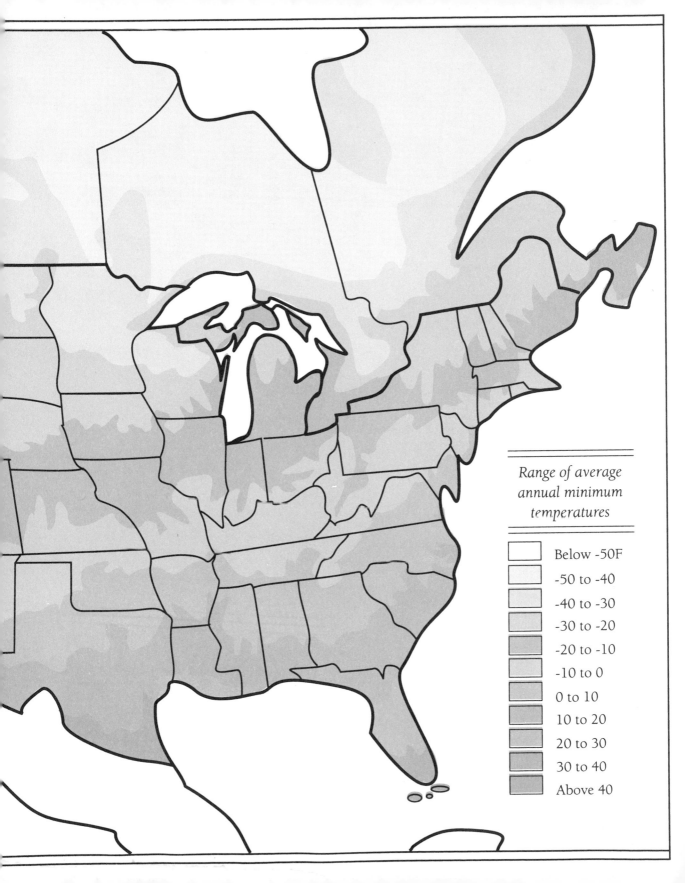

*Range of average
annual minimum
temperatures*

Below -50F
-50 to -40
-40 to -30
-30 to -20
-20 to -10
-10 to 0
0 to 10
10 to 20
20 to 30
30 to 40
Above 40

INDEX

LIQUID AND DRY MEASURE EQUIVALENCIES

CUSTOMARY	METRIC
¼ teaspoon	1.25 milliliters
½ teaspoon	2.5 milliliters
1 teaspoon	5 milliliters
1 tablespoon	15 milliliters
1 fluid ounce	30 milliliters
¼ cup	60 milliliters
⅓ cup	80 milliliters
½ cup	120 milliliters
1 cup	240 milliliters
1 pint (2 cups)	480 milliliters
1 quart (4 cups; 32 ounces)	960 milliliters (.96 liters)
1 gallon (4 quarts)	3.84 liters
1 ounce (by weight)	28 grams
¼ pound (4 ounces)	114 grams
1 pound (16 ounces)	454 grams
2.2 pounds	1 kilogram (1,000 grams)

OVEN TEMPERATURE EQUIVALENCIES

DESCRIPTION	°FAHRENHEIT	°CELSIUS
Cool	200	90
Very slow	250	120
Slow	300–325	150–160
Moderately slow	325–350	160–180
Moderate	350–375	180–190
Moderately hot	375–400	190–200
Hot	400–450	200–230
Very Hot	450–500	230–260